CALIFORNIA
Foraging

CALIFORNIA
Foraging

120 wild and flavorful edibles
from evergreen huckleberries
to wild ginger

JUDITH LARNER LOWRY

TIMBER PRESS
Portland·London

Frontispiece: High meadows of mountain mule's ear produce edible seeds and flower stalks within sight of dramatic Sierra Nevada scenery.

Photography credits appear on page 328.

Published in 2014 by Timber Press, Inc.

The Haseltine Building
133 S.W. Second Avenue, Suite 450
Portland, Oregon 97204-3527
timberpress.com

6a Lonsdale Road
London NW6 6RD
timberpress.co.uk

Printed in China
Text and cover design by Benjamin Shaykin

Library of Congress Cataloging-in-Publication Data

Lowry, Judith Larner, 1945–
    California foraging: 120 wild and flavorful edibles from evergreen huckleberries to wild ginger/Judith Larner Lowry.
        pages cm
    Includes bibliographical references and index.
    ISBN 978-1-60469-420-8
    1. Plants, Edible—California. I. Title.
    QK98.5.C18L69 2014
    581.6′3209794—dc23

2013048763

To Grayson James Koehler and his parents, Molly and Matt Koehler, and to the memory of Margaret Ellen Grindley, huckleberry pie maker supreme

Contents

Preface

One foggy summer day near the coast, I discovered an unexpected treasure trove of California hazelnut bushes. They were loaded with sweet, mild nuts that were ripe and ready to eat. I found a comfortable place to sit, a rock to crack the shells, and settled in for a session of hazelnut appreciation. To other hikers on the trail, I was hidden from view by the hazel's leafy branches.

Soon, I heard two parents cajoling their children onward up the trail. The children sounded tired and complained about being hungry and bored. I thought momentarily of having them join me in my cozy fort under the hazel and sharing the bounty.

While I considered it, they disappeared up the path. Maybe I should have called out to them: *There is delicious food here. Come join me.*

I didn't then, but I am calling out to you now. There is delicious food all around us.

Two unexpected strands have come together during the writing of this book. One, an even greater deepening of my appreciation for California's native flora, I expected and welcomed. The other strand has taken me by surprise.

For most of my adult life, I have been an advocate for California's native plants. At my mail-order native plant seed and nursery business, we specialize in growing seed crops of native wildflowers, grasses, shrubs, and trees, some of them threatened with local extinction.

Through the years, my realization that many of these native plants are also food has felt like startling new information about old friends I thought I knew well. I first started to value California's native plants for their drought tolerance and appropriateness to California's climate and soils. Then they became a crucial part of my developing and deepening sense of home in the Golden State, and I wanted to live surrounded by them. Their importance as habitat for native bees, butterflies, birds, and other creatures added yet another layer to my appreciation of the grounding details of sharing life with the plants that evolved here.

Early on, I learned that many of the seeds we gathered from the wild were grain crops for California Indians. The wildflower meadows that drew me with their beauty represented to many native peoples a harvest of healthful seed foods, produced with no added fertilizer, pesticides, water, or plowing. That's how the journey of this book began, with the seeds.

California buttercup flowers dropped their highly edible seeds, prized for making pinole, onto a stone wall, so I could easily brush them into a bag.

When I hear people talk about the importance and value of diversified sustainable farming operations, I look at the wildlands and think about what a diversified sustainable farming operation they already are. Or once were, and could be again.

At our seed-growing garden, I proclaimed a zero-tolerance policy for weeds, the better to learn how the native species grow when unimpeded by teasel, fennel, velvet grass, or other rampant invasive plants. My proclamation of this weed-free zone was made partly in jest, since there is no way to totally eliminate weeds. This I know from experience. But we didn't allow them much of a presence here until my interest in eating naturalized European and Eurasian forbs, otherwise known as weeds, caused me to occasionally stay the weeder's hand. The response was surprising, even to me, though I have watched this story so many times before, the old disappearing under the onslaught of the new.

In one season, black nightshade, curly dock, and borage grew where they hadn't been before. Sheep sorrel and chickweed appeared from out of nowhere.

Huge colonies of lambsquarters sprang up overnight. The native clarkias, tar-weed, and red maids may have been thinking, *Oh no, not here, too,* as my demonstration garden became a place of somewhat uneasy alliances.

Soon, I was eating these weeds from elsewhere with gusto. Treating weeds as food crops required a close and constant attention and a rigorous control of weedy reproduction. I learned how to have my borage and control it too, making pesto, stews, and stir-fries using a combination of both weedy and native greens. I learned something about the proud histories of weedy greens, especially their roles in intriguing national dishes, like green sauces made in Germany with borage leaves, or salsas made with black nightshade berries in Guatemala.

I began to savor this second strand: harvesting and eating the edible weeds to protect the native plants, while managing and harvesting the native plants in ways that increase their numbers. This pattern now guides my gathering days in the wild. It could be called sustainable foraging, and I hope it will guide yours too.

Black nightshade rewards the forager with ripened shiny black berries even while unripe green berries are still present.

By imparting an interest in foraging to you, it is my hope that you will fall in love with wild edibles, their tastes, and their histories, forming alliances and culinary relationships all your own. That you will discover a pattern of interaction that benefits both you and the plants. And that the mantle of indifference toward land and plants that has replaced our evolutionary closeness will slip easily off your shoulders, as you welcome a new, knowledgeable intimacy with wild food plants.

And now a few words about the organization of this book. The introduction provides an understanding of the rich nature of foraging in general, beginning with definitions, and then offering important guidelines, from safety issues to plant identification tips to legal matters. A brief discussion of the regions of California will help you locate both yourself and edible wild plants of interest to you. A Seasonal Gathering Guide will tell you what plant part you can find, when.

Also included in the introduction is a brief pitch for the advantages of planting wild food plants as part of gardens around your home. A discussion of developing your own sustainable foraging ethic builds on this concept, which is woven throughout the book.

The majority of the book is a section called Edible Wild Plants of California, with more than 120 California native and naturalized non-native edible species, organized alphabetically by common name. The index will help you find plants under their scientific, or botanical, names.

Each plant entry includes one or more photographs with informative captions, a list of common names the plant is known by, the scientific name currently in use, and the edible parts of each plant, followed by an introduction to the plant, discussion of its identifying characteristics, where and when to gather, how to gather, how to use, responsible harvests as part of a sustainable foraging ethic, and any precautions needed in the use of the plant.

At the end of the book, websites, books, and organizations are listed that will be helpful to both beginning and experienced foragers. Also included is a list of public botanic gardens throughout California, where labeled native plants can be viewed, a great way to learn.

Introduction: Foraging in the Golden State

California lies before you, replete with opportunities to discover its healthful, delectable, and unique wild foods—from the Coast Ranges, to the mountains, the deserts, the Central Valley, the Great Basin, the northwestern rain forest, and everywhere in between.

Many of these plants are an integral part of California's history, as well as irreplaceable participants in the precious food web of our region. Foraging is an interest that can draw you into many other worlds, including the culinary arts, nutrition, botany and ethnobotany, natural history, anthropology, ecology, taxonomy, and ecological restoration. Elements of all these disciplines are found within this book.

The word *foraging* contains a surprising number of meanings, even contradictory meanings, ranging from the lighthearted activities of the curious nature lover to the more serious searches undertaken by soldiers and civilians in response to food shortages during wars, a common dictionary definition. Usually implied is the common element of looking for something to eat that you're not certain you will find.

This uncertainty, for some, is the sauce that flavors wild foods. Without the control that modern agriculture wields over food crops, the existence of edible plants that survive without farming assistance can be reassuring on many levels. The poetry and excitement of that encounter is part of the appeal of wild harvests. Author Wendell Berry describes the foraging finds of one character in his Kentucky novel, *A Place on Earth*, as "the harvest of a ramble and not a search or a labor," adding that for this character the activity "bespeaks a peaceableness between her and the world."

Yet under the rubric of carefree wild plant harvest lies another important and contradictory layer. Though one meaning of foraging expresses the serendipity and grace of unexpected encounters, California's native peoples, important wild food–using models, were and are such skilled and knowledgeable plant managers that they returned year after year to familiar camas fields, berry patches, brodiaea colonies, or pond lily wetland seed farms. The continuing productivity and health of

A member of the mint family, mountain pennyroyal has a delightful fragrance and makes a good mountain tea.

those harvesting grounds were encouraged through their actions. Because of a painful history, their land management strategies are no longer prevailing in much of our wildlands, and populations of many of these wild foods have accordingly declined. From native peoples, we can learn to harvest sustainably, replanting cormlets, seeds, and tubers as we go, weeding and pruning for plant health.

Foraging is many things to many people: how we evolved, a way to connect with our ancestors, and a lens through which to understand the universe. These distinctions will frequently blur, as you create your own ever-changing definition of foraging, based on your particular set of experiences.

Awaiting you are some world-class culinary experiences and health-enhancing meals, as well as unexpected life lessons that will keep you coming back—good reasons to bring your children with you into the woods.

Upon finding a sought-after plant, from the leaves of yerba buena to the corms of wild hyacinth, the forager is flooded with a delicious sensation almost unimaginable to the nonforager. Whether you head out with certain plants in mind or simply open yourself to whichever plant you come upon, encountering edible wild plants

Camas bulbs can be harvested before plants go to seed, from spring to midsummer.

carries with it a feeling of being blessed. A smidgeon of smugness may even creep in, a hint of patting yourself on the back. The happy feeling of receiving an undeserved gift elicits gratitude.

It is your adventurous resolve and your burgeoning knowledge of the plant world that have put this food—this prickly pear pad, wild onion, or camas bulb—on your plate. Conversely, if the plant you seek isn't there, you learn to handle that circumstance with equanimity. It's all information, grist for building your knowledge of the plant world. And that feels good.

Foraging Guidelines

How do you learn what you need to know about responsible foraging? When you are foraging, the overriding principle is: *Do no harm*, either to yourself, to your loved ones, or to the land whose secrets you seek to untangle.

The aim of this book is to convey some of the knowledge and skills necessary to identify a plant, to guide you in harvesting it carefully and responsibly, and to describe appropriate procedures for its consumption. Following are general foraging guidelines and principles.

Learn how to identify a species.
Foraging begins with learning how to solidly identify a species. As has been true throughout human history, one human being teaching another is still the safest and most effective way to learn about eating wild plants. Refreshingly, foraging is one part of life that still relies to a great extent on the direct transmission of information from one person to another.

Learning about edible plants may begin with kids playing together after school or waiting for the bus, and showing each other the sweet nectar found in clover flowers or discovering together the tang of sourgrass. It may continue during casual strolls with knowledgeable friends who take you to their favorite patch of stinging nettle, show you how to harvest it painlessly, and tell you how to prepare it like spinach. It can burgeon into field trips to gather pine nuts in the mountains or camas bulbs in meadows.

Learning from professional teachers can include field trips to find and identify plants, as well as workshops that demonstrate techniques of cleaning and cooking edible wildflower seed, using native and weedy greens to make pesto, or how to build an earth oven or make a digging stick. Classes may meet monthly for an entire year, highlighting at each session the plants available at that time, how to identify, harvest, and use them.

Along with person-to-person transmission of knowledge, books have been the way to learn about foraging, particularly since the writings of twentieth-century authors like Euell Gibbons, Tom Brown,

and Brad Angier. Books are authoritative and useful on the trail. They are also great tools for armchair foraging, which has merits all its own.

And the seemingly infinite number of Internet websites pertaining to wild foods indicates the enormous interest in the topic.

As a rule, you should use more than one source to nail down a plant identification. Remember that the enemy of solid identification is wishful thinking. Take a look at this short interview between an enthusiastic new forager and a curmudgeonly old forager:

NEW FORAGER: Except for the number of petals, this plant looks just like the picture in the book, so maybe this flower is just having an off day. It's probably the same one. I guess I'll try it.

OLD FORAGER: Don't do it.

NEW FORAGER: Haven't you ever taken any risks by experimenting with a new or unknown plant of uncertain identity?

OLD FORAGER: Yes, I have. Should you? No.

NEW FORAGER: Did you ever get sick?

OLD FORAGER: Once.

NEW FORAGER: Was it bad?

OLD FORAGER: It's not something I want to experience again. Here, let me look at that plant. Be glad I'm here to tell you about it, because—it's not the same plant!

California Foraging presents the essential aspects of each plant's appearance and characteristics to help you identify the plant in question. If you want to learn the process of determining a particular plant's scientific name, seek out books and classes

Golden chia, which offers a popular seed, has purple blooms on square stems.

on botanical taxonomy. You can learn how to identity a specific plant by studying the plant's habit, leaves, and flowers. In that process, you follow a yes/no process to arrive at the two-part scientific name (binomial) of the genus and species of the plant in question.

The bible for California taxonomy is *The Jepson Manual: Higher Plants of California*, second edition, edited by Bruce Baldwin et al., and the online version, the Jepson Herbarium, Jepson eFlora. If the taxonomical lingo in *The Jepson Manual* seems difficult, don't conclude that foraging isn't for you. Human beings are hardwired to develop a sense of what a given plant looks like and to be able to find and identify it, at least to genus level, without being able to explain it using technical language. This, after all, is what our ancestors did. In addition, shorter plant books are available, covering particular regions, like *Marin Flora* for inhabitants of Marin County, which are less daunting for beginners.

The many public gardens, botanic gardens, and native plant nurseries in California where native species are grown and labeled are also useful for working on your identification skills.

Start small.

Begin each foraging experience with a small taste of a new plant, to ensure that you have no unusual sensitivities to that plant. Allergic reactions to a plant are not always fatal but occur along a continuum, from an unpleasant stomachache to a trip to the emergency room, all of which you want to avoid.

Mushrooms are the most frequent causes of problematic experiences, and since they are a separate field of knowledge, they are not included in this guide. Use books specializing in mushrooms for that purpose, and avail yourself of the on-the-ground, person-to-person teachings of professional mycologists, through mushroom societies and field trips.

This book does discuss poisonous plant look-alikes and plant chemicals that require attention, such as oxalates, inulins, and saponins, which are included in the individual plant entries under the Caution subheading. Such plants require different kinds of processing before consumption, from leaching to boiling to roasting.

Pay attention to other safety issues.

Avoid areas that may be polluted, like roadways and places where dogs are walked. Avoid agricultural fields, lawns, and median strips where fertilizers and herbicides may have been applied. You can often tell if an herbicide was used by the white-blond look of the thoroughly dead plants. A telltale abrupt line between the pale, sprayed area, nearer the road, and the still green and growing unsprayed area next to it, indicates that the area was sprayed.

Wash all foods thoroughly before eating. Soaking greens in three gallons of cold water with one cup of vinegar is an effective way to deal with potential contamination.

Learn where you can forage legally in California.

To forage on private land, you need permission from the owner. Some private landowners will be grateful to have you point out the edible foods growing on their land, and, in exchange, may allow you to harvest there.

The many types of protected, publicly owned lands in California are one of our glories, but regulations pertaining to foraging on public land vary from park to park. Check with individual entities before planning a foraging excursion. Such information is usually available online; go to the website of the specific park, national forest, state park, county park, county open space, state forest, state tidelands, or reserve in question.

California state parks are the most restrictive and have stringent penalties, since no plant or plant part can be harvested unless it is posted as harvestable at the headquarters of that particular unit. Penalties are up to six months in jail or a $1,000 fine.

National parks have a variety of allowances and prohibitions, which do frequently permit the individual, for personal use, to harvest a specified quantity of berries or mushrooms. An interesting example is the allowance of ten gallons of tanoak acorns per person per day at Redwood National Forest.

There is also the land surrounding your house, where you won't need permission, assuming, of course, that you haven't used any chemical fertilizers or herbicides on your own property.

The Foraging Regions of California

The geography of California is dizzyingly complex and variable. *The Jepson Manual* recognizes fifty different geographic units, from provinces to districts. For the purposes of this book, we use six different major regions: the Coast Ranges, the Sierra Nevada and Cascade Range mountains, the deserts, the Central Valley, the Great Basin, and the northwest rain forest.

The California Floristic Province is a useful bioregion defined in *The Jepson Manual*. It is where most of the endemic (meaning found only in California) species grow and where most of the people live. It includes 70 percent of the state and a huge number of habitats, from foggy coast to hot inland valley, from chaparral to grassland to redwoods to oaks, from foothill to mountain. It could also be defined as everywhere in California except the deserts and the Great Basin. It extends from the northwest rain forest, with winter rainfall up to 100 inches, to the Central Valley, with a mere 5 inches of precipitation in its southernmost parts. It also includes the north coast, the central coast, and the south coast.

The defining characteristic of the California Floristic Province is a Mediterranean climate, which means that the bioregion is known for cool, rainy winters and hot, dry, rainless summers. However, coastal summers can experience significant

These winged seeds of gray pine contain delicious pine nuts.

fog, which in forested areas can sometimes add up to as much as 30 inches of rainfall annually, coming in the summer.

The California Floristic Province includes the northwestern rain forest, with its cool, moist winters with rainfall up to a stunning 60 inches, and hot summers, except by the coast. This area continues into southern Oregon, and has the most predictable climate in the region.

Also included within the California Floristic Province are the Sierra Nevada and Cascade Ranges, from the foothills on the western, rainy sides, up to the highest alpine peaks. It does sometimes rain (and even snow!) in mid to late summer in the Sierra Nevada, so it doesn't have a classic Mediterranean climate.

One of the two floristic provinces not included in the California Floristic Province is the Great Basin, which is east of the Sierra Nevada and the Cascade Range, its vast open spaces continuing east and north into Nevada, Utah, and Oregon. The northern Great Basin in California includes the Warner Mountains and the Modoc Plateau. The southern part contains the White and Inyo Mountains and the eastern Sierra Nevada, which border California's deserts.

The other floristic province not part of the California Floristic Province includes the Mojave and the Sonoran Deserts, the two deserts found within California's borders east of the California Floristic Province and south of the Great Basin. The Mojave includes more mountains than the

The many golden stamens of giant blazing star contribute to the spectacular appearance of the flowers, a source of edible seeds.

Sonoran, resulting in a greater temperature range, including frost in winter, and a greater moisture range, from 1 to 10 inches, again mostly in winter. The Joshua tree is an indicator species of that desert, so if you see a Joshua tree, you're in the Mojave Desert. About 2,000 species of plants are found in the Mojave. Joshua Tree National Park is a place where the two deserts meet.

The Sonoran Desert is south and east of the Mojave, and larger, lower, and hotter. It has palo verde, ocotillo, California fan palms, and no Joshua trees. Lower and fewer mountains, and summer rain, called a monsoon season, make the climate closer to a subtropical desert.

Within these six regions are numerous wetlands, rivers, streams, creeks, hills, valleys, and mountain peaks, with different soil types, topographies, exposures, and winds. With such complex topography, it is not surprising that California has over 6,000 native plants and subspecies, over 2,000 of which occur only in the state, or that California is listed as one of the world's Twenty-Five Biodiversity Hotspots by Conservation International.

The Range of Foraging Opportunities in California

At one end of the spectrum are the many weedy greens that have made it on their own from other continents to ours, from the Atlantic Coast to the Pacific, or from south of the border north. Examples are the aforementioned curly dock, purslane, borage, and chickweed. Important parts of the cuisines of their native countries, these plants seek out places where European patterns of land management followed by neglect have provided them with the disturbance conditions they like. These species are identified in the book as those that can be harvested freely.

Some books on foraging focus solely on these weedy greens from elsewhere, found in vacant lots, old farm fields, roadsides, weedy lawns, and abandoned pastures. Unfortunately, all too many of these weeds have found their way into our remaining wild or partially wild lands. This is where you, the forager, come in.

There will always be more of these wild greens, and they are often easy to incorporate into your culinary day. Pull them up by the root if they spread through rhizomes, being careful not to scatter the seed. The forager in this way can help to avoid a world that is filled only with weedy greens, which sometimes seems a real possibility.

In the middle are the native species included in this book, which once were abundant but now are less so. Each plant entry in the book discusses the historical and ecological reasons for this situation and how you can make a positive contribution.

At the other end of the wild foods spectrum is a plant too rare to be included in this book, though it is said to be delicious. I refer to the almost mythical desert plant called sandfood, *Pholisma sonorae*, a mysterious root parasite found in the Sonoran Desert. "To learn the secrets of this shy plant," ethnobotanist Amadeo Rea said, "you must sit and meditate. Maybe in an hour, or even two, the little purple crown might appear to you out of the ground."

Underneath it will be a long, thick, sweet edible stem that few have tasted. According to ethnobotanist Wendy Hodgson, some of this plant's former dry habitat has been converted to high water–using asparagus fields, a replacement of a drought- and sand-adapted local species with a high-water-use, high-fertility-requiring vegetable from faraway. Gary Nabhan writes that the act of harvesting sandfood caused its seed to be scattered deep below the surface of the sand, even 6 feet down, near the roots of the host plant, enabling sandfood's survival.

This forager's Holy Grail has been seen by very few, and is an example of a plant that your developing sense of responsibility would discourage you from harvesting, should you be so lucky as to find it. There are other plants that you may never see in the wild at all, and being human, you may long to try them. Consider the following option.

Establishing Your Own Wild Food Garden

Many foragers will find at least a few edible species right outside their door. Use this opportunity to observe, harvest, and either contain or encourage them. Perhaps you want to understand more about a wild species before you harvest it from the wild, or maybe you have decided that it will never be proper to do that but you are intrigued by it and long to experience it. Seek out such plants from your local native plant nursery and begin to integrate a wild food garden into your landscape. Begin with species that are local to your region.

A garden of wild food plants is not a contradiction in terms but a blurring of distinctions. It's a win/win situation, which the forager may or may not choose to embrace. Many edible native plants are not currently available in the nursery trade, but I predict this is going to change. Interest in healthful, unusual, local foods and in their sustainable production is creating a food revolution worldwide. At the same time, nutritionists are starting to take a serious look at wild food plants.

It is now thought that plant domestication has eliminated many important phytonutrients (over 8,000 have been identified) that are essential for our health. Western serviceberries, for example, have five times more antioxidants than the domesticated strawberry. Purslane, a wild green, has fourteen times more omega-3 acids than spinach. Wild huckleberries have more than twice as many antioxidants as domesticated blueberries.

Responsible Harvesting: Developing a Sustainable Foraging Ethic

The diverse and productive California landscape encountered by the Spaniards and following settlers was the product of many centuries of intelligent and subtle land management by the indigenous peoples. Some activities we know about, like burning, pruning, replanting; others are lost in the mists of time, tantalizing us with unanswered questions.

When we forage we become increasingly conscious of our long-term relationship with the plant world, and we want to keep the gift moving. In a give and take that becomes second nature, we earn the right to harvest wild plants by becoming responsible for their increase. Here is the goal: Imagine the satisfaction of returning to the harvesting site year after year to find the plants looking better and more numerous each time.

Each plant entry in this book provides guidance on how to promote that plant's thriving. Spend time with the plant in question, observing it, thinking about its health, its reproductive strategies, and possible threats to its posterity. Providing this kind of attention is already a giveback to plants that will potentially feed you.

Some native peoples say that by no longer using these plants, we have hurt their feelings. As a consequence, like ignored infants, they fail to thrive, a metaphor for neglect.

Strategies leading to increase include, for root foods, the replanting nearby of reproductive parts, like tubers, corms, and bulbs. For seed crops, the sowing of some of your harvest nearby also helps plants meet their goal of spreading. Choose spots where taller plants will not outcompete new seedlings and where the soil and conditions are similar to the original site—at the edge of the original site is often a good place. Scrape a bit of soil over the seeds for protection and for retention of the moisture necessary for good germination.

In our demonstration garden, seed collection is always followed by a cleanup of weeds and pruning of dead plant parts. In this way, new growth has a chance to rejuvenate the plant. Fire or flood traditionally accomplished this process; now it's up to the gardener. Follow this practice in your own garden, and if tip-pruning will increase fruiting spurs of plants in the wild, make tip-pruning part of your harvesting technique.

Weeding is always and forever valuable. Many times I have seen invasive species getting a start near a stand of valued native

The edible flowers of bigleaf maple bloom in March and April.

plants, and in those cases, quick action resolved the threat. Remove the entire plant, particularly if it spreads through rhizomes, like cape ivy or sheep sorrel. Don't try to compost rhizomatous species, which can start spreading in your compost pile. Many weed seeds aren't killed in compost unless the pile reaches 140°F. Covering the compost pile with a tarp for as long as a year can make it safe to include these invasive weeds.

Harvesting Amounts

How much to harvest is the question that differs for every species in every situation. Guidelines that quantify harvesting amounts, providing rules of thumb that recommend taking no more than 5 percent, for example, can't take into account the numerous variables in every situation, such as: How many other foragers will be following in your footsteps? Is a hillside facing erosion problems? Is the area experiencing development? To promote foraging, as I am doing, requires an act of trust. It's not hard to imagine that large numbers of irresponsible foragers could have a devastating impact on some species. How can I justify promoting the eating of native plants, given the 38 million people now living in California?

One reason is that current thinking about the dynamics of biodiversity in California incorporates and even requires intelligent human actions. Hands-off policies in some situations are not so slowly but very surely resulting in a greatly simplified landscape, with correspondingly fewer wild food plants. Human attention, care, and love are required in most places in California.

It is often observed that the opposite of love is not hate but indifference. The results of such indifference are visible in every median strip, vacant lot, untended park, weedy roadside, financially stressed open space, and abandoned farm field.

We need Californians to first pay attention to and then fall in love with the plants of the Golden State. The experience of gathering, preparing, and eating these wild foods arouses gratitude and delight in the forager. With attention directed and gratefulness awakened, can the requisite affection be far behind?

Seasonal Gathering Guide for California

Somebody somewhere in California is foraging for tasty edible wild food today. California, with its enormous range of temperatures, topography, soils, moisture, wind, and land-use history, provides wild foods to harvest almost year-round. Different combinations of these regional factors as well as particular locations will create different foraging opportunities. It all begins with and turns on moisture.

The rain and snow of fall, winter, and early spring bring the germination and growth of edible greens. These plant parts are at their most tender and mildest before the longer, warmer, drier days coax out the edible shoots that become flower stalks, which in some cases can be eaten like asparagus. And finally the edible flowers appear, some producing pollen that is also important food.

Before the heat and drought of summer cause seed ripening, the immature seeds of some species can be eaten like peas. Seeds, fruits, and nuts ripen with summer's heat, while the root foods store energy as plants go dormant, either from the lack of moisture, shorter days, increasing cold, or a combination of these.

For further information on harvesting times for edible wild plant parts, turn to the individual plant entries that follow this chart.

Plant

Plant	Green Plant Parts *shoots, leaves, stems* 	Edible Flowers *buds, flowers, pollen* 
angled onion	November–March	March–April
beavertail cactus	May–June	March–April May–June
bigleaf maple		March–May
black nightshade	November–December	
bladderpod	March–May	January–April
blue camas		
blue dicks		
blue elderberry		April–July
blue flax		
blue palo verde		March–May
blue wildrye		
borage	year-round	March–October
bracken fern	February–May	
bull clover	February–May	March–May
butterfly mariposa lily		
California bay laurel	year-round	October–May
California blackberry	January–February	
California black oak		
California bottlebrush grass		
California brome		
California buttercup		
California hazelnut		

Seeds

*immature (peas) and ripe
(dry hard seeds for pinole)*

Roots

*bulbs, corms, tuberous
roots, rhizomes*

Fruits, Nuts, Sap

Seeds	Roots	Fruits, Nuts, Sap
	September–April	
		FRUITS June–July
		SAP January–February
		FRUITS July–September
	March–April September–October	
	June–August	
		FRUITS July–September
July–August		
April–July		
May–August		
	April–September	
		NUTS October–November
		FRUITS June–August
		NUTS October–November
July–September		
May–August		
May–June		
		NUTS June–August

Plant	Green Plant Parts *shoots, leaves, stems*	Edible Flowers *buds, flowers, pollen*

California juniper		
California oatgrass		
California oniongrass		
California wild grape	April–May	
California wild rose		April–May
candy flower	January–April	February–May
cattail	April–July	May–June June–July
chalk buckwheat	May–July	May
chaparral yucca	January–February	February–March
checkerbloom	November–April	March–June
chickweed	November–July	
chuparosa		March–June
common mallow	year-round	February–May
common tarweed		
cow parsnip	December–January January–March	
coyote mint	December–June	April–July
creek monkeyflower	November–March	
curly dock	October–April	
desert ironwood	December–October	April–May
Douglas fir	March–June	
evergreen huckleberry		

Seeds	Roots	Fruits, Nuts, Sap
immature (peas) and ripe (dry hard seeds for pinole)	*bulbs, corms, tuberous roots, rhizomes*	

Seeds	Roots	Fruits, Nuts, Sap
		FRUITS Winter–Spring
May–July		
May–June		
		FRUITS August–October
		FRUITS June–November
May–August		
April		
January–March		
July–September		
July–August		
May–June (immature) June–July (ripe)		
		FRUITS July–October

Plant	Green Plant Parts shoots, leaves, stems 	Edible Flowers buds, flowers, pollen 
farewell to spring		
fawn lily		
fennel	February–January	September–January
foothills palo verde		April–May
giant blazing star		
golden chia		
golden currant		
golden prettyface brodiaea		
goldfields		
gray pine		
hairy bittercress	November–March	
harvest brodiaea		
Himalayan blackberry		
holly leaf cherry		
honey mesquite		
Indian ricegrass		
Kellogg's yampa	**LEAVES** February–April **SHOOTS** April–June	
lady fern	March–May	
lambsquarters	December–March	**YOUNG BUDS** March–April
lemonade berry		
madrone	June–August	
manzanita		

Seeds	Roots	Fruits, Nuts, Sap
immature (peas) and ripe (dry hard seeds for pinole)	bulbs, corms, tuberous roots, rhizomes	
July–August		
	June	
October–January		
May–June (immature) June–July (ripe)		
August–September		
May–July		
		FRUITS June–July
	August–September	
April–June		
		NUTS July–October
	July–September	
		NUTS August–September
		FRUITS July–September
June–August		
May–June		
July–September	April–July	
May–July		
		FRUITS May–July
June–November		FRUITS June–November

Plant	Green Plant Parts shoots, leaves, stems 	Edible Flowers buds, flowers, pollen 
meadow barley		
meadowfoam		
milkmaids	December–February	
miner's lettuce	November–March	
Mormon tea	year-round	February–May
mountain mule's ears	April–May	
mountain pennyroyal	June	July–August
mountain sorrel	June–September	
narrowleaf mule's ears	May–June	
nasturtium	year-round	July–September
Nevada stickleaf		
Nootka rose	March–May	May–July
northern California black walnut		
ocotillo		March–June
Oregon grape	February–March	April–May
perennial pickleweed	year-round	
Point Reyes checkerbloom	April–August	
prickly pear	March–May and after rains	February–April
purple sage	October–June	
purslane	year-round	
pussy ears		
red huckleberry		
red maids	January–March	March–May

Seeds	Roots	Fruits, Nuts, Sap
immature (peas) and ripe (dry hard seeds for pinole)	*bulbs, corms, tuberous roots, rhizomes*	
June–August		
April–May		
September–October		
June–August		
August–October		
June–August		
		FRUITS June–October
		NUTS July–September
		FRUITS August–September
May–July		**FRUITS** May–October
June–August		
	April–October	
		FRUITS July–August
April–May		

Plant

Green Plant Parts
shoots, leaves, stems

Edible Flowers
buds, flowers, pollen

Plant	Green Plant Parts	Edible Flowers
redwood sorrel	December–March, or year-round	
redwood violet	November–May	March–April
salal		
saltbush	February–May	
sheep sorrel	February–May, or year-round	
Sierra mint	April–September	
silverweed	April–September	May–September
singleleaf pinyon pine		
soaproot	October–March	May–June
sourberry		
springbank clover	October–February	March–June
stinging nettle	November–April	
sugar bush		
sugar pine		
swamp onion		
tall coastal plantain	February–April	
tanoak		
thimbleberry		
thistle sage		
tidy tips		
Torrey pine		
tree mallow		

Seeds

immature (peas) and ripe (dry hard seeds for pinole)

Roots

bulbs, corms, tuberous roots, rhizomes

Fruits, Nuts, Sap

Seeds	Roots	Fruits, Nuts, Sap
		FRUITS August–September
May–July		
	September–November	
		NUTS September–October
	July–October	
		FRUITS October–February
	December–June	
		FRUITS May–August
		NUTS September–October
June–October		
		NUTS September–November
		FRUITS June–July
May–November		
April–May		
		NUTS June–October
May–August		

Plant

Plant	Green Plant Parts shoots, leaves, stems	Edible Flowers buds, flowers, pollen
tule	January–April	March–April
valley oak		
vetch	January–June	
vine maple		April–May
wapato		
watercress	February–April	
western serviceberry		
wild ginger	year-round	
wild hyacinth		
wild radish	September–January	January–March
woodland strawberry	year-round	
wood rose	December–February	April
yellow pond lily		
yerba buena	February–September	
yerba santa	February–July	

Seeds	Roots	Fruits, Nuts, Sap
immature (peas) and ripe (dry hard seeds for pinole)	*bulbs, corms, tuberous roots, rhizomes*	
August–September	August–September	
		NUTS October–November
	June–August	
		FRUITS July–August
	year-round	
	July–September	
July–September	April–May	
		FRUITS March–June
		FRUITS May–June
August–October		

Wild Edible Plants
of California

Wildflower fields like this one on the Carrizo Plain were managed by California's native peoples as a source of both beauty and edible seeds.

angled onion

Allium triquetrum

wild onion, onionweed, wild onion lily, three-cornered leek

EDIBLE leaves, bulb, flowers

This weedy perennial, well-known in Europe's Mediterranean landscape, has all the oniony flavor needed to liven up dishes like early spring wild greens.

Early every spring, angled onion turns up reliably. It tastes of strong onion and leek with a definite hint of garlic. Its leaves are similar to those of young domesticated onions, but a bit wider and more pungent. The smell of this non-native plant is noticeable from farther away than some of California's species of native onions, many of which are too uncommon to be foraged.

How to identify

Angled onion presents masses of nodding white flowers on plants up to 14 inches tall. To identify, give the grasslike, keeled stems

The whole angled onion plant can be eaten, much like scallions.

and leaves a sniff test. Also, cut the stem to see its triangular keeled shape with a ridge on the underside, hence the common name. The bell-like, six-pointed flowers have green veins; the flowers of this onion species have no pink in them.

Where and when to gather

The angled onion likes semidomesticated weedy yards, vacant lots, and roadsides in full sun. It grows throughout the California Floristic Province, and has a long harvesting period on the Pacific Coast. The succulent green leaves can be eaten as soon as they emerge with the fall and winter rains. The bulbs can be harvested when the leaves die back in summer.

The white flowers of angled onion bloom in late winter and early spring.

How to gather

I recommend pulling up the entire plant to use like young green onions. During the rainy season, the plant will usually pull readily from the soil. Cut the leaves to a few inches above the ground, leaving the root in place, if you think this plant needs to be encouraged. The flowers can be snipped with scissors or fingers.

How to use

To use the leaves and immature bulb like green onions, put briefly in cold water and then chop finely. They can be sautéed separately or incorporated into stews, omelets, stir-fries, tuna salad, and pastas. Longer cooking brings out the sweetness and tames the pungency.

Future harvests

In areas where there is concern about native species, the spread of angled onion is undesirable, so harvest it by removing the entire plant. In New Zealand and Australia, for example, the governments sponsor a fight against angled onion's continuing spread. In weedy areas where angled onion may be the only edible wild plant, you may want to leave some behind to spread.

beavertail cactus

Opuntia basilaris var. *basilaris*
beavertail prickly pear

`EDIBLE` buds, flowers, fruit, pads, seeds

The spectacular, showy beavertail cactus, like the other prickly pear cacti of the Mojave and Sonoran Deserts, produces five edible parts—buds, flowers, fruit, pads or stems, and seed.

Widespread in the deserts of California, beavertail cactus has gray-green, succulent, fleshy stems called pads (or nopales, or joints). The flower buds, perched side by side along the top rim of the blue-gray oval leaves, are tasty eating before they bloom. Beavertail pads and buds are some of the most delicious among prickly pear cacti. The small flower buds taste like tender artichoke hearts, and in fact are excellent cooked with butter and garlic. The flowers and fruit that follow the buds are also significant foods.

How to identify

Identifying characteristics of beavertail cactus are the blue-gray color of the flattened stem segments and its small size,

The edible buds of beavertail cactus line the rim of the succulent edible pads, then bloom in March and April.

usually less than 2 or 3 feet. The individual pads are from 3 to 14 inches long and 3 to 6 inches wide, and are shaped like ping-pong paddles without handles (or beavertails). In spring, this plant responds to the high temperatures and drought of its environs with showy pink to magenta flowers, which are hard to miss in the desert. The blossoms emit a fragrance like sweet watermelon. The spineless fruit, about 1 inch long, is green or tinged with purple and dries to tan.

Where and when to gather

Look for beavertail cactus in many different habitats, from sandy, gravelly valleys to dry, rocky slopes, from Mexico to the California deserts. It grows in both the Mojave and Sonoran Deserts. Buds are ready to gather in March and April. Flowers open from March through April, and fruit can be gathered in June and July. Pads are most tender in May and June.

How to gather

Because of the absence of large spines, gathering beavertail pads is less daunting than with other prickly pears. Yet the almost invisible, hairlike spines (glochids) present in all parts of this plant must be carefully and thoroughly removed. Buds can be easily plucked with gloved fingers or tongs. The glochids should be scorched off over a flame or removed by rolling the pads vigorously in a towel, in gravel, or in sand. Wetting the pads down first makes the job easier.

How to use

The pads and buds are the outstanding edible features of beavertail cactus. Buds can be eaten raw, steamed, baked, or roasted. The buds, raw or cooked, can be dried and stored, eaten with pasta or with chili and onions, or dipped in sauce or garlic butter. The flowers can be eaten raw or cooked. Pads should be harvested while young, the glochids removed, and then cooked by sautéing, boiling, or roasting until any sliminess disappears. They can be used in many dishes, from stir-fries to tortillas. They can be sun-dried, stored, and reconstituted later, and also eaten raw. The fruits of beavertail cactus are not juicy like other prickly pears, but they can be eaten raw, baked, or dried.

Future harvests

Only harvest beavertail parts where you find a good stand of these slow-growing cacti, and leave some fruit or buds on each plant. Removal of a pad or two is a form of pruning, and can result in two or three pads appearing where one previously grew.

Caution

Before I learned about glochids, I once ate a raw beavertail bud without removing the glochids. I noticed them, but fortunately experienced only brief minor discomfort. I would not do that now. Juice made from the beavertail fruit should be consumed in small quantities, since sometimes an unusual reaction can occur, described as a chilling sensation.

bigleaf maple

Acer macrophyllum

Oregon maple, broadleaf maple, white maple

EDIBLE flowers, sap

Bigleaf maple produces flowers that are delicious eaten raw or fried, and everyone who tries making maple syrup from these trees is impressed.

A deciduous hardwood tree with leaves that turn golden in the fall, bigleaf maple is a magnificent shade tree. It is the largest maple in the west, though we don't often see it reach its full height of 100 feet tall anymore. It also produces flowers that are delicious eaten raw or fried. Maple syrup from bigleaf maple is currently being investigated for production. It has a unique flavor, and it's ours, found within our own state, rather than being shipped from thousands of miles away.

How to identify

In the spring, the flowers of the different maples are small but beautiful when examined closely. The bigleaf maple has the largest, most ornamental flowers of

The luxuriant flowers of bigleaf maple are edible, blooming in March and April.

the maples, consisting of sweet-smelling greenish yellow flowers in pendant racemes 6 inches long.

The silhouette of a maple leaf is so familiar that it's become almost a taxonomic term, as in "maple-leaf-shaped," which basically means a simple hand-shaped (palmate) leaf with pointy tips. Bigleaf maple leaves can be up to 12 inches long, and are a beautiful deep-orange color when they first emerge in the spring, presaging the golden color they will turn in the fall before dropping.

Where and when to gather

Bigleaf maples grow from British Columbia south through the Coast Ranges of California to San Diego County, on the west slopes of the Sierra Nevada to 5,000 feet, and on the south slope of the San Bernardino Mountains. They can be found in valleys, on stream banks, and near rivers, where they achieve their greatest height and greatest lifespan of up to 300 years. Snip the flowers in March and April. Tap the sap in late winter—January and February—as

The large, flexible leaves of bigleaf maple cast a comfortable shade.

leaf buds begin to open, ideally on a warm and sunny day following a few days of freezing temperatures.

How to gather

Were you ever in a sugaring house in Vermont? It would be difficult to reproduce the steamy atmosphere of that traditional facility, but amateur sap-makers in California use the same equipment. To tap the sap, make a hole with a drill bit no larger than 2 inches in diameter and no deeper than 2 inches into the tree. Use a spout that won't rust, preferably of stainless steel. When finished, clean the holes with fresh water, and leave them unplugged to heal on their own. Use pruning shears to snip maple flowers.

How to use

Use the flowers as you would elderberry flowers—battered and fried, candied, or incorporated into puddings. Boil the sap till it becomes concentrated. Bigleaf maple has approximately the same concentration of sugar in its sap as the eastern sugar maple, though the flavor of the syrup is slightly different. For both species, it takes about forty to fifty gallons of sap to produce one gallon of syrup. The tricky part is to encounter the same conditions of freezing nights and warmer days that are more common back east.

Future harvests

Tap a specific maple tree only once every two or three years. Tap only trees at least 8 inches in diameter and in good health.

black nightshade

Solanum americanum

American black nightshade, glossy nightshade, small–flowered nightshade

`EDIBLE` leaves, berries

For many years, the innocent and edible black nightshade, probably from South America, has been confused with a toxic plant called deadly nightshade, *Atropa belladonna*, which has distinctly different leaves, flowers, and fruit.

Black nightshade leaves are widely eaten greens through many parts of the world. And the ripe berries, with a taste somewhere between blueberry and tomato, make a unique and well-loved sauce, pie, or salsa. On the north and central coasts, where cool, foggy summers can make it hard to grow tomatoes, black nightshade

A volunteer black nightshade thrives in a central coast garden, revealing its white flowers and edible leaves.

Black nightshade is simultaneously decked with unripe green berries, which should not be eaten, and fully ripe shiny black berries, which are delicious.

is a find. Why has black nightshade been falsely accused? It's a familiar story of the repetition of undocumented, untested information. The differences in appearance between the two species are clear, the most obvious being that black nightshade has tiny white flowers, whereas deadly nightshade has larger tubular purple flowers.

How to identify

Black nightshade is an annual that can act like a biennial or a perennial, depending on when it germinated and the temperature and rainfall occurring during its lifetime. It grows about 2 feet high and 3 feet wide, and is usually wider than it is tall. The alternate leaves are medium green when young, dark green when older, and ovate with toothed margins. Small,

white, five-petaled flowers are surrounded by a calyx (united sepals, or the leaflike structures cupping the flower) that is not attached to the fruit. The berries that follow grow in bunches and are shiny and smooth, first green, then deep black and glossy when ripe. They are about the size of an English pea, about ¼ inch in diameter.

Where and when to gather

Black nightshade grows throughout the California Floristic Province. The berries ripen in July and August. Gather only completely ripe berries, black with no green lines remaining. In November and December, black nightshade germinates, appearing almost overnight. Young leaves, identified by their lighter green color, can be harvested for greens until the plant flowers. Greens from plants growing from the previous summer may be bitter. On the coast, where fog supplies the moisture for seed germination, new young plants continue to appear in August, ripening berries in September and October.

How to gather

Berries are picked by hand individually. It is not uncommon to find flowers, unripe fruit, and ripe fruit on the plant at the same time. Collect only the completely black fruit. Young leaves are snipped or plucked from the plant.

How to use

Eat ripe, cooked berries in jams, pies, sauces, applesauce, salsas, and chutneys. Or eat them raw in salads. Add to garnish roasted vegetables just at the end of cooking. The taste and texture are like very small cherry tomatoes, with an extra-rich, deep, tart but slightly sweet flavor all their own. Boil young leaves for 15 minutes.

Future harvests

When black nightshade appears on its own, it usually requires some control. So you can feel free to eat it. Some gardeners treat volunteer plants as regular garden vegetables.

Caution

Initially, eat leaves and berries well cooked and in small quantities, to ensure that you have no allergic reaction to them. Only eat young leaves and fully ripe berries. The black, round fruits of the true deadly nightshade could conceivably be mistaken for the fruit of black nightshade, but the flowers, never. So identify the plant by the flowers, not solely by the berries.

bladderpod

Peritoma arborea; Cleome isomeris, formerly *Isomeris arborea*
spider flower, burro fat, shrimp plant

EDIBLE flowers, immature seeds

Bladderpod's flowers are edible, and so are the sweet "peas" (or immature fruits) that follow.

Bladderpod, a distinctively pungent ever-green shrub, is found in both California's deserts and southern coastal scrub. With its cheerful yellow flowers, it may be the only plant blooming, or even looking alive, in some parts of the Mojave Desert in winter and early spring. This attractive species is one of the hardiest plants, blooming even after several years of severe drought. The unripe fruits are sought-after delicacies. Harvesting the fresh, juicy peas in the brown-gray landscape is a startling situation, and is testimony to the advantages of the long taproot of this plant.

How to identify

A rounded shrub growing 3 to 6 feet high and equally wide, bladderpod has showy yellow flowers with four petals each and leaflets in threes. The flowers form inflated pods of 2 to 3 inches in length with a seam along the side and a point at the tip. The foliage has been described as evil-smelling on some shrubs, yet on others an odor is barely noticeable.

Where and when to gather

Bladderpod is common in the lower half of the state, up to 4,000 feet elevation. It has one subspecies that loves the desert and another that grows on the south coast, so it can be gathered by both desert and coastal foragers in southern California. Bladder-pod blooms from January through April in the desert, producing pods while it is still in full bloom, so flowers can be gathered from winter through spring, and occasionally after that. This plant, with its long, exuberant bloom period, produces edible blossoms and peas at the same time, which are easy to spot and to harvest. Peas can be gathered from March through early May.

How to gather

The peapods and flowers are easily snipped from the plant.

Bladderpod blooming in the desert is a favorite of native bees.

How to use

The flower buds can be prepared like capers. The flowers must be cooked for four hours to remove the bitterness and become sweet. They can then be mixed with cooked onions and salt and eaten on a tortilla, a favored dish of some native southern California and Mexican tribes. Harvest the immature seeds in the pods as you would garden peas, splitting the pod along the side and shelling them. I find that these peas, though juicy and sweet, have a very strong taste when raw, so they are best boiled for about fifteen minutes.

Future harvests

Harvest moderately from any one area. A bladderpod shrub in March and April is a pollinator oasis, attracting humming-birds and native bees in huge quantities, so remember to share with them.

blue camas

Camassia quamash

small camas, quamash, sego, Indian hyacinth

EDIBLE bulb

The dense, white bulbs of camas can be slow-cooked down to a deliciously sweet, creamy, caramelized cake.

Camas historically was one of the most important root foods for many of our continent's western indigenous peoples. It has been enjoyed in our region for at least 7,700 years. Archaeologists have found evidence of skillfully dug pits 6 feet long, which were filled with heated stones, and had a channel for pouring water into the pit to create the steam needed for slow-cooking. Camas played a dramatic role in the settling of the western regions of our country. Indicative of the importance of camas were the Nez Perce Wars of 1877, partially the result of the destruction of the Nez Perce camas fields by white settlers—who also found camas to be delicious.

In referring to the many tantalizing taste overtones of camas, fans mention baked sweet potato with a hint of fig, baked pear, sweet chestnut, maple sugar, vanilla, or pumpkin. Cooked camas lends itself to many cuisines and can be eaten alone or used to sweeten other foods.

How to identify

Look for the "Skye blue petals that resemble lakes of fine clear water," as Meriwether Lewis described the camas fields. Camas's tall, showy flower stalks hold from ten to thirty large blue flowers on a spikelet, surrounded by several grasslike leaves. The flowers on the leafless flower stalk open sequentially from the bottom, four or five flowers at a time. Long, narrow petals vary in color from pale to dark lilac-blue. The seed capsules are relatively rigid. The round bulb, from 1 to 2 inches wide, has a paper-thin irregular coating of dark brown tissue.

Where and when to gather

Camas can be found in northern California, including the foothills of the Sierra Nevada and in the Modoc Plateau in northeastern California. Patchy occurrences have also been found in Marin and Mendocino Counties. Fond of full sun and some moisture, it grows along seasonal watercourses, wet meadows, swales (long, narrow depressions that retain water), and annual floodplains. Opinions differ as to when to harvest camas. Some harvest it before it flowers when the sugars are still thought to be stored in the edible roots. Others think the bulbs last longer if harvested in September and October, which is when I gather it.

A blue camas flower appears in April near a creek in Mendocino County.

How to gather

Although it is easier to dig camas from March to April, just before blooming, and the bulb, still connected to its flower, is more easily distinguished from death camas at this time, these bulbs don't keep as well as those dug later, after the flowers have died down. Camas dug in September and October are at maximum weight and can be kept for a long time. The bulbs are found 2 to 6 inches below the surface.

How to use

Camas contains inulin, a starch requiring lengthy cooking to convert to fructose and become digestible. The Indians of the west, famous for their earth-oven cookery, steamed camas bulbs for thirty-six hours, so the starch was slowly converted, the bulbs turning brown as they reached their peak of delicious sweetness. If you eat the bulbs earlier than that, you may get indigestion.

In the absence of earth ovens, try cooking camas in a steamer within a slow cooker after first boiling them in water for one hour to shorten the cooking period. Add water up to the bottom of the bulbs in the cooker or casserole. Cook for at least twelve hours, adding more water as necessary. If they are gummy, they're not cooked enough. Slice and cook in hot oil with salt.

Indigenous peoples formed cooked camas into cakes for drying, the most popular traditional way of storing it. The cakes varied from finger-sized to ten-pound

The bulbs of camas are a sight that produces joy in those who've tasted them.

loaves. Cooked camas can be added to puddings and cakes. It is spectacular used in South Asian desserts like ras malai, keer, and rice pudding, especially those using rosewater.

Future harvests

Like other edible members of the lily family, camas was traditionally gathered in a sustainable manner, which should be emulated today. The larger bulbs were removed for eating, while offsets clinging to the sides of the larger bulb were replanted in the loosened soil to grow into a future harvest in two to four years. I highly recommend growing camas at home, for the beauty of its bloom, to savor its bulbs, and to hone identification and sustainable foraging skills.

That same year of 1877, the Bannock and Shoshone peoples found that settlers had been pasturing hogs in the crucially important camas fields they thought had been ceded to them by treaty, which let to the Camas Prairie War of Idaho. The direct cause of that war was hunger for camas. Current high levels of feral pigs, possibly the descendants of those earlier camas field destroyers, are still uprooting what is left of California's camas fields; I've seen this myself. Encourage control of these rapidly increasing mammals.

Caution

Death camas, or common star lily, is a native plant that produces a toxic bulb. This species, *Toxicoscordion fremontii*, has small, creamy-white flowers in loose clusters, easily distinguished from the blue flowers of blue camas. The beginner should harvest camas bulbs only when the flower or seed stalk is still attached.

blue dicks

Dichelostemma capitatum

pig-nut, purple head, brodiaea, cacomites, wild hyacinth, Indian potato

`EDIBLE` corm

This perennial wildflower, with its tasty bulb, is one of the most popular species in the group known as Indian potatoes.

Blue dicks used to turn the hills and meadows of many parts of California blue in the spring. Such a sight is too infrequently seen these days. Its older name, pig-nut, indicates how vulnerable this and other native bulbs (or corms) are to the wild boars now thriving unchecked in many parts of northern California. The bulb is a surprisingly strong grower, one of the most vigorous of the Indian potatoes, and could, with our help, make a comeback. Taste it once, properly cooked, and you'll want to be part of its revival.

How to identify

Like other Indian potato plants, blue dicks can grow from 10 inches to 3 feet tall. The flower color ranges from blue and

Blue dicks has a wide range in California. This specimen is growing on Mount Tamalpais in Marin County.

Indian Potatoes

The term Indian potatoes refers to several genera of western native bulbs, usually in the lily family, whose underground roots in the form of bulbs or corms were traditionally harvested as root foods. Information about indigenous practices of sustainably harvesting Indian potatoes has informed current thought about the complex land management practices of California's tribal peoples.

This group of wild plants is renowned for the beauty of their flowers as well. The species of Indian potatoes described in this book, just a sampling of all that are available, include camas, blue dicks, butterfly mariposa lily, golden prettyface brodiaea, harvest brodiaea, wild hyacinth, and pussy ears.

Gathering and storing
Indian potatoes

Historical and ethnographic accounts strongly indicate that indigenous land management practices helped to maintain the health of the Indian potato fields.

Indian potatoes are usually harvested when the flower seed begins to ripen. If the seed stalk is still present, follow it with your fingers into the soil. Using a digging stick with a sharpened point, a crowbar, trowel, or shovel, dig in a few different spots around the seed stalk, 2 to 3 inches out from the plant. Use the digging stick to lever the bulbs out. The bulbs will be found from 2 to 8 inches down, and the challenge is to avoid destroying them while digging.

Indigenous Californians returned annually to the same areas to harvest with their pointed wooden digging sticks. That process kept the soil loosened and aerated, made harvesting easier, preventing destruction of the bulbs, and helped the young plants to grow. Heavy clay soils at the end of California's dry season can be hard enough to break a trowel, but a digging stick in the hands of an experienced gatherer is a perfect tool. Prairies full of Indian potatoes traditionally were burned frequently to increase fertility and prevent the invasion of shrubs or trees.

blue-purple to lavender and pink. Blue dicks has curved flower stalks (scapes) up to 2 feet tall. The flower, which consists of about eight small, bell-shaped blossoms closely pressed together at the top of the stem, can range in size from 2 inches across to less than 1 inch. The corm is very productive, with numerous cormlets attached to the mother corm. The cormlets often have a sharp elongated tip. The grasslike leaves frequently wither by flowering time.

The key to sustainable harvesting of Indian potatoes consists of saving the large mother bulb for eating, removing the immature bulblets that are lightly attached to the bulb, and replanting them in the loosened soil. Some areas should be left alone for two to four years after harvesting and replanting. Once harvested, the bulbs of some species can be stored, skins intact, in the refrigerator for up to seven months. The natives traditionally mashed them into cakes, which were dried and stored, or they ate them immediately.

Unrefrigerated, they will begin to sprout as early as October, putting down roots from the base and sending up the first narrow leaf blade from the bulb's creamy heart, just as they would in the soil. In this way, native bulbs are reliable indicators of the time of year.

How to prepare Indian potatoes

Rub corms or bulbs (these are botanically different but are prepared the same way) in a towel until the dry, brown, hairy overcoat is loosened and comes off, leaving the shiny white bulbs, or peel individually. Boil water and add the bulbs. Depending on the size, cooking can take as little as ten to fifteen minutes at a full boil. Remove, slice thinly, and add salt and pepper to taste.

Or brush the cleaned bulbs with oil and bake in the oven at 275 to 300°F for twenty to thirty minutes, depending on the size of the bulbs. Be careful not to overbake. Roasted like this, the bulbs develop a delicious nutty flavor and an almost chestnutlike floury texture, making them hard to resist. They can also be boiled and then sautéed in hot oil.

Cooked in earth ovens until they caramelized, Indian potatoes were prized for their sweetness. To simulate an earth oven, add ⅛ inch of water to a roasting pan and cover it with aluminum foil. Cook until soft, and remove the delicious gooey mass with a spatula. Crockpots are also useful for slow-cooking Indian potatoes.

Where and when to gather

Blue dicks has a wide distribution in grassy and scrubby areas throughout California, including the deserts and mountains, excepting the east side of the Sierra Nevada. The plant blooms from February to June. Harvest the corms when the plants begin to set seed, from June through July.

How to gather

If you come across blue dicks in the spring and plan to return to harvest the corm in the late summer, use a digging stick or crowbar to loosen the surrounding soil, taking care to not harm the corm. Otherwise, returning in the fall when the soil can be rock hard, you are likely to miss or damage the bulb. Only harvest corms of this once-common species in a spot where there are numerous plants, and then only if you can watch a particular plant through the seasons, keep the soil loose, and eventually harvest it properly.

How to use

Remove the thin outer coat from the blue dicks corm, and then boil, steam, or roast it. The Indian potato can be mashed after boiling and made into little cakes. Serve as appetizers or snacks. I like to boil and then sauté them. Cook for thirty minutes to two hours, depending on the size of the corm. Long cooking is necessary to bring out the flavor and sweetness, but camas is the only Indian potato that requires more than a day of cooking in an earth oven.

Future harvests

Research indicates that indigenous harvesting techniques of replanting cormlets, loosening the soil, and controlled burns can increase populations of blue dicks and other native bulbs. After replanting the small cormlets, if possible, return to remove weedy grasses and keep the soil loosened, to encourage the plant's growth.

blue elderberry

Sambucus nigra subsp. *caerulea*

Mexican elderberry, music bush, tree of music, mountain blue elderberry

`EDIBLE` flowers, berries

Blue elderberrry's large white flower heads in spring are followed in summer by clusters of juicy, deep blue berries high in vitamin C.

California's blue elderberry is related to elderberry species around the world, and its berries are considered among the best. Taxonomical opinion may sometimes lump the mountain blue elderberry with the shrub from lower elevations, but those growing in the mountains are thought to have particularly sweet berries.

The flowers of blue elderberry have flat-topped circles of countless tiny ivory-colored flowers with a slight green tinge. Bury your nose in the lush flower heads for a delightful sweet fragrance. These flowers also make a good tea, and are used to make fritters and pancakes. Watch the flower heads face fully toward the sun in

Blue elderberry provides a festive spring bloom display from northern to southern California.

late spring, then slowly turn over to face the earth, as they droop from the weight of the ripening green berries. Such languid summertime observations help you to be on the spot to get your share when the berries ripen, since everybody from quail to bears loves elderberries.

How to identify

Blue elderberry is a deciduous, semiwoody, large shrub to small tree with compound green leaves comprising five to nine leaflets per stem; the entire leaf is 6 to 8 inches long. It can be a single-trunked small tree or a multitrunked shrub. Specimens that have been cut to the ground will sprout up with numerous flexible shoots. Their twigs are pithy inside, offering a good nesting place for native bees and the valley elderberry longhorn beetle, a federally threatened species. The hollow stems with the pith removed also make good clappers and flutes, so the shrub is sometimes called the music bush. The fruit is berrylike with

The ripening berries of the blue elderberry are a familiar sight along California's roadways and woodland edges.

three to five seeds inside. The berries' blue to purple-black ripe skin develops a bloom that changes them to a luscious deep powder blue.

Where and when to gather

Elderberries are found in many parts of California, from suburban backyards and along freeways to remote woodland edges. They can grow in full sun or part shade. They grow in the Sierra Nevada to 8,000 feet elevation.

Berry-ripening and bloom times depend on where in California you live. In the Central Valley and other warm inland areas, elderberries are in full bloom in April and May, with fruit ripening from early July to August. On the coast, flowers can be cut for fritters in late May through July, with fruit ripening from late July to August. In a California summer, elderberries are blooming or ripening somewhere.

How to gather

Cut berry-covered flower heads at the base and store in bags or cartons until ready to remove the berries from the stems. Or, run a large-toothed comb through the berry clusters, dropping the berries onto a sheet or box below.

How to Use

Remember, eat only the flowers and berries, and eat the berries only when fully ripe. Stems, leaves, and twigs are toxic and should not be included in any elderberry preparation. To separate the berries from the stems, put the whole flower head in the freezer. When frozen, the berries separate easily from the stems.

Though sampling a few very ripe, very blue-black berries is enjoyable, using elderberries in baked goods, especially muffins, brings out the best in them. Also they are delicious in pies, pancakes, and waffles, and in sauces, syrups, and jellies. For winemaking, combine elderberries with wild grapes to add acidity.

Drying the berries brings out their sweetness and flavor, eliminating the slight tinge of bitterness found in the fresh fruit. They become elderberry raisins with little trouble. Spread them on a tray and leave in a warm place, safe from other foragers, but not directly in the sun. Even casual storage in a paper bag produces good elderberry raisins that can be incorporated into muffins even five years later.

Future harvests

These deciduous shrubs thrive with regular coppicing (cutting to the ground) every five years or so. New shoots will grow into shrubs 3 to 5 feet tall in just one year. The pruner's saw is the tool of renewal for the music bush.

blue flax

Linum lewisii
prairie flax
`EDIBLE` seeds

Blue flax shares many of the beneficial qualities of the better known related European species of flax, which has been used to make clothing and food for at least 30,000 years.

Blue flax is a slender perennial wildflower with flowers of a rich sky blue color that grace our woodlands and prairies. The seeds of blue flax are somewhat mucilaginous, producing a mucouslike gel when they come in contact with water. This characteristic slows carbohydrate metabolism and blunts spikes in blood glucose, promoting cardiac and digestive health. Their pleasant, nutty taste makes them fun to gather and use for your own wild flaxseed.

How to identify

Blue flax has an open, medium blue flower, veined in darker blue. Each five-petaled flower is over 1 inch wide, and lives just a day or two. Each stem produces several flowers, blooming from the bottom upward. The seeds of blue flax are produced on the lower flowers, while those above continue to bloom. The brown seeds are flattened to rounded, becoming slimy when wet. The stem is leafy when the plant is young, gradually losing most of its leaves as it matures. The small leaves are narrow, alternate, linear, and about ¾ inch long. The plant grows about 2 feet tall, with several stems growing from a woody root crown.

Where and when to gather

Blue flax grows in open woodland and grasslands throughout the California Floristic Province and also in the eastern Sierra Nevada, the White and Inyo Mountains, and the desert. It usually grows in scattered bunches. It flowers May to July. Keep an eye on the late summer bloom to establish when the seeds are ripe; they will be impermeable to a fingernail.

How to gather

Cut flower stems with ripened and ripening seeds and place in paper bag, allowing the seeds to drop to the bottom.

How to use

Toast the seeds. Grind them, adding to baked goods, or use as a seasoning.

Blue flax has flowers, buds, and ripening seed at the same time.

Future harvests

Sow some of the seeds you have gathered nearby in a similar sunny or partly shady spot.

Caution

Do not eat flaxseed raw. The seeds contain cyanide, which is destroyed in the cooking process. Always drink ample liquids with any species of flaxseed, because of the high amount of soluble fiber in it, and to bring out the beneficial mucilaginous quality.

Pinole: California's Seed Foods

As a seed collector, it took me some years to realize that many of the native plant seeds I was wild-collecting to grow native plants were also food. During the Spanish settlement era in California, the word pinole, a Hispanic version of the Aztec word *pinol* or *pinolillo*, was used to refer to the whole panoply of roasted and then ground seed foods enjoyed by Mexican and California Indians, and the term is still used today. I continue to be surprised by just how many different species of plant seeds were used to make pinole in California.

By adding these delicious and nutritious seeds to your foraging repertoire, you also gain knowledge about the life processes of plants. Each species is unique in its manner of flowering, ripening, and dispersing seed, though members of the same genus, such as clarkias or wildryes, are often quite similar.

From the dozens of plants that were used to make pinole, I have narrowed the list to the most accessible, tasty, and easy to collect and clean. One exception may be the native grasses, which in some cases require more work. Like most grains from grass species, two more or less persistent bracts (leaflike structures surrounding the seed) must be separated and removed from the seed before eating. (See California's Native Bunchgrasses, page 69, for details of preparation.)

Nongrass species (forbs) are usually easier to clean, because many species have seeds that drop free of seed capsules on their own. Placed in a canvas or paper bag (plastic can cause mold), they will release their seed, which will fall to the bottom of the bag. After a good shake of the bag, the dry and inedible chaff can then be lifted off and discarded, or used for mulch in your garden.

As well as porridge, you can also use native seed foods in crackers, cookies, and muffins. Crackers in particular show off the different shapes, colors, and flavors of the seeds. Nut cookies with toasted chia and red maids seeds have long been a staple of our open houses, workshops, and holiday baking.

Golden chia seed is one famous example of the delicious native plant seed foods available in California. Others covered in this book (and there are many more) are blue flax, blue wildrye, California bottlebrush grass, California brome, California buttercup, California oatgrass, California oniongrass, common tarweed, farewell to spring, giant blazing star, goldfields, Indian ricegrass, meadow barley, meadowfoam, mountain mule's ears, Nevada stickleaf, purple sage, purslane, red maids, tall coastal plantain, thistle sage, tidytips, and yellow pond lily.

Seed biology for the pinole enthusiast

Ripe seed usually has a hard, tough seed coat, which is usually but not always dark in color, and usually but not always hard enough that a fingernail has difficulty penetrating it. All this becomes obvious when observed in the wild rather than when read on the page.

Some seeds will fall readily out of the seed capsule, which will be dry, brittle, and usually tan or brown. Some seed heads, like chia, need to be bent over or turned upside down to help the seed drop out where you want it. Red maids and miner's lettuce share the characteristic that the seed leaves clasping the flower and then the maturing seed stay green, moist, and flexible, even when the seed inside is shiny, black, ripe, and ready to gather. Other seed capsules split explosively along a seam when ripe, sounding rather like a gun going off, which is called dehiscing. Plants with dehiscent seed capsules need a deep bag or basket to contain the dehiscing seeds.

Many wild seeds ripen indeterminately, which means that the seeds at the bottom of the flower stalk may have ripened and fallen out, while the flowers at the top of the flower stalk are still ripening seed or sometimes even still in bloom.

This sequential ripening is part of nature's strategy to enhance chances for successful reproduction.

One great secret of seed gatherers is that, if the plant has begun the maturation process, some seed can still ripen after the seed stalk is picked. This means that you don't have to be present at the exact moment of its complete ripening, which can be logistically difficult. In other words, you can gather when the seed is still somewhat immature. Harvest the seed stalks and leave them in a paper bag to ripen and dry completely. The seeds will eventually fall to the bottom of the bag. Dried seed can be stored for long periods of time without spoiling.

Few of these seeds have been analyzed nutritionally. One that has is small-flowered blazing star, *Mentzelia albicaulis*. It only produces a few tablespoons of seed per plant, yet seed caches found in storage jars in archaeological sites indicate that plant populations were high enough to produce hundreds of pounds of this seed. The fact that so much human energy was allocated to gather this tiny seed speaks highly for its edibility and nutritional properties, which include high-quality lipids, protein, and carbohydrates.

blue palo verde

Parkinsonia florida, formerly *Cercidium floridum*

greenbark acacia, lluvia de oro, shower of gold

`EDIBLE` unripe fruit, seeds

Blue palo verde manages to provide edible flowers, peas, and seeds in the desert, while standing virtually leafless most of the year.

A large shrub or small tree of the desert, blue palo verde has distinctive pale olive-blue-green twigs that inspire its common name. In early spring, when its golden-yellow flowers appear, it earns its Spanish nickname *lluvia de oro,* or "shower of gold." By the time summer's heat has wilted the leaves and flowers, the large seeds begin to ripen. Before they ripen, try the immature green seeds, which are delicious when eaten raw or cooked, and look and taste very much like sweet, tender garden peas. The sweet-tasting flowers are also edible raw, and the dried seeds can be used to make sprouts.

How to identify

Blue palo verde grows relatively quickly to 30 feet tall and wide. From a distance along the edges of a wash, it forms large multitrunked mounds that, because of their closely intertwined limbs, give a pale

The dried seedpods of blue palo verde may hang on from the previous year as late as April.

green appearance even when leafless. This distinctive blue-green bark has photosynthetic capabilities, which allow it to survive being leafless most of the year. Small spines at the leaf nodes are also green.

When its leaves do make their brief appearance, they consist of tiny, wedge-shaped, compound blue-green leaflets, one to three per leaf. Blue palo verde's bright yellow flowers have five petals and ten stamens. The fruit is a pod with one to three seeds in a tan, brittle seed capsule, which is larger than the seedpod of foothills palo verde. The seeds are flattish, dark brown, irregularly circular, and about the size of a pea. Sometimes a paler brown area surrounds the dark brown center.

Blue palo verde thrives in a dry wash in Joshua Tree National Park.

Where and when to gather

Blue palo verde is found in the Mojave and Sonoran deserts in southern California, particularly in open sandy places below 1,200 feet with at least seasonal moisture. It can usually be found near a wash or spring. It blooms March through May, so gather flowers then. The green seeds form shortly thereafter from April through June, and the ripe seeds appear in June and July and can hold on until the following spring. Foothills palo verde has a wider distribution and tolerates drier conditions.

How to gather

Carefully snip off the flowers, avoiding the thorns. The young seedpods open along a seam, resembling garden peas in the pod. Use your fingernail to trace this seam, just as you would open a pea pod, and similarly rejoice in finding the juicy green peas within. Gather the mature seeds and clean in a similar manner.

How to use

The flowers can be eaten raw. The mature seeds were traditionally dried and ground into flour. But the green "peas"—the immature green seeds—are the best part to use and can be eaten raw or steamed. The dried beans are considered survival food, but make tasty sprouts when kept moistened for a few days.

Future harvests

This widespread desert tree makes an intriguing landscape plant, so don't hesitate to plant it in your yard if you live in the desert. Blue palo verde is an important nurse plant for some cacti, providing shade, shelter, and rain drip while the cactus is young. Because blue palo verde is relatively short-lived, when it dies, it leaves room for the cactus to thrive.

blue wildrye

Elymus glaucus

`EDIBLE` seeds

If the idea of harvesting your own cereal grains from native grasses appeals to you, include the fast-growing and abundant native blue wildrye in your foraging.

This slender plant is widespread in California and elsewhere in the west. Unlike most native bunchgrasses, blue wildrye is a perennial grass whose flowering stalk is more noticeable than its leaves. Prolific and adaptable, its easily gathered edible seeds are larger than most. Its seedstalk has a characteristic look like a golden braid. When the seeds ripen, they almost ask for your fingers to grasp the inflorescence at the bottom and pull, sliding off the seeds into your hand for tomorrow's breakfast. Quick to germinate and grow, the plant is frequently used for restoration on stream banks and slopes.

How to identify

Blue wildrye is more flowering stalk than leaf. The flower stalk can be up to 5 feet tall, with the flowering part about 5 inches

Seeds of blue wildrye ripen in June and July.

Giant Wildrye

Blue wildrye's massive Sierran relative, giant wildrye, *Elymus condensatus*, was also harvested as a grain by the Paiute people on the east side of the Sierra Nevada. In his *Mountains of California*, John Muir recounts catching a rare glimpse of such a harvest near Lake Moraine: "There was a field of wild rye, growing in magnificent waving bunches six to eight feet high, bearing heads from six to twelve inches long. . . . I found them [the grains] about five-eights of an inch long, dark-colored, and sweet. Indian women were gathering it in baskets, bending down long hand-fuls, beating it out, and fanning it in the wind. . . . One caught glimpses of them here and there, in winding lanes and openings, while their incessant chat and laughter showed their heedless joy."

Blue wildrye is a common native bunchgrass that produces relatively large edible seeds.

long. The leafy part of the grass is seldom more than 1½ feet tall. Leaves range from blue-gray to green, with a waxy white coating, and are over 1 inch wide. The flowers are closely pressed to the flower stalk.

Without the flower stalks and seeds, the "bunch" itself (the leaf blades) has a somewhat weedy look, being rather coarse and broad across and not very dense. Each plant produces three to five flower stalks. These plants start to go dormant fairly early in the season, so some dead leaves are frequently present, a characteristic of some non-native weedy grasses.

Where and when to gather

Tolerant of sun and part shade, blue wildrye grows on the edges of open woodlands and with oaks, and also in meadows and near streams. Blue wildrye flowers from April to May in central and southern California, ripening seed from mid-May through June. It blooms in June and July in northern California, ripening seed in mid-July through August. Though it responds well to years of good moisture, it usually produces seed even in times of drought.

California's Native Bunchgrasses

Three-fourths of California's native bunch-grasses are perennial, which means that when some of their grass blades die and dry up during our dry summers, the crowns remain alive. When the sun gets lower, the days shorter, and whether the fall rains do or do not come, the new leaf blades and seed stalks begin to grow, giving them an advantage over annual grasses, whose seed requires moisture to germinate. Their huge fibrous root systems are already mature, extending down and out to 15 feet, holding and enriching the soil.

Annual grasses from Europe, Eurasia, and Africa, with shallow root systems that die midsummer, have invaded most California grasslands. This change means that the soil is no longer held by perennial root systems. The demise of our native bunchgrasses and the possible reversal of this decline is complicated, but the forager can begin to learn about these native grasses, know them by sampling the seeds they supply, and become an agent of their survival and renaissance. Native prairies, important food-gathering areas for indigenous peoples, cast a spell. Succumb to it.

Bunchgrasses grow from a central crown that remains relatively constant in size once it reaches maturity. This is true throughout the arid and semi-arid west. The sod-forming grasses used in lawns, in contrast, send out short underground roots (stolons) that produce a new grass plant for each stolon.

When you have determined that the seed of the bunchgrass is ripe, strip the flower stalk by sliding your partially closed fingers up the flowering stalk, and letting the seed drop into a paper bag or a tightly woven basket. Or else snip the entire stalk into a bag or basket, and beat, shake, or otherwise disturb the contents until the seeds loosen from the stalks and fall to the bottom of the bag.

A bit of grass terminology will help here, to explain what needs to be removed and what is edible. Grass flowers are

How to gather

Clasp the seed stalk between your fingers and thumb and slide your hand up with enough pressure so that the seed detaches. Drop the seed into a paper bag or box and proceed to the next stalk. Or, break off the seed stalk and place it in a canvas or paper bag, where the seed will detach on its own.

How to use

Use in mush, and in muffins, breads, goma-sio, and other baked goods. Roasted and ground as for gomasio, it has a toasty, pop-cornlike odor and taste, reminiscent of the smell of a movie theatre concession stand. Pinole in California and gomasio in Japan are both toasted, ground seeds used to characteristically arranged in spikelets, each spikelet having one or more florets. The spikelets are further grouped into panicles or spikes. A spikelet consists of two (or sometimes fewer) bracts at the base, called glumes, followed by one or more florets. A floret consists of the flower surrounded by two bracts, one external (the lemma) and one internal (the palea). The bracts called glumes and the bracts called the lemma and the palea make up the chaffy part of the grass seed that needs to be removed, leaving the edible part of the grain.

When I made my first bowl of breakfast mush from California brome, *Bromus carinatus*, I felt I had discovered a whole new world of possibilities. Nothing has been so stripped of nutrients as commercial breakfast cereals. It is a thrill to find, gather, clean, cook, and eat for breakfast whole grains that have been grown for you by California's own tough, perennial bunchgrasses.

To prepare, toast the seed, even if the bracts are still attached, in a frying pan, shaking it back and forth until lightly browned. Let cool and put in a clean coffee grinder; many folks keep a grinder just for cereals and spices. Grind briefly and place the ground seed and remaining chaff in a pot of water. The chaff will float to the top, and the dark seed, your breakfast, will sink to the bottom. Pour off the brownish water and repeat the process several times. Soak the seed for a couple of hours, drain the water, then cook with twice the amount of water as grain, until the grains have absorbed moisture, softened, and plumped up. Eat as breakfast porridge with honey and other condiments. You can also use the dry flour or cooked mush combined with wheat flour to make bread, muffins, cookies, biscuits, or crackers.

accompany other foods or to eat on their own. To clean the seeds, see California's Native Bunchgrasses, above.

Future harvests

Blue wildrye, with its advantageous height and its quick early growth, is a fairly widespread native grass. Sowing seed into nearby areas is likely to produce new plants. I am always heartened by the sight of these wild grains, which ask for no help to produce their crop.

borage

Borago officinalis
starflower, bee bush, bugloss

EDIBLE flowers, leaves, seeds

Borage is a tasty and extremely healthful wild green. Its leaves can be harvested both before and during flowering.

This plant both requires control and richly rewards our attention. Its bright blue flowers have a sweet flavor that is distinctly reminiscent of cucumber. Its flavorful leaves are the basis of many special dishes in several European cuisines. For example, it is used as a filling in Italian ravioli, as an ingredient in alcoholic (gin) drinks, in soups, and in a well-known German green sauce, Grüne Sobe, served over eggs or used as a salad dressing. Borage contains high amounts of many vitamins and minerals, so it has numerous medicinal uses. It is also esteemed for the healthy oil, GLA (gamma-linoleic acid), produced from its seeds. I used to regret, but I no longer do, the appearance of borage here and there, as I can easily and enjoyably consume almost all that I see.

How to identify

Borage sends up many rich blue, star-shaped flowers each spring, summer, and fall that make it easy to identify the plant. Though they are usually blue, some pink and white flowers can also occur. The flowers and the large, tough leaves are covered with tiny bristles that are less noticeable in younger plants. The bristles have no lasting sting and are not of concern.

The flowers have five narrow, triangular petals that are cupped by star-shaped flower leaves (bracts) between each petal. They frequently curve to face downward, exposing the distinctive pattern of flowers and bracts. Growing about 2 feet tall, the thick stem is the prickliest part of the plant. The plant begins its growth with its large, coarse leaves, 3 to 5 inches long and 3 inches wide, flat against the ground. The leaf veins are deeply incised.

Where and when to gather

Borage can be found throughout the California Floristic Province. Gather flowers as they bloom from late March through September and October. The leaves may be harvested before the plants flower and during as well. In central and southern coastal regions, borage blooms for much of the year, and the leaves can be harvested year-round.

How to gather

Pluck flowers just below the blossom to include only the blue petals. The leaves remain behind, clasping the flower and the stem. For wild greens, cut the plant's large, substantial basal leaves with a knife. You may want to use gloves because of

The unusual cucumberlike, sweet taste of the blue borage flower can flavor drinks and salads.

the leaves' bristles, or you can ignore the minor, temporary discomfort they cause.

How to use

Borage flowers are frequently used as decorations for salads, and also for baked goods, to which they offer their pleasantly sweet cucumber flavor. Place in ice trays, pour water over, and freeze, and use in lemonade and punchbowl drinks.

Wash and chop the leaves into $1/2$-inch pieces for eating raw combined with other wild greens, or cooked into sauces with onions. As they cook, their bristles soften and become undetectable. The flavor is easy to like. They can also be used to flavor pickled preserves, and they make a healthful raw component of weed pestos. The leaves also make a pleasant tea.

Future harvests

The spread of this species is of some concern. Its population seems to burgeon suddenly, after some years of appearing in only modest amounts, so do not worry about overharvesting. Borage self-seeds vigorously, so it is here to stay. Since the leaves are still delicious even when the flowers are blooming, it is a valuable wild green. Its continual spread could and should be alleviated by enthusiastic borage users. Offer to keep your neighbor's land borage-free as well, leaving a few plants to reseed.

bracken fern

Pteridium aquilinum var. *pubescens*
western bracken fern, brake, eagle fern

EDIBLE sprouts

One of the most common ferns in the world, found from California to Vermont to Japan, bracken fern provides a delicious fiddlehead— a tightly curled, young shoot—used in many types of dishes.

If you notice masses of bracken fern's tall reddish brown dead stalks in fall and winter in nearby pastures and woodlands, make a note of the location so you can return in the spring to harvest this superb fresh vegetable. With a unique taste— a combination of kale, asparagus, and almonds—it is eaten by millions of people. The trick is to find the fiddleheads as

they emerge straight from the ground and to harvest them before they unfurl. Unlike the fiddleheads of most ferns, they rise individually from underground rhizomes rather than from the crown of the plant.

How to identify

Bracken ferns are easy to spot, since their dense stands of plants 2 to 3 feet tall and

Bracken fern grows in large colonies throughout California.

equally wide have persistent dead leaves through the dormant season. Dormancy can be brought on by drought in the California Floristic Province and by cold winters in northern California. Each frond is leathery, about 3 to 5 feet long, composed of many subdivided leaflets, and shaped like a triangle with the widest part toward the stem. Their horizontal underground rhizomes are up to 6 feet long and covered with tiny black hairs.

Where and when to gather

Bracken fern grows in moist and dry, sunny and shady locations in many parts of the California Floristic Province, excluding the Central Valley. It can produce new fiddleheads for months, from February through May. It is frequently seen in pastures, near woods, in meadows, and on hillsides.

How to gather

Cut the fiddlehead when it is 6 to 8 inches long, before it has unfurled. It should still have a tight curl in the stalk. Use a knife, or snap it off with your fingers. Put it immediately into cool salty water.

How to use

Boil them in hot water, remove, and plunge again into cold salted water. The fiddleheads can also be sautéed after this step. Do not eat them unfurled or raw.

Future harvests

A shortage of bracken fern doesn't seem likely, but still, respect a good fiddlehead patch when you discover one. You're not the only one who likes them, so share with

Harvest the young sprouts of bracken fern before they unfurl.

the deer, cottontails, and ants. Many farmers and ranchers remove bracken ferns routinely from their land to make room for grass for grazing animals, so if you ask, they are unlikely to protest your harvest.

Caution

It is well-accepted that bracken fern fiddleheads are delicious, and equally well-accepted that they contain a carcinogenic substance (called ptaquiloside) known to cause cancer in lab rats. However, it is less well-known that this substance is water-soluble and can be almost totally eliminated by the way the fiddleheads are cooked. Since many things we eat contain carcinogens but are harmless if properly prepared and eaten in moderation, it is worth understanding and enjoying the proper way to eat bracken fern's curled new sprouts. Put simply, never eat them raw or after they have unfurled.

bull clover

Trifolium fucatum

sour clover, cow clover, pepper clover

EDIBLE leaves, flowers, young seedpods, seeds

The annual bull clover is well documented as one of the most important edible clovers, and also one of the easiest of native clovers to identify.

Native clovers, now somewhat uncommon and infrequently seen, are frequently mentioned in the ethnobotanical literature as being consumed with great enjoyment. Many California tribes broke winter's fast with a harvest of these juicy fresh greens, marking the joyous occasion by a special dance honoring them. We know that over half of California's thirty species of clover were harvested by the state's native peoples, some eaten raw, some baked, some steamed, and some eaten in conjunction with other foods, such as bay laurel nuts and/or salt. Some were eaten before flowering and some after.

How to identify

Bull clover has unusually large, 2-inch-wide, creamy white to yellow to pink flowers tipped with black. As the seeds ripen, they are enclosed by a puffy, succulent, shiny seedpod of pink and yellow. The foliage is also distinctive, with the usual three leaflets sporting clear-cut markings on each leaf that, as the leaflets develop, merge together to form one perfect triangle. The stems are hollow.

Where and when to gather

Bull clover is found in many plant communities, from coastal prairies and valley grasslands to pine forests, foothill woodlands, and chaparral. It equally favors both riparian (near a river, lake, or stream) areas and dry prairies, but is perhaps most delicious when growing in moist soil. Native peoples of California have been recorded as eating the leaves, flowers, and seeds of different species of native clovers in late winter and early spring, from February through April. Gather before and after they begin to bloom from February to June.

How to gather

Early accounts describe native peoples grazing the clover directly from the plant, as well as clipping and bundling it up to be carried home. Snipping with your fingernail works well for trailside snacking. To gather in quantity, use a knife or pruners. Harvest the leaves of bull clover before the plant flowers, taking leaves from different plants rather than destroying any one plant.

One of the most beautiful native clovers, bull clover was also one of the most frequently eaten.

How to use

Eat bull clover before and during flowering, either raw, baked, or steamed, with or without salt. Cooked or raw clover can be wrapped around bay laurel nut balls for a traditional hors d'oeuvre. Dip the plant parts in salt water to prevent digestive upset.

Future harvests

Non-native snails and slugs also devour native clovers with enthusiasm and may be significantly responsible for their decline. Anything that controls or discourages snails and slugs is good for clovers. Workers in native clover restoration projects use a combination of snail control methods, from using an organic compound that repels snails to hand removal to controlled burns. To plant bull clover, scatter seed in appropriate places that have few weedy grasses. Don't use non-native clovers as cover crops, since they are competitors of native clovers.

Caution

When first eating clover, sample a small amount, to test how your body responds. Combining clover leaves with bay nuts, soaking them in salt water, or boiling makes clovers more digestible. Most people don't have a problem consuming moderate amounts of bull clover.

butterfly mariposa lily

Calochortus venustus

white mariposa, sego lily, fairy lanterns, star tulip, globe lily

`EDIBLE` bulbs

The bulbs of the butterfly mariposa lily, a spectacular wildflower with a wide range in California, can be eaten like other Indian potatoes.

There can be no more beautiful group of flowers than those of the species of native bulbs called mariposa lilies. These graceful flowers are so elegant that they have been given the Spanish name for butterfly, *mariposa*. Butterfly mariposa lily has much variety in its flower color and in the exquisite design and coloring of the glands decorating its bowl-shaped flower. Because the bulb is edible, it's as though the most exquisite orchid also provides tasty nourishment.

How to identify

This member of the lily family grows from a solid bulb that is covered with a fibrous coat. A bulblet is produced within the axil of the basal leaf. Stem leaves appear early

The petals range from white to pink, but the yellow and maroon markings at the base of each petal are typical of butterfly mariposa lily.

in spring, grasslike and slender, dying down about the time the flowers emerge. The tall mariposas resemble a tulip but with broader, shorter petals. Petals are thick and lustrous, with a wide range of colors, from white to rose, dark red, or yellow. A dark blotch low in the flower bowl may be repeated at the top of the petals. The square gland is covered with short yellow hairs. The plant grows 1 to 2 feet tall, with several flowers per stem blooming in succession.

Where and when to gather

Butterfly mariposa lily grows in a wide range of soils, from sandy to rocky, including serpentine soil, in sunny meadows and open woodlands, and on steep banks. It can be found from 1,000 to 8,000 feet in the Sierra Nevada, in El Dorado to Kern Counties to the Coast Ranges of the San Francisco Bay Area, and south to Los Angeles County. The flowers are seen from April through June. The bulbs can be gathered while the flowers are blooming or later in the year, but they can be difficult to find and dig once the soil has dried up.

How to gather

These bulbs grow about 6 inches deep in the soil and are harvested like other Indian potatoes (page 64).

How to use

Peel the bulbs. Then boil, steam, roast, sauté, or bake for at least twenty minutes. Sauté the bulbs in oil after boiling, or mash. The bulbs should be well cooked to develop their sweetness and texture. The bulbs cannot be stored for more than about a week.

When the grasses have dried in early summer, look for the flower of butterfly mariposa lily.

Future harvests

Like other Indian potatoes, the bulb can be harvested knowledgeably in such a way as to add to their numbers. Practice growing mariposa lily in your garden from commercially grown and purchased corms, so you can learn how to properly harvest it. Since the plant is already vulnerable to careless flower pickers, invasive species, feral pigs, and countless other threats, foragers should first earn their stripes at home. If you succeed in increasing the numbers in your own garden, you can serve unusual vegetables to your guests while amazing the neighbors with the beauty of your butterfly lilies. Some *Calochortus* species are rare, threatened, or endangered and must be left entirely alone. Native peoples have first right of harvest on good gathering grounds, always.

California bay laurel

Umbellularia californica

bay tree, California laurel, Oregon myrtle, spicetree

EDIBLE leaves, buds, nuts, husk

The leaves of this native tree are frequently used as seasoning, but the nuts are less well-known, a unique ingredient awaiting discovery by modern cooks.

Both Californians and Oregonians are proprietary about this widespread tree of many uses and legendary beauty. Its mossy trunks give a fairytale aspect to deep woods, and the objects made from its lumber are many and highly esteemed. The wood is still gaining in popularity, being increasingly used for flooring (the steps of my study) and for the sides and backs of acoustic guitars. The intoxicating aroma of California bay laurel's dark green leaves may be familiar to most, because its leaves are sometimes sold interchangeably with those of the European bay laurel (*Laurus nobilis*).

The nuts of the bay tree were traditionally toasted and enjoyed by indigenous peoples, and have an enticing coffeelike aroma, a powerful taste, and a satisfying crunch. I recently ate my first bay nut truffle, delicately flavored with maple syrup.

How to identify

California bay laurel is a handsome evergreen tree with shiny, green, lance-shaped leaves about 3 inches long, each with a very short leaf stem (petiole). The plant assumes different shapes depending on where it grows, from a neatly pruned, almost topiary look where coastal winds sculpt it, to a tree almost as broad as tall in the deep woods. When aging, it sports venerable pendulous branches, with mosses finding a hospitable niche on its scaly bark.

The heady, pungent fragrance of the leaves—somewhat resembling eucalyptus though sweeter—is an unmistakable tip-off to the tree's presence. The bark is usually reddish brown. The flowers appear as tiny clusters of greenish white, snugged up against the upper leaf axils (junctions of leaf and stem). The fruit somewhat resembles a greenish olive, the fleshy outer covering turning purple and softening as it matures. The tan kernel inside is the edible part.

Where and when to gather

California bay laurel is a common tree found growing in canyons, valleys, and chaparral in the Coast Ranges of California, and from Oregon to Baja, and also on the west slopes of the Sierra Nevada below 4,000 feet. The buds appear in winter, in the leaf axils, and can be gathered in early spring, appearing as tiny umbels of

The ripening bay laurel nuts are gathered in October and November.

greenish white blooms. The nuts ripen in October and November. The leaves can be gathered year-round.

How to gather

Bay nuts can be picked directly from the tree when the husk is soft, or gathered from the ground when they have fallen. Unlike acorns, they are usually not susceptible to insect invasion, so gathering them from the ground is not a problem. Bay leaves, when dried to a pale gold, either still on the tree or on the ground, have a mellower flavor than the dark green leaves and are preferred by some.

How to use

Remove and discard the fleshy husk that surrounds the bay nut. Roast the nuts in the shell in the oven at 350ºF for about forty-five minutes, stirring them occasionally to make sure they don't burn. Once they are cooled, crack the shells, releasing the nuts. Eat the nuts whole or grind them in a grinder. Grinding them releases enough oils that the meal can be formed into small balls about the size of a walnut. To make the classic Pomo dish *behe chune*, wrap native clover around these nut balls. Adding sweetener to the bay nut meal brings out a flavor that resembles chocolate. With maple syrup, they make an intriguing shortbread.

Add bay leaves to stews, soups, and roasts, to contribute a rich flavor to a dish. Almost twice as strong as the European bay leaf, California bay laurel leaves require fewer to make an impact. Remove from the dish before serving. The buds can also be used for a more delicate seasoning.

Future Harvests

Though California bay laurel is a host for sudden oak death (SOD) and can spread it (it is a vector for the disease), the trees themselves don't seem harmed by it, and are currently doing very well, even profiting from the decline of the oak trees around them. On your own land, don't allow bay trees to overtop nearby oaks, or they may drip contaminated moisture onto them. Don't move bay leaves from one place to another unless they show no signs of SOD (see California Oak Mortality Task Force in Resources).

California blackberry

Rubus ursinus

native blackberry, California dewberry, Pacific dewberry, trailing blackberry

`EDIBLE` berries, sprouts

California has its own native species of blackberry, which many consider to be superior to the also delicious yet dauntingly invasive Himalayan blackberry.

The California blackberry is less invasive than the Himalayan blackberry, has a sweeter, tangier, sometimes smaller berry, has less painful thorns, ripens earlier, and is altogether a more well-mannered supplier of summer fruit. Also, the berries don't need to be as completely ripe to be tasty. The sourness of an even slightly unripe Himalayan berry causes a powerful wince, whereas the sweeter California blackberry is one ancestor of the milder loganberry and the boysenberry. Rich in antioxidants, the berries have a low glycemic index. The young cane sprouts

California blackberries are juicy and delicious, fresh or in baked goods.

California blackberries (right) are smaller and narrower than the Himalayan blackberry (left); California blackberries have a sweeter, stronger flavor.

traditionally were eaten in soups and stews.

How to identify

The main stems are round, usually slender, and clamber close to the ground rather than rising straight up and arching over. The leaflets are green above and below, while the Himalayan blackberry leaves are white underneath. There are male and female plants, so some plants don't bear fruit. The female flower has long, narrow petals, unlike the Himalayan berry, which has wider oval flowers. The berry is ½ to 1 inch long, black to purple, and oblong. The berries are red until they ripen into their characteristic black color.

Where and when to gather

California blackberry can be found throughout the California Floristic Province. It blooms from April to July, with flowers on the bush at the same time that fruit is ripening, from June to August.

How to gather

These delicate berries need to be gathered carefully, one by one, since all berries on the flower panicle rarely ripen at the same time. Because of their size, this is a fairly rapid process. Place them carefully in a small bucket hung around your neck, so both of your hands are free to maneuver. Long-sleeved shirts or even thin gloves are recommended, to protect you from thorns

The flowers of California blackberry bloom from June through August along the coast.

and berry stain, though pickers don't often use them. Harvest young sprouts in early spring as they emerge from the ground.

How to use

Few people need to be told how to use the native blackberries that make it back to the kitchen. Many aficionados create blackberry pies, tarts, crisps, muffins, pancakes, jams, jellies, juice, and wine. Some fans just like to stand in one place and gorge on the freshly picked flavorful berries. Add peeled, chopped sprouts to soups and stews.

Future harvests

The California blackberry frequently loses out to its competitive cousin from Eurasia. Learning how to distinguish the two is a good beginning toward squelching the exuberance of the Himalayan blackberry and ensuring the future of California's own.

California black oak

Quercus kelloggii

black oak, Kellogg's oak

`EDIBLE` nuts

California black oak is thought by some to have the most delicious acorns of all California oak trees.

Of the nineteen species of oaks in the state, thirteen are known to have provided traditional food for native peoples. Sometimes acorns from nearby local oak species, the most well-known to a group, are the most highly esteemed, or it may be that the scarcest and hardest to obtain are considered the prizes. But black oak acorns are favored by animals and birds as well as people, so they're not often found lying untouched on the ground.

The new leaves of the black oak are a soft, tender pink, and are as beautiful as wildflowers in the spring. In the fall, the leaves turn a bright yellow or orange against the tree's dark gray bark before

The magnificent California black oak graces savannahs and woodlands throughout the state.

Acorn Processing

Acorns, the fruit of the oak tree, have long been an important food for California's native peoples. Each tribe had its own ways to process acorns, all a result of the need to remove the bitter and indigestible tannic acids (tannins) from the nuts. After gathering, the acorns were cracked with a stone and peeled. The nuts were ground in rock mortars to make a fine meal, and then placed in a depression in sandy soil. Water was gently and evenly poured through the fine grains, slowly and continually leaching out the tannins, which turn the water brown. Once the acorn meal was leached and no longer tasted bitter, it could be made into a variety of dishes, from soup to mush to cakes or biscuits roasted in ovens. Sometimes it was eaten with various kinds of pinole, sometimes plain.

My preferred modern version of leaching requires a large mason jar, which is filled half with ground acorn meal and half with cold water. Shake thoroughly and refrigerate. Once a day for three to ten days, depending on the species of acorn, pour off the water, which turns brown from the tannins. When it stops turning brown, taste the meal. If it is neutral-tasting, it is ready to use.

Demonstrations of acorn processing are available throughout the state (see Resources).

they drop. With its munificent bounty and wide geographic distribution, the California black oak is an important tree crop, well worth knowing.

How to identify

The oblong black oak acorn, with its almost blunt tip, is nearly half covered by its cap. It is 1¼ inches long and ¾ inch wide. The leaves, bright green above and pale green below, are deeply lobed, with each of the six or so lobes ending in a sharp point. The sharp point helps to distinguish between the lobed leaves of the valley oak, with their rounded tips, and the lobed leaves of the California black oak, with the pointed spines. Leaves can be as long as 8 inches, and 2 to 6 inches wide.

Where and when to gather

California black oak is adaptable, occurring in a wide variety of soils from Oregon south to San Diego, but it does like moisture. It is found growing at 2,000 to 8,000 feet. Black oak acorns, which take two years to ripen, will finish their lengthy maturation process in October and November.

How to gather

Either knock the trees gently with a wooden pole, shake the limbs, being careful not to damage them, gather from the ground as soon as they fall, or pluck directly from the trees.

How to use

Peel, grind, and leach out the tannins (see Acorn Processing, previous page). Cook as a mush, or use in breads or as a component of other baked goods.

Future harvests

The future of California's oaks is a widely discussed topic. The trees require protection from timber harvest, invasive species, and development. A new problem is the disease called sudden oak death. For more information, see the website for the California Oak Mortality Task Force, in Resources).

Keep the young oaks coming by joining the jays and squirrels and planting some of your acorn harvest in the ground. When choosing a location, keep in mind their large ultimate size, so that they will not be removed prematurely. Once established, oaks can grow surprisingly rapidly.

California bottlebrush grass

Elymus californicus

EDIBLE seeds

The large seeds of California bottlebrush grass and ease of harvest make it a good candidate for breakfast porridge.

The seeds of most of California's native bunchgrasses are small compared to the seeds of grasses from other parts of the world. One of the larger grass seeds is produced by the uncommon bottlebrush grass, a tall, graceful woodland grass with a fairly small distribution. California bottlebrush grass is one of those species whose ability to reseed and maintain vigor and a long life is impressive within its narrow range along the central California coast. Its seeds should be collected as part of adopting and nurturing a patch in one of the openings in the coastal woods where bottlebrush grass thrives.

How to identify

California bottlebrush grass has an unusually long and showy seed stalk that grows 3 to 6 feet tall. The flowering spikes, three to six per plant, are from 4 to 10 inches long. Flower clusters jut out from the stalk at almost right angles, each with a hair-like appendage. As the grass's seeds ripen

The long, graceful, distinctive seed head of California bottlebrush grass contains some of the largest bunchgrass seeds.

and become heavy, the flower spikes arch over toward the ground. The wide, flexible leaf blades of the grass range from 2 to 4 feet tall.

Where and when to gather

California bottlebrush grass is found in the Coast Ranges from the San Francisco Bay Area to the Santa Cruz Mountains. You will find it in coniferous forests and mixed evergreen woodlands where fog and shade prevail. Although it does grow in conditions where it gets only part sun, it is one of a relatively small number of bunchgrasses that can thrive and set seeds in deep shade. This perennial grass blooms from June through August and sets seed from July to September.

How to gather

Break off the long, dried seed stalks or snip with scissors into a bag. Rub them between your fingers until the seeds detach and fall to the bottom of the bag. Or grab the seed stalk and pull, running your index finger and thumb up the sides of the seed stalk so the seeds detach in your hand, then drop them into a container.

How to use

The seed is used for porridge and as an ingredient in baked goods. Remove the chaff, toast the seeds, and simmer with water until the grains have absorbed the water and are soft (for more information, see California's Native Bunchgrasses, page 68).

Future harvests

With an uncommon species like California bottlebrush grass, collect sparingly. Consider adopting a patch of bottlebrush grass, ensuring that weedy species are pulled, increasing the territory of bottlebrush grass in that clearing. Sow some of your harvest nearby in a similar location, one with shade, moisture, and fog drip. It spreads readily.

California brome

Bromus carinatus

mountain brome, California mountain brome

`EDIBLE` seeds

For another breakfast opportunity offered by native bunchgrasses, try California brome, an unassuming but productive native bunchgrass. Once you learn how to clean and prepare the seed of California brome, you'll enjoy it as an excellent breakfast cereal.

When served as mush with honey at an heirloom seed conference, California brome won raves. Gluten-free, like all the native bunchgrasses, the flour does not rise, but it makes great crackers, mush, and biscuits— a worthy vehicle for butter and honey.

California brome is called both a short-lived perennial and a biennial. Because it germinates readily and grows rapidly, it is used to prevent erosion on road cuts and banks, acting as a nurse plant for slower growing grasses by providing shelter for

California brome is a short-lived native bunchgrass with edible seeds.

The florets of California brome are tinged with red.

their young seedlings. And, of course, it requires no fertilizer or plowing.

How to identify

Learning about native grasses, their ecology, and identification is a tranquil world of nitpicking and validating that God is in the details. California brome would be a good place to begin the study. Bring a native grass identification book with you to the fields, identify each plant, and firmly tape specimens into a notebook. You may be surprised how quickly you become familiar with the look of a particular native grass.

California brome is not a particularly distinctive-looking bunchgrass until it sets seed. It is green like grass is supposed to be, with flowers in panicles, growing about 2 feet high. They are soft to the touch and don't stick in your socks. Each plant lives only three to five years and grows 2 to 4 feet tall. The roots of California brome are fibrous, grow very quickly, and become deep and widespread. Young plants are erect, but older stems grow along the ground. Stems are robust with hairy sheaths.

Where and when to gather

California brome is a taxonomically complicated species, similar to many different grass species found all over the California Floristic Province. A closely related or possibly identical species called mountain brome, *Bromus marginatus*, can be found in the mountains and foothills where at least 16 inches of rainfall occur. California brome grows in open woods and forests, shrublands, grasslands, meadows, and open places. You'll know the seeds are ripe when the plant and the seeds have turned pale beige. Seeds mature in May and June at low elevations and by late August at high elevations.

How to gather

Avoid any seeds that have black smut on them. When you have determined that the bunchgrass seed is ripe, strip the flower stalk by sliding your partially closed fingers up the flowering stalk, and letting the seed drop into a paper bag or a tightly woven basket (for more information, see California's Native Bunchgrasses, page 68). Or else snip the entire stalk into a bag or basket, and beat, shake, or otherwise disturb the contents until the seeds loosen from the stalks and fall to the bottom of the bag.

How to use

For a bunchgrass breakfast, toast the seed, let cool, grind briefly, and place the ground seed and remaining husk in a pot of water. The husk will float to the top and the dark seed, your breakfast, will sink to the bottom. Pour off the brownish water and repeat the process several times. Soak the seed for a couple of hours, drain the water, then cook with twice the amount of water as grain, until the grains have absorbed moisture, softened, and plumped up. Eat with honey and other condiments for breakfast. You can also use the dry flour or cooked mush combined with wheat flour to make bread, muffins, cookies, or crackers.

Future harvests

California brome is a hardy survivor. Scatter seeds in a likely spot when you find it growing in the wild, particularly if the stalks are leaning over and about to drop their seeds onto a trail or road where they won't be able to grow. Avoid areas with the slower growing native grasses, like California oatgrass, because California brome might overwhelm them.

California buttercup

Ranunculus californicus

EDIBLE seeds

The seeds of this charming wildflower can be made into a tasty pinole.

California buttercup, a well-known perennial wildflower, is found in lowland, moist meadows throughout the state. It has counterparts throughout the country that have long been held under the chins of children to establish whether they "like butter." Glossy yellow petals reflected on the skin indicate that butter is enjoyed. No part of this plant is edible except the seeds, which were widely enjoyed in California as toasted, ground seed meal.

How to identify

This perennial grows as high as 1 foot, with a spread from 1 to 2 feet wide. The five shiny, bright yellow petals are no more than 1 inch wide, with five sepals (flower leaves). The leaflets are wedge shaped, and the upper stem leaves are deeply lobed and toothed. The pale green seeds are flattish disks 1/8 inch in diameter that rest against each other as they ripen, until they turn brown and drop.

California buttercup, a cheerful yellow-blooming perennial, seeks out situations with some seasonal moisture.

Where and when to gather

All species of buttercups require moisture through the flowering and fruiting stage. In some wet areas, it dominates; in other less wet areas, it can grow with a full complement of native grass species. Flowering in February through April along the coast, this species has a fairly long seed-ripening period, beginning in May and continuing through June; away from the coast, it's shorter. The seeds can be picked a bit before they ripen, and will finish ripening in the bag.

How to gather

Hold the seed head between your fingers and pull the seeds off. They are ready to harvest when pale brown. Where plants grows thickly, cut a handful of plants at the base of the stems, store in paper bag, and let dry in a warm place until the seeds drop off and fall to the bottom of the bag. Lift the vegetative debris from the bag, shaking it a bit as you extract it. You can also put sheets on the ground around drying California buttercup, so that the flowers release the seed onto the sheets.

How to use

Roast the seeds in a frying pan, stirring rapidly till toasted, for thirty seconds to one minute. Use seeds toasted to make porridge, or grind toasted seeds into a flour and mix with wheat flour to make cakes, cookies, muffins, or breads (see Pinole: California's Seed Foods, page 62).

The seeds of California buttercup can be picked slightly green, before they naturally drop from the plant, and will finish ripening later.

Future harvests

California buttercup is a hardy perennial, but since it likes moist, sunny places, it must compete with numerous other species with the same preferences. If you've adopted a buttercup seed-collecting area, keep a sharp eye out for fennel, teasel, vinca, and other invasive species. California buttercup goes dormant in early to midsummer, making them vulnerable to weedy species. Still, buttercups are with us yet.

California hazelnut

Corylus cornuta subsp. *californica*
California hazel, California filbert

`EDIBLE` nuts

California hazelnuts are sweet-tasting nuts that appear on a graceful, thornless, deciduous shrub growing in a variety of situations.

California hazelnut can ripen its nuts on the foggy coast as well as in California's woodlands. Early to late summer is the time to gather these rich, mild nuts, which taste similar to the European filbert. Some California tribes made a practice of keeping hazelnuts on hand so that they could be ground into a milky liquid that is a nutritious, digestible supplement for newborns, convalescents, and the elderly. Their culinary uses are many, and the thin shell makes it possible to crack and enjoy them while hiking. Native hazelnuts are resistant to a fungus that is a serious problem for the imported European hazelnut, or filbert.

The leafy bracts clasping California hazelnuts turn rosy and begin to split apart as the nut ripens inside.

The nuts dry and sweeten if stored in the shell.

How to identify

California hazelnut thrives in thin soil in sun or in deep loam in shade. Its leaves are soft and fuzzy, heart-shaped, and from 2 to 4 inches long. In the fall, they turn gold before they drop. Both male and female flowers are found on the same plant; look closely in January to find the tiny red flower on the node above the long, dangling male catkin and then watch it turn into a nut. Each nut is enclosed in a papery cup made of two fused bracts. As it ripens, the cup turns a rosy hue and begins to split open, revealing the shiny, tan nut underneath—a thrilling sight to the hazelnut lover.

Where and when to gather

Our native hazelnut grows in many habitats, but especially in moist, shady places in the mixed evergreen woodlands of the outer Coast Range from San Francisco Bay to Oregon. They are also found in the Cascade Range and in the foothills on the west side of the Sierra Nevada.

California hazelnut can also be found growing in full sun in sandy soil close to beaches, with all their salt spray and fog. This uncommon plant community, called hazel scrub, grows 3 to 6 feet tall, with the nuts conveniently forming right on top of the short shrub, right at hand and easily visible. A good harvest year is a sight to behold. Gather from mid-June to August. They sometimes hang on the tree until September.

How to gather

Until you develop a "hazelnut search image," you may stare in vain up into the leafy reaches of a hazel bush, seeing no nuts. Then suddenly, they appear. Once you see them, they're everywhere. Your brain has now developed a search image, or what in this case could be called "hazelnut eyes."

The riper the nuts, the more easily they detach from the twig. The trick with hazelnuts is to harvest them when they are ripe enough to detach easily from the shrub but not so ripe as to have been harvested by others. The tiny hairs on the bracts that cup the nut can be mildly irritating to some, so you may want to wear gloves.

Crack a few nuts open to be sure they are ripe. If you pick too early, you can end up with a beautiful-appearing nut with nothing inside. If too late, you may find a shriveled, though frequently still very sweet, pea-sized nutmeat.

How to use

A small hammer or nutcracker can be used to crack the nuts; on the trail, a rock on a rock will suffice. A table-mounted nutcracker speeds things up. Crack the relatively thin shell first, then pick out the nutmeat, which is an irregular shape varying from $1/4$ to $1/2$ inch in diameter. Native hazelnuts are much faster to process than tough-shelled native walnuts. Use California hazelnuts wherever a mild, sweet nut is appropriate—in baking, for snacking, with granola, for nut butters, and to make nut milk. With the bracts removed but unshelled, the nuts will last a long time, three to five years in a cool, dry place.

Future harvests

Jays, woodpeckers, and squirrels bury hazelnuts for future meals, and then forget to retrieve some of them. If you'd like to join the animals' work, bury individual nuts blunt side down in appropriately humusy, shady places where leaves and other natural debris make good hiding places and nurseries for seedlings.

California juniper

Juniperus californica

EDIBLE berries (cones)

You can easily recognize California juniper by its pale blue berries, which are well known for their use in flavoring gin.

California juniper is one of the group of staunch desert plants that impress us with their evergreen foliage and stoic endurance of harsh conditions. The shrub is often seen in the company of singleleaf pinyon pine and Joshua tree. You can easily recognize it by its scaly leaves and berries. Sampling naturally dried berries right from the bush helps quench thirst and brings to mind creative cooking possibilities using the juniper berries as seasoning, particularly for steak and stews. They are known for cutting the gaminess of wild meats like venison.

How to identify

This rounded evergreen shrub typically grows to 15 feet high, but the largest California juniper in existence is twice that height. The plant's blue berries are about 1 inch long and dry into platelike scales. A member of the cypress family, California juniper has prickly leaves with a braided appearance, on stiff, irregular branches.

The light blue fruit of California juniper is easy to spot.

California juniper can handle the tough conditions of the Mojave Desert.

It's not pleasant to rub up against the shrub.

Where and when to gather

Found in dry areas below 5,000 feet, California juniper ranges from Shasta County south to Mexico and on the western slopes of the southern Sierra Nevada. It is commonly found growing with pinyon pines from the western edge of the Colorado Desert and Joshua Tree National Park to Kern County. California juniper berries remain on the tree and can be harvested through the winter months and even into the spring. New berries come along in May and June. They are at their sweetest when gathered at three years of age.

How to gather

The berries and stems can be removed from the shrub with pruning shears.

How to use

Grind the dried berries and use for baked goods or mush, and as a trailside snack. Twigs and berries can be used to make a tea, which can also be used as a marinade for meat, stews, and sausage. Crush with a mortar and pestle just before adding to the dish.

Future harvests

California juniper is currently thriving.

Caution

Avoid juniper berries if you are pregnant or experiencing bladder or kidney problems.

California oatgrass

Danthonia californica

California danthonia

`EDIBLE` seeds

The nutritious seeds of California oatgrass can be toasted and ground into a delicious pinole reminiscent of popcorn.

Finding California oatgrass reminds us of the vast sweep of coastal prairie that was once a crucial part of the ecology of California and of the aboriginal diet. A relatively short bunchgrass in stature, California oatgrass was a dominant species in many parts of our region's native prairies. Though native grasslands are much reduced in size today, California oatgrass is still a survivor. Tug on the leaf blades to feel the strength with which its fibrous roots penetrate the soil and prevent erosion. European oatgrass, with which it is sometimes confused, is an annual with shallow roots that will pull right out of the soil. When grazed moderately, or mowed, California oatgrass can form an almost continuous lawnlike colony that produces high-quality forage for animals. This native species is among the many that contribute to overall land health. Its edible seeds can also contribute to yours.

The light-colored ripe seed can be seen growing at right angles to the seed stalks, while the bunchgrass below remains partially green.

How to identify

California oatgrass is a fibrous-rooted perennial grass 6 to 12 inches tall and equally broad, with characteristically flattened spikelets at the end of long, arching seed stalks. It has hairy leaf axils. An intriguing aspect of California oatgrass is an uncommon feature called cleistogamy, which refers to its ability to produce self-fertilized seeds hidden within the lower seed stalk. Slit that portion of the seed stalk lengthwise with a fingernail, and you'll find several fertilized seeds sitting within the stalk.

Where and when to gather

From Del Norte County north to southern Oregon and down the central coast to Santa Barbara, look for California oatgrass where grazing, mowing, or burning have maintained open grasslands within fifty miles of the coast. It often survives in fire roads and along rivers with seasonal flooding.

California oatgrass is one of the first native grasses every year to ripen its seed. When the local hills have turned golden in May and June, you will notice its long seed stalks arching over the ground, the cluster of seeds at the end of the stalk ripening to a pale beige. You may chew the seeds while they are still green for a sweet, fresh-tasting snack, but collecting the dried seed in quantity is best when the seed is fully ripe, in May and June.

How to gather

Gather sheaves (bundles of cut stalks) of oatgrass by cutting the seed stalks just above where they emerge from the grassy crown of the plant. Or gather seeds by pulling the seed stalk through lightly grasped fingers, so that the seeds release in your hand and you can put them in a paper bag. Some prefer cutting the seed stalks, putting them in a paper bag, leaving the bag in a warm place, and letting the seeds fall off the stalks on their own. You can also wet the seed stalks and leave them to dry on a tarp in the sun for a few days, which hastens seed drop.

How to use

Outdoors, hold the sheaf in one hand, and light the seeds on fire over a cast-iron frying pan so that the chaff burns up completely and the seeds, lightly toasted, drop into the pan. When the seeds cool, put them in a blender and grind them into a dry powder, which can be used over rice or as a nutritious, unique additive to bread or muffin recipes. Or simply toast on the stove in a frying pan before grinding (for more information on preparing bunchgrass seeds, see California's Native Bunchgrasses, page 68). The dried seed can be stored for long periods of time without spoiling.

Future harvests

A good stand of native grasses requires protection from weedy plants, particularly European and Eurasian grasses. In our state, native grasses provide habitat for a number of rare species, including the Ohlone tiger beetle and numerous birds and insects.

California oniongrass

Melica californica

California melic grass, melic grass

`EDIBLE` seeds

The attractive California oniongrass has showy flower spikes loaded with edible seed, sometimes producing twice in one season.

The melics, or oniongrasses, are an interesting group of western bunchgrasses. One of these, California oniongrass, has the rich look of an agricultural grain, with distinctively large seeds that make the interested seed harvester look twice when thinking about breakfast. California oniongrass seed is easy and satisfying to harvest,

When ready to harvest, oniongrass seedstalks turn silvery.

and is another useful addition to the pal-ette of native seed breakfast porridges.

How to identify
These perennial bunchgrasses grow 1 to 2 feet tall and from 6 to 24 inches wide. The satiny leaf blades are a bright medium green, upright, and sometimes curling over at the top. The flower stalks grow close together and have purple bands on the flower spikelets, which are almost ½ inch long. This delicately clumping bunchgrass keeps its bright green foliage in winter and spring. When dormant in the summer and fall, the leaflike structures clasping the seeds turn silvery, and persist even after the seeds have dropped off.

Where and when to gather
California oniongrass is a tough, handsome bunchgrass native to the grasslands and oak woodlands of the northern and cen-tral Coast Ranges and the Sierra Nevada foothills. You may find it in full sun or part shade in open hillsides and conifer-ous forests under 6,000 feet. The plant will go dormant in summer, while retain-ing its attractive silvery seed heads. When rain comes, it may produce a second crop of seeds in the same season. The first seed harvest is in late May.

How to gather
Strip the seed stalks with the fingers and drop into a bag or box (see California's Native Bunchgrasssses, page 68).

How to use
Burn off the bracts adhering to the seed, grind, float off the chaff in cool water, and boil for porridge.

Future harvests
California oniongrass is fairly popular among those growing native grasses in gar-dens and in grassland restoration proj-ects. Its adaptability serves it well, grow-ing even on serpentine soil, an infertile soil type with low amounts of calcium and high amounts of magnesium that is widespread in California. It also grows in sun or part-shade, and reproduces from seed, bulb, and rhizome.

California wild grape

Vitis californica

EDIBLE fruit, tendrils, leaves

Gathering the tangy-sweet fruit of California's wild grape in the fall is a nourishing experience.

The deep purple skin of California's wild grape makes it a good source of anthocyanins. Using wild grape as rootstock saved the California wine industry when a serious disease threatened the non-native vines. California writer Mary Austin described moving as a young girl to southern California, where from homesickness she languished and fell ill, until she discovered some vibrant local populations of California wild grape. Gorging on the fruit, she ate her way back to vigorous health, while beginning to experience the essential feeling of connection with her new California home that led to her most influential book, *The Land of Little Rain*. When I read that book, I think of eating wild grapes.

How to identify

Like cultivated grapevines, California wild grape spreads by grasping tendrils. The palm-shaped leaves are toothed, and the inconspicuous greenish flowers form racemes (clusters of separate flowers). Smaller than cultivated grapes, the fruit is similar to wild grapes in the rest of the

California's wild desert grape grows in arroyos and near desert streams, with the same exuberant habit as the California wild grape.

country, with deep blue skin with a bloom. Its leaves turn rich shades of red and gold in the fall. A related species, the desert wild grape, *Vitis girdiana*, produces fruit with no bloom on its skin.

Where and when to gather

California wild grape grows from San Luis Obispo County north through the inner Coast Ranges. It flourishes near creeks and rivers in the Central Valley, in the foothills of the Sierra Nevada and east of the Sierra, in northwestern California, in the foothills of the Cascade Range, and in central western California.

The desert wild grape is found from Inyo and Santa Barbara Counties south, in canyons following streams in the desert. There are nice stands of the desert wild grape in the Indian Canyons in Palm Springs.

Blooming May through June with inconspicuous greenish flowers, California wild grape is ripe and ready to be gathered in late summer and early fall, August through September. The leaves can be gathered in April and May, while tender.

How to gather

Snip entire bunches of grapes off the stems with a knife or pruning shears. Gather tendrils with a sharp tug. Cut off grape leaves before fruit forms. Though the grape seeds are nourishing and somewhat tasty, they're a bit too large to be delicious, so they can be removed while preparing the grapes. If you're eating the grapes as a trailside snack, simply if inelegantly spit them out. Learn to extract the juice and skin with the tongue when desired, disgorging the seeds. Practice makes perfect.

How to use

Eat the ripe fruit raw, including the skins and seeds. Or crush and strain out seeds and skins, using the juice to make wine, grape juice, or jelly. Wrap rice and other foods in young native grape leaves and steam.

Future harvests

The vigorous twining habit of wild grapes can be a danger for the trees they climb on. But it's hard to grudge them territory, when their terrain, the rich, multilayered habitat that used to extend for several miles on either side of creeks and rivers, has been so diminished. Birds and other animals do a good job of spreading wild grape seeds, and we can probably count on them to continue to do so. Still, when spitting out the seeds, aim for areas that don't yet have vines crawling over them.

The rich dark blue fruit of the California wild grape is flavorful and healthful, ripening in late summer and fall.

California wild rose

Rosa californica

wild rose, rosa del Castillo, rosa de Castilla, rose of Castile

EDIBLE flowers, fruit

Well known for their scurvy-preventing vitamin C and high amounts of calcium and other nutrients, wild rose hips have long been gathered and enjoyed.

The sun-loving California wild rose is a vigorous plant with long-lasting pink blossoms that have a sweet fragrance and classic rose features. The rose hips are the red-orange fruit of the rose, from oval to round, which contain white seeds. They can be dried and powdered or used fresh in a variety of ways, including for making jelly. South Asian desserts flavored with an extract made from rose petals are delicacies, and the oil from the flowers, requiring tons of flowers to produce a tiny amount of oil, are among the costliest of perfume ingredients.

How to identify

The flowers have no more than five flat open petals, ranging from pale pink to deep

The fragrant flowers of California wild rose are considerably simpler than those of the domestic rose.

magenta, with numerous yellow stamens, and occur at the ends of curving stems, either singly or several together. The bright red, round rose hips appear in the fall. The thorns along the stems are prickly and painful, though not as daggerlike as those of many cultivated roses. The green leaves consist of multiple toothed leaflets.

Where and when to gather

Found in full sun or in part-sun openings in the woods throughout the California Floristic Province, and in the foothills of the Sierra Nevada, the California wild rose is notable for the length of its bloom time. It flowers from April to October, ripening fruit from June to November. In some situations, it is still in luxuriant bloom in September and October, at the same time that its scarlet rose hips have formed. The hips may persist through the winter if not harvested.

How to gather

In April, the sweet-tasting rose petals can be gathered even when slightly wilted, without interfering with the ongoing and future production of rose hips. Hips are easily plucked from the ends of the branches when ripe.

How to use

The flowers can be gathered to make teas, jellies, or rosewater. Remove the seeds from the ripe fruit before using, because in large quantities, they can irritate the stomach. The rose hips produced by the wood rose, though smaller, produce fewer and smaller seeds that don't require removal. Eat the fruit of the rose raw or boil it with sugar to make jam, jelly, syrup, or tea.

Future harvests

Native roses, whose hips are beloved by birds and mammals, are reliably spread by them. Most species are also thicket-formers, spreading from underground roots. Using these two forms of reproduction, they are not easily threatened, except by habitat loss and other, more vigorous thicket-formers, such as the Himalayan blackberry. As good wildlife food, their fruits sometimes still available in the winter, these and other wild roses should be allowed to grow in their luxuriant profusion, providing both cover and food for birds and animals.

candy flower

Claytonia sibirica

Siberian miner's lettuce, peppermint candy flower, pink purslane

EDIBLE leaves, flowers, seeds

A perennial relative of miner's lettuce, candy flower is a welcome snack or salad green, and cooks up into a tasty potherb.

With two famous edible relatives, miner's lettuce and spring beauty, found in northern and eastern parts of the country, candy flower, a less well-known perennial wildflower, has a lot to offer in its own right. Aesthetically, its small, white and pink- or purple-striped edible flowers create a dainty fairyland effect in moist places and in part-shade from February to May. Its spade-shaped leaves are a bit tougher and less mild than those of miner's lettuce but still good. Candy flower is remarkable for the longevity of its bloom and the length of time it is edible. In northern California, its leaves emerge with the fall and winter rains, and can be eaten for an impressive

The petals of this low-growing perennial wildflower can be purple or pink. The pink form is reminiscent of striped peppermint candy, hence the name candy flower.

four to five months. The seeds are edible as well.

How to identify

Its leaves are smaller than miner's lettuce, while its pink or purple and white flowers are bigger. The immature leaves of both have a spadelike shape, but candy flower foliage retains that shape as it ages, while miner's lettuce leaves become almost circular, with the flower stalk emerging from the center of the leaf (perfoliate). Like spring beauty, candy flower spreads from corms, but unlike its eastern relative, these reproductive bodies are insignificant in size and are not eaten.

Where and when to gather

Candy flower has an unusual distribution, being found on the west coast from Alaska to California, and in California from northwestern California, to the Cascade Range, and in the San Francisco Bay Area. From there, it jumps to Siberia. On the coast of California, it grows sparsely with other forbs (nonwoody, nongrass herbaceous species like annual and perennial wildflowers) in full sun in coastal meadows, especially where water accumulates, as well as in moist woodlands, along creeks, and in wetlands. Sometimes it carpets the ground thickly in open woodlands, especially moist woods with red alder. It blooms under willows and at the dripline of oaks. The leaves are more delicious before bloom, but can still be enjoyed while young and before the plant goes to seed, January through April. Harvest through the winter, from January through March. Because the flowers have such a long bloom time, February through May, seed ripens for a long period of time as well, from May through August.

How to gather

Use a sharp knife or scissors to cut the leaves, including the long stalk. Rinse in chilled water and then refrigerate as soon as possible. Include the edible flowers to make a salad that will remind you of the fresh, cool environs where candy flower grows. The flowers ripen on the flower stalks from bottom to top, so mature seeds that are black and shiny may be at the base, while flowers are still in bud at the top of the stalk. Cut the whole plant and invert it in a paper bag, where the seeds will drop to the bottom.

How to use

Eat the leaves raw or cooked, steamed or boiled. Decorate salads or other cold dishes like ice cream with the dainty flowers. Candy flower's significant quantity of shiny black seed can be prepared according to the great California pinole tradition (see page 62).

Future harvests

This species is a profligate reseeder that spreads well on its own. Ants delight in moving the seed around, gophers move the bulblets, and neither seems to need our help, because these perennial plants return and spread year after year. Don't introduce it where it could outcompete less vigorous woodland species, like milkmaids.

cattail

Typha latifolia

soft rush, broad-leaved cattail, bulrush, common bulrush

EDIBLE shoots, flowers, pollen, rhizome

Generous with its gifts and ubiquitous in shallow fresh water, the cattail is an outstanding edible swamp vegetable.

This plant is many vegetables in one, but let's focus on its three most rewarding uses: the succulent heart of the lower stalk, also called the core or shoot; the vegetable provided by the edible male flower spike; and the golden, nutritious pollen the male flower produces. The core of the new leaf stalks is delicious, with many uses. The immature male flower spikes are a famous wild food often compared with corn on the cob. Cattail pollen is worth its weight in gold, enriching pancakes, waffles, muffins, rice, and sponge cakes with its golden color and nutritious flavoring, elevating them from ordinary to sublime. Begin harvesting cattail parts in the spring, starting at the bottom with the leafshoots, and working your way up.

How to identify

Cattail leaves, bunched together at the base, can be almost 10 feet tall. The stalk is solid with airholes, and the flower consists of two distinct parts, the long, narrow male part on the top, which has edible flowers and also edible pollen; and the female part,

Located at the very top of the cattail plant, the male flower spike while immature makes a good vegetable.

the seed producer, just below it, which resembles a corn dog on a stick and is of minor culinary importance.

Cattail could be confused with tule, since they grow together and have similar growth habits, but tule has small, sedgelike brown flowers in panicles at the top. Cattail flowers are quite unique, often compared to hot dogs, one stacked on top of the other. When the green leaves turn brown in summer, they remain so for a good third of the year, while tule leaves stay green much longer, and the stalks are hollow.

Where and when to gather

Cattail is frequently found in freshwater marshes and marshy places throughout coastal California. You may find cattails in different developmental stages at the same time in a single pond or in different ponds nearby. Before the plants flower or even start to form flower stalks, when the plant is about two-thirds formed, May through July, the outer part of the growing leaves can be removed to leave the succulent inner core, or heart, of the shoot. In May and June, the immature male part at the very top of the flower stalk can be harvested as a vegetable. It will still be sheathed by leaves. A week or so later, it will be full of pollen, which lasts only a few weeks.

How to gather

To harvest the shoot, pull on the inner part of the leaf stalk so it detaches from the outer leaves, without pulling up the root.

Use the part that is easily cut through; discard the tough part. To harvest the top flower section, the male part, to eat as a vegetable, bend it over until it snaps off. To harvest the pollen, also cut the male flower off, put in a glass jar, and take it home to clean the pollen. Dry the flower stalks immediately and thoroughly, then bang the stalks against the inside of a glass bowl three times a day for several days to remove the pollen, which you then put through a sieve.

How to use

To prepare the shoots, peel off the outer layers of the leaf stalks until the soft inner core is revealed, chop, and use as cucumber or quickly cooked in a stir-fry. The top section of the flower stalk (male part) can be steamed, then removed with a knife from the inner woody core, mixed with butter and salt, and used in omelets, fritattas, and quiches, or it can be eaten plain. Once the pollen is dry, it can be stored for a year or two in the freezer and used to enhance the quality of baked goods. It gives waffles and pancakes a rich flavor and golden color, and it is a tasty way to flavor rice.

Future harvests

Cattail is doing so well that in some areas it is considered invasive. It is native to many parts of the world and is currently engaged in spreading to the other parts. In most situations, do not hold back on harvesting cattails.

chalk buckwheat

Eriogonum latifolium

sourgrass, coastal bluff buckwheat, coast eriogonum, coast buckwheat, seaside buckwheat

`EDIBLE` flower stalks, seeds

The stems of this attractive evergreen perennial have a zesty crunch and can be served as sourgrass sticks for an interesting appetizer.

While many oral traditions regarding wild foods have been lost, today's children still manage to convey to each other some knowledge of edible wild plants. These child-friendly plants are often called sourgrass, whether they are an actual grass or not, which chalk buckwheat is not. In early summer, the stems of the plant are enjoyed by local children and others. The plant is in the same family (Polygonacaea) as the grain known as buckwheat, though its seeds, which were traditionally used as a grain by native peoples, are too time-consuming to clean for that use today. The dense, white, chalky coating on its leaves accounts for the name chalk buckwheat.

How to identify

Chalk buckwheat grows 1 to 2 feet high and equally wide. The round to oblong leaves are wavy margined and woolly to varying degrees. They cluster at the base of the stout stems and are of a distinctive blue-gray with white bloom. The flower stalks

This low-growing perennial has a multitude of sour stalks that can be eaten before the buds (shown here) appear.

Chalk buckwheat's flowers are beginning to ripen seed.

are 6 to 8 inches long and leafless, bearing pretty flowers in heads of round, white to pale pink balls over 1 inch wide.

Where and when to gather

Chalk buckwheat grows on steep, rocky coastal bluffs, dunes, and grasslands, from central California to Oregon below 500 feet. Other *Eriogonum* species, such as *E. fasciculatum* (from southern California) and *E. umbellatum* (from the mountains), are found in many parts of California and a few outside of the state. Buckwheat species usually require good drainage and full sun. The leaves and stems of most species can be gathered in late spring to early summer, May to July, before the flowers bloom.

How to gather

Snip off the flower stalks above the last set of leaves.

How to use

Eat stems raw, in salads, or lightly steamed or boiled. They can also be pickled.

Future harvests

This species reseeds well on its own. Six or eight stalks, or even twice that, won't be missed from most good stands of chalk buckwheat.

chaparral yucca

Hesperoyucca whipplei

Our Lord's candle, Spanish bayonet, quixote plant, yucca

`EDIBLE` buds, flower petals, flowering stalk, root, seeds

Chapparal yucca is a prized shoot food, tasting like as well as resembling a giant asparagus. Its creamy white flower petals are an elegant addition to many dishes.

Chaparral yucca is no longer considered by botanists to be a yucca, but it still resembles one, with its stiff, succulent, pointed stems radiating out from the center of the plant (in a rosette) and its stunning 6- to 15-feet-tall flower stalks, depending on the age of the specimen, with many cream-white blossoms. Unlike true yucca, this plant thrives outside of the desert, forming an important part of coastal scrub in central and southern California. Like a meal for a giant, chaparral yucca flower stalks provide a large amount of biomass and should be harvested only when you know you will use the entire stalk. The head, or base, of the flowering stalk can also be removed and roasted. But for a meal with less impact on the plant, the fragrant flowers can be harvested petal by petal; they are sweet and enjoyable to eat, especially cooked with onions.

How to identify

The tall club-shaped flowering stalk reaches upward from the gray-green or blue-gray leaf rosette, their white, waxen flowers dancing in the wind. The numerous white flowers (one naturalist counted 6,000 of them) open facing the ground. The plant needs to be five to seven years old to produce a flower stalk. The plant dies after flowering, but frequently has

These chaparral yucca plants thrive on a steep hillside.

produced new young plants by then, the offsets clustered near the original rosette, ready to take over for it.

Where and when to gather

Chaparral yucca is found growing in the lowlands, in the chaparral belt, and in coastal scrub from southern California to San Benito County. Cut flower stalks in January and February. Gather flower petals in February and March. Seeds ripen in April.

How to gather

The price for harvesting the bounty of chaparral yucca is braving the sharp-pointed leaf stalks that guard them. Wear thick pants and gloves, and proceed with care. Pluck petals off the flower and rinse thoroughly. Yucca moth larvae can be inhabiting many of them. Let them crawl away into the chaparral or leave the cut flowers or stalk near another chaparral yucca.

How to use

The flowers of chaparral yucca are delicious stewed. Sauté with onion, and use in quiche, omelets, or pasta. They can also be boiled. The young flower stalk, which can be turned into a large amount of food, is cut into pieces and pit-roasted or oven-roasted. The young seedpods before they ripen are also cooked and eaten.

Future harvests

The plant expends a prodigious amount of energy to produce the massive flower stalk and flowers. Since it dies afterward, you will not damage the plant by removing its flower stalk for eating. Still, removing an entire flower stalk should be a once-in-a-lifetime event, limited to planted areas or areas about to be bulldozed.

checkerbloom

Sidalcea malviflora subsp. *malviflora*

wild hollyhock, dwarf checker-mallow, dwarf checkerbloom, prairie mallow

`EDIBLE` leaves, flowers

Checkerbloom deserves the description "pretty enough to eat." The sturdy, deep green leaves are delicious mild greens, both raw and cooked.

Checkerbloom is among the prettiest of the spring-blooming native perennial wildflowers. The large, open pale to deep pink flowers are found throughout California in meadows in sun, part-shade, or at woodland edges. The shallowly lobed basal leaves give way to deeply lobed leaves on the flowering stem, and both are tasty, with many culinary uses.

How to identify

The open pink blossoms of checkerbloom are sometimes mistaken for clarkia, but clarkias are annuals and have lance-shaped, long, narrow leaves, while checkerbloom has round, lobed leaves. Though the deer would disagree, clarkia leaves are not edible. Also, large-flowered species of clarkia bloom in early to midsummer,

Checkerbloom's leaves and flowers are edible.

hence the name "farewell-to-spring." Checkerbloom flowers much earlier, in early spring. As members of the mallow family, checkerbloom has flowers that form characteristic little "Gouda cheese" seedpods, each triangular seed fitting neatly into the whole round seed head.

Where and when to gather

Checkerbloom prefers areas where the summers are relatively cool, so don't look for it in the desert. The leaves may be best in early winter, but in the California Floristic Province, winters may be mild enough to keep the leaves going for several months, from December through February. The plants shrivel and go dormant in late spring to midsummer.

How to gather

Leaves and flowers can be easily snipped off with scissors or a fingernail.

How to use

The leaves, when raw, are good in chopped salads and in salsa. Add them to a pesto with cheese and nuts. They also can be steamed, baked, or boiled, becoming slightly mucilaginous, which makes them a good thickener in stews.

Future harvests

The sight of the heart-lifting pink blossoms of checkerbloom is also a kind of nourishment, so do nothing to interfere with future springtime blossoms. Harvest the leaves sparingly, and check the site for invasive weeds that could begin growing while checkerbloom is dormant in late summer, preventing its return to life with the fall and winter rains.

chickweed

Stellaria media

chickenwort, craches, maruns, winterweed

`EDIBLE` flowers, leaves, stems

The modest little herb called chickweed is one of the widely used naturalized greens that some gardeners consider a pernicious weed while others enjoy it in salads.

Creeping unassumingly along the ground, chickweed sends its small oval leaves sprawling in all directions and can be readily harvested for salads or potherbs. Backyard chicken caretakers may be aware of the long-recognized benefits to their flock of this annual weed, and humans also benefit from consuming its full complement of vitamins and minerals. Raw or cooked, it frequently appears on its own in late winter to early spring, disappearing by summertime.

How to identify

With its sprawling habit and bright green oval leaves with pointed tips growing opposite each other, chickweed is somewhat similar to a native woodland herb called modesty. Modesty, however, is a woodland groundcover growing in the shade and is not edible. Chickweed can form a dense mat from 2 to 6 inches tall. It quickly produces tiny, white, five-petaled flowers that look like little stars. The stems have a band of hairs along one side.

Chickweed is still flowering while its edible leaves hug the ground.

The pointy-tipped leaves of the ground-hugging chickweed accompany the narrow white petals of its tiny flowers.

Where and when to gather

Chickweed grows throughout California, particularly where cool, moist winters stay above freezing. It will flower and set seed at the same time, and can be harvested from winter to spring.

How to gather

Pull the entire plant out of the ground, which is not difficult because the roots are shallow. Cut the stems above the roots with kitchen scissors. Try to gather the plant before it flowers, since seed production begins quickly.

How to use

The mild taste of chickweed lends itself to salads and sandwiches until the plant flowers. The more mature leaves that follow are best quickly boiled or added to stews and soups.

Future harvests

Chickweed comes and goes quickly and, with its prolific seeding and quick germination, may even appear again the same year. In spite of its humble appearance, it is a good idea to control the spread of chickweed. So you can freely harvest this pleasant and time-honored green in quantity.

chuparosa

Justicia californica

beloperone, hummingbird bush

`EDIBLE` flowers

In the California desert, the stunning scarlet tubular flowers of chuparosa with their sweet nectar are a draw for humans and hummingbirds alike.

Chuparosa is an easily identifiable showy desert shrub, whose name derives from the Spanish verb *chupar*, "to suck," indicating one use of its red flowers with their sweet nectar. The flower, which has a cucumberlike flavor, can also be eaten. Though not a food to gorge on, because the flowers are small and don't grow as densely as, say, those of creosote bush, restrained consumption adds an enjoyable experience to a desert hike along a creek or wash in the spring.

How to identify

This deciduous shrub, 3 to 4 feet tall, is easily identified by the bright red flowers found in the leaf axils and by its intricate branching pattern. The flower's fused petals create a long, narrow tube, a perfect match for the long, narrow beak of a

The bright red flowers of chuparosa are a vivid sight in April.

Chuparosa lights up the Mojave Desert in Joshua Tree National Park.

Chuparosa's tubular flowers are perfect for the beak of a feeding hummingbird. Look closely to see the incision in a flower made by an insect in search of nectar.

hummingbird. The leaves are oval and usually scanty; the gray-green to silver stems take on the work of photosynthesis.

Where and when to gather

Chuparosa grows along creeks and seeps (narrow openings where water oozes slowly out of the ground) in the deserts of southern California, like near Indian Canyons in Palm Springs. Its main bloom time occurs after the winter rains, from March to June, but some blossoms may be found throughout the year.

How to gather

Pluck the flower carefully from the stem, and remove the green leaves from under the blossom.

How to use

Use as a trailside snack. For an intense jolt of sweetness, either sip the nectar from the open blossom or eat the entire flower.

Future harvests

Sharing the flowers with the hummingbirds and bees that love them is recommended. Harvest lightly from several bushes rather than taking a lot from one individual. Chuparosa is a familiar sight in California deserts, holding its own.

common mallow

Malva sylvestris
cheeseweed, tall mallow

EDIBLE leaves, immature fruit

Depictions of this striking perennial member of the mallow family can be found on tomb paintings in Egypt, where the plant is still an important component of traditional soups and stews.

The large, toothed leaves can be used, like okra, to thicken soups, as well as raw in salads, and in countless other inventive ways, some having to do with the mallow leaves' mucilaginous properties. Mallow is also thought to have anti-inflammatory properties. With its large reddish purple flowers, common mallow can be grown as an attractive garden plant. The leaves are sensational in a weed pesto.

How to identify
Common mallow is a large, weedy, widespread, upright perennial, growing 3 to 4 feet tall, with hairy, sometimes purple, stems and thick, round to kidney-shaped lobed leaves. It begins life looking graceful, and then becomes ragged looking through the season. Like many mallows, it has showy hollyhocklike flowers. The flowers of this species are dark purple-pink with darker stripes.

A mallow pea has formed from the attractive flower of common mallow.

Common mallow is an impressively robust member of the genus *Malva*.

Where and when to gather

Common mallow thrives in the driest ground, and is often found on construction sites, in vacant lots, and along roadsides. Harvest throughout the California Floristic Province in January through March. On the coast, it can germinate with the fog-drip in August and be gathered while young for the next several months, until it flowers.

How to gather

Snip the leaves and flowers with kitchen scissors. Pluck immature mallow peas with your fingers. Remove the leaves cupping the seeds (bracts) or leave them on.

This plant has no poisonous attributes or look-alikes. It is a sought-after host plant for some butterflies, like the painted lady. So you may find caterpillars forming in and munching on the older leaves. If you've already picked a leaf with a caterpillar on it, just put that leaf with its caterpillar on the ground next to the plant.

How to use

The young immature, or unripe, seeds of mallow inside the seed leaves can be eaten like peas, either raw or cooked, while they are still soft, green, and juicy. Once they dry and harden into dark brown, ripe seeds, they are no longer eaten this way. Use the young leaves as salad greens and as spinach. Use larger, older leaves in soups and stews, in tempura, in stuffed "malva grape" leaves, in smoothies, and in chicken soup. Combine with other wild greens, native pine nuts, Parmesan cheese, and olive oil for a wild weed pesto. The young mallow "peas" can also can be boiled with three times the amount of water and sweetened and whipped to make an authentic marshmallow.

Future harvests

The common mallow is doing extremely well. If you find one this year, you'll find five the next year. Make and freeze lots of pesto.

common tarweed

Madia elegans
elegant madia, wild wheat, Indian wheat
EDIBLE seeds

The pungent odor of a field of tarweed and the distinctive savor of its seeds are uniquely Californian experiences, as is the activity of harvesting and preparing the seed.

Once California had many acres of different species of these handsome yellow or white annual wildflowers, all providing seed for the native harvest and all called tarweed because of their intense, bracing odor. They can still be found in sunny meadows where invasive species have not crowded them out. Those who know tarweed seem divided into those who love it and those who do not. The Tarweed Appreciation Society is a small tongue-in-cheek group of native plant lovers who have a fondness for tarweed. The members forgive the plant for the black tarry resin on the leaves that comes off on hands and clothes and is difficult to remove, for the sake of its utterly unique smell, its beauty, and its tasty, spicy, black seeds.

The seed of this attractive species has been widely used for food for centuries.

How to identify

Common tarweed is an annual wildflower growing from 2 to 5 feet tall. In the aster family, it has lemon-yellow blossoms that open in the fog or at the beginning or end of the day, and stay open all night. In full sun, they partially close. The showy flower has a daisylike appearance. The lemon-yellow petals have a faint tint of chartreuse, and sometimes there's a deep maroon circle at the base of the petals. The foliage exudes a unique oil.

Where and when to gather

In July and August, the yellow suns of their flowers, growing on thin stems, seem to float disembodied in the coastal fog. The seeds ripen in August and September on the coast, and earlier inland.

How to gather

To harvest the seed, the Hupa tribe in northwestern California burned the hills while the plants were still green but after the seeds had matured. After burning, they gathered the toasted tarweed seed from the charred plants. Enormous skill was required to control the fire so that it burned the plants just the right amount, because the thin seeds are easily scorched. The contemporary tarweed seed gatherer should become acquainted with the look of the ripe seed and pluck each seed head individually. The hairs on tarweed chaff act like Velcro, making it difficult to separate from the seed. Try to keep seed and chaff separate while harvesting.

How to use

Toast the seed in a pan, and add whole to baked goods, use as a topping or breading, or grind to make a flour (see Pinole: California's Seed Foods, page 62).

Future harvests

This once-common annual wildflower is losing ground to weedy grasses and weeds like yellow star thistle. Sow extra seeds where you can keep an eye on their progress, removing encroaching weeds. Check out biological control programs to prevent the spread of yellow star thistle.

cow parsnip

Heracleum maximum

Indian rhubarb, Indian celery

EDIBLE stalks, leaves, seeds

A favorite of grizzly bears (it comprises 15 percent of their diet from spring through fall), cow parsnip has a unique, spicy fragrance and crunchy, tasty stems.

There is something thrilling about the exuberant early winter appearance of cow parsnip, with its mammoth, toothed leaves and thick light green stalks rising up through native grasses in the rain. It is one of the largest native perennials, with a growth habit reminiscent of celery, its long, hollow stems emerging from a nonwoody crown.

Though it has been named after several well-known European vegetables (parsnip, celery, rhubarb), this native perennial has its own special taste and crunchy texture. The pleasing crunch of the hollow stems is accompanied by the fresh fragrance of the entire plant—sweet, unique, like celery with an indescribable, lively, tangy undertone.

Cow parsnip's large flowers, leaf stalks, and seeds are edible.

How to identify

The large, flat, white, compound flower head, consisting of dozens of tiny, white, toothed flowers, bears a resemblance to the flowers of other members of the carrot family, such as Queen Anne's lace. But cow parsnip distinguishes itself by its large, maple-leaf-shaped leaves. It's a substantial-looking plant, growing from 3 to 8 feet tall. The flower stalk is fuzzy.

Where and when to gather

Cow parsnip grows in many different habitats in the California Floristic Province. Coastal scrub, with its sometimes somber plant palette, is enlivened by the huge flowers of cow parsnip appearing in March through June. Gather stalks from January to March, before the flower stalk begins to form its buds. Once bud formation begins, only the very top of the stalk will be edible.

The seeds ripen in July and August. Leaves appear in October through February.

How to gather

Cut the succulent stems near their base. Remove the leaves and buds to eat the shoots of both flowerstalks and leafstalks.

How to use

Peel the thin outer membrane from the leaf and flower stalk, and eat the stalk raw, steamed, or boiled. Cook young leaves in soups and stews. Use dried seeds for seasoning; their strong taste makes a distinct contribution to stews and soups.

Future harvests

Cow parsnip, with its perennial roots and large size, is holding its own. Cut to the ground after seeds ripen, it will return the following year. It reseeds vigorously.

The sturdy flowers with their umbrellalike shape make cow parsnip easy to identify.

Cow parsnip flowers bloom and seeds ripen at the same time.

Caution

Wear a long-sleeved shirt and avoid touching your eyes when harvesting cow parsnip. Wash your hands thoroughly after gathering. Some people are allergic to substances contained in cow parsnip called furanocoumarins. They can cause sensitivity to sunlight but are easily removed with soap and water.

Cow parsnip is sometimes thought to resemble another member of the carrot family, poison hemlock, *Conium maculatum*, the plant reputed to have sent Socrates to his grave. The leaves and growth habit of the perennial cow parsnip are readily distinguished from the annual poison hemlock. The white flowers might confuse you in the beginning, but check out the leaves. Poison hemlock has many fernlike or parsleylike finely dissected leaves, triangular in shape, that begin going dormant quite early in the summer. The leaves of cow parsnip resemble maple leaves and are large and few. The flower and leaf buds are massive.

Poison hemlock is an annual dependent on reseeding, with a minimal root system that does not survive more than one season and is nothing like the sturdy roots of cow parsnip. Once you get used to these two species, their differences are obvious. Still, have an expert verify your initial identification. Water hemlock, *Cicuta maculata*, another member of the parsley family, should also be avoided. Unlike cow parsnip, it has hairless stems.

coyote mint

Monardella villosa

western pennyroyal

`EDIBLE` leaves, flowers

The fragrant leaves and flowers of coyote mint make a pleasant digestive tea, particularly enjoyable around the campfire.

A pretty native perennial belonging to the mint family, coyote mint grows on rugged, sunny, well-drained slopes and hills where it is set off by other California perennials that like a similar setting, such as wild buckwheat and lupine. Its shiny, dark green leaves, neat mounding habit, and soft, fuzzy purple flowers add color and presence to the plants growing on a dry hillside. At the same time, they expand our repertoire of enjoyable, healthful native beverages. Popping the fragrant leaves or flowers into your water bottle provides a pleasant minty flavor that will refresh you throughout the day. In the evening, you can pour hot water over the leaves for a soothing after-dinner tea.

Coyote mint is a pretty sight when in full bloom in April through July.

How to identify

Leaves are lance-shaped and dark green, with an unmistakably minty fragrance. They are green both above and below, with short hairs. The plant is 1 to 1 ½ feet tall and 1 to 2 feet wide, with a woody base. The flowers are purple, up to 1 inch across; four long stamens create a fuzzy appearance.

Where and when to gather

Coyote mint grows in northern and central California, on banks and slopes in chaparral or at the woodland's edge. It likes full sun or part shade. Gather the leaves through June, and the flowers in April through July.

How to gather

This little plant is a bit too tough for fingernail snipping, so cut with pruning shears. Cut to enhance its naturally neat, mounding habit.

How to use

For tea, pour boiling water over the leaves and flowers and steep for 10 minutes. Strain and drink plain or with sweetener. Coyote mint can be dried for future use. Use it to make syrups or jellies as you would any member of the mint family.

Future harvests

Harvest in small amounts from several plants, rather than large quantities from a single plant.

Caution

Avoid if pregnant.

creek monkeyflower

Mimulus guttatus

seep monkeyflower, seep spring monkeyflower,
valley monkeyflower, yellow monkeyflower

EDIBLE leaves, stems

When young, the new leaves of creek monkeyflower have a sweet, crisp, lettucelike succulence, so you can enjoy them raw.

As the name indicates, creek monkeyflower is found in moist areas. Though this perennial native wildflower has seeds that are only dustlike in size, it somehow manages to secure a hold for itself among many powerful wetland plants, like sedge and iris. When young, its new leaves have an enjoyable texture and a hint of bitterness, which is thought to be healthful, an indicator of the phytonutrients that are often missing from the modern diet. When mature, the leaves should be boiled. Its

Gather the succulent greens of creek monkeyflower before its large yellow flowers appear, drawing bees and other pollinators.

large yellow flowers, said to resemble monkey faces, offer a welcoming platform for bees and other insects.

How to identify

A perennial growing from 1 to 3 feet tall, depending on its competition and available moisture, creek monkeyflower is easily identified by its light green, scalloped leaves and its large, showy, yellow flowers. Unlike most of its monkeyflower relatives, it has soft rather than woody stems and springs forth anew from the ground every year.

When and where to gather

Look for creek monkeyflower near creeks, seeps, and wetlands throughout the California Floristic Province. The leaves taste best before it blooms, so gather from December through February. New leaves will appear with the fall and winter rains.

How to gather

Cut the leaves from the stem, leaving enough for the plant to continue its life cycle.

How to use

Add young leaves to salads, sandwiches, and snacks. Boil older leaves and stems until no longer bitter, and use like you would other wild greens, or quelites. They may require boiling in one or two changes of water.

Future harvests

Given a modicum of support, creek monkeyflower tends to return year after year in its home territory. Sharing habitat with extremely tough plants and even invasive species like vinca, it both returns from the previous year's roots and spreads from seed. Scattering seed nearby works well. Weeding out the invaders works even better.

curly dock

Rumex crispus

curled dock, sour dock, bitter dock, winter dock, narrowdock, yellow dock

EDIBLE leaves

The mild lemony taste of curly dock is pleasing when the young leaves are eaten raw, and becomes creamy when cooked.

Our continent has its share of *Rumex* species, but curly dock, naturalized from Europe and Asia, has such a long history of use here that it almost sets the standard for wild edible greens. Its long, narrow leaves are high in vitamins A and C. Don't judge this excellent potherb by its overly mature leaves. With curly dock, timing is all, and following its dramatic life cycle is a lesson in plant growth. The dramatic seed stalks from the previous year will help you locate nearby young, tender dock plants for salads. And as the plant matures, you'll have no trouble finding its large, older leaves to use in a multitude of ways.

How to identify

The rich, dark green mature leaves of this perennial are elliptical, rise from the ground, and have one light noticeable vein in the middle of the leaf (midrib). They have crisped or curled leaf margins, with

Curly dock produces a prodigious amount of reddish seed capsules.

much variability, that can be as long as 1 foot. Pull the plant up when it is done flowering to examine its yellow root, which confirms your identification of this plant also called yellow dock. In early summer, curly dock produces masses of flowering stalks with numerous tiny flowers consisting of three green and three red seed leaves (sepals).

Where and when to gather
In coastal counties in California, dock plants usually germinate with the fall and winter rains, or send up new leaves from the taproot. So harvest greens from October through March. Leaves mature through the winter and by spring in the California Floristic Province are frequently too tough to enjoy. Foggy days along the coast can provide enough moisture for new plants to germinate, providing greens in early and late August through October, when they're at their best. Desert docks begin growing in the Mojave Desert with the winter and spring rains. Moisture and temperature will determine when to harvest, but generally early spring, March and April, sees the beginnings of the flower stalk, signaling the end of leaf edibility.

How to gather
Leaves can be plucked by hand or cut with kitchen scissors.

How to use
Like many widespread weedy greens, dock is an honored ingredient in recipes from the lands of its origin, such as Turkey. Uses for dock are related to leaf age: the young, tender leaves are excellent in salads and pestos; older leaves are good additions to soups, stews, and lasagnas, and can be boiled or steamed like spinach. The leaf stems (petioles) can be chewed raw.

Future harvests
Many dock species from Europe and Asia, including curly dock and broad-leaved dock, are categorized as injurious weeds, so don't hesitate to harvest them, and be careful that you do not spread the seeds. Keep your own patch well under control.

desert ironwood

Olneya tesota
tesota, palo fiero, ironwood
EDIBLE flowers, pods, seeds

Desert ironwood is a stalwart desert tree that yields profuse, sweet, edible pink-lavender flowers, tasty immature seeds, and dried seeds that can be popped like popcorn.

Desert ironwood enhances its immediate environment with nitrogen, shade, and organic matter to such an extent that the plant has protected status as a "keynote species." And it can do all this throughout a lifespan of about 1,500 years. The presence of ironwood in desert scrub, its natural environment, increases the number of local bird species by 60 percent. It is a nurse plant to the vulnerable young seedlings of innumerable species as well, providing shade and protection from the desert's extremes of cold and heat, as well as fertility from the nitrogen-fixing nodules on its roots. For many desert peoples, its seeds, which taste like peanut butter, were an important protein source. Its wood is so dense and hard that it sinks in water like a stone.

The leaves of desert ironwood are present for a longer season than those of any other desert tree.

This desert ironwood is growing in an alluvial fan in the Sonoran Desert.

How to identify

A wide-crowned large shrub or small tree, desert ironwood has compound leaves, with broadly rounded leaflets of pale bluish green to 3 inches long and ½ inch wide. The leaves drop in summer, leaving the tree briefly bare. It is characteristically large enough to create a canopy where it grows, and is the only desert tree with leaves in midwinter.

In late spring and early summer, desert ironwood will transform an alluvial fan or dry wash in the Sonoran Desert with the haunting fragrance of its blue-purple-rose, wisterialike, long clusters of flowers. After the blossoms drop, so do the old, dark-green leaves, which are almost immediately followed by light green new leaves. The light tan pods are 1 to 2½ inches long, and contain one to three black seeds per pod.

Where and when to gather

Found only in the Sonoran Desert of southeastern California below 2,500 feet, as far west as Palm Springs, desert ironwood favors sandy washes and alluvial plains. Its flowers are found in profusion from late April through May. The fresh peas can be gathered from May through June, and the pods of dried seeds in June and July.

How to gather

Snip flowers into a bag and use at once. Light brown seedpods will contain bright green immature seeds, which should be collected when the seeds are sweet and nutty. Dried mature seeds should be gathered into a paper bag or box. Either shake from the tree onto a tarp or pluck directly from the tree, which can go surprisingly quickly. Do not, however, gather pods directly from the ground.

How to use

Desert ironwood flowers can be eaten raw or candied. The fresh green pods are best eaten either in the pod or shelled like garden peas. Blanch immediately in boiling water for at least 2 minutes. Cool and eat, or freeze. Mature seeds can be soaked overnight, rinsed and dried well, then toasted in a frying pan to pop like popcorn.

Serve with butter and salt. Or, after soaking overnight, they can be rinsed daily and kept slightly moist until sprouts emerge. Squeeze the seed coat, releasing the sprout, then use raw or cooked.

Future harvests

With its many useful attributes and importance to desert scrub habitat, ironwood needs protection and planting. Only use salvaged lumber, never cut desert ironwood for charcoal or timber, and control buffelgrass, whose spread leads to the increased fires that desert ironwood cannot withstand. Consider using it as a landscaping plant wherever possible.

Douglas fir

Pseudotsuga menziesii var. *menziesii*

EDIBLE needles, exudate (sugar)

The needles of the mighty Douglas fir make a mild, exceedingly pleasant tea, woodsy with a hint of lavender.

Douglas fir is one of the defining conifers of the west and a mainstay of the timber industry. Its needles and the needles of many other conifers have an array of health benefits, including a high percentage of vitamin C. One cup of Douglas fir tea contains more than five times the vitamin C found in a lemon, as well as significant vitamin A. Under certain conditions, Douglas fir produces a sweet, white substance called Douglas fir sugar, or wild sugar. It is exuded from the branch tips, and was once a popular sweetener, containing an unusual form of sugar called melezitose.

How to identify

Douglas firs in their middle years are tall, pyramidal forest giants with drooping limbs and deep green single needles with a white streak down the middle. The new growth spreads out at the branch tips in a chartreuse fan. The cones are small, the size of an egg, with three-lobed bracts sticking out between the thin, closely

A pleasant, healthful tea can be made from the new growth of Douglas fir.

layered scales. When old, Douglas fir has deeply furrowed gray bark on a tree that is either the mightiest of the mighty when given its favored spacing of 50 to 100 feet from other trees, or a very tall telephone pole with a radiating topknot of branches when grown close to other forest giants. The trees can be found blasted by coastal winds into picturesque shapes or planted in monocultures like tall ears of corn.

When and where to gather

Douglas fir grows from the central coast of California to the west side of the Sierra Nevada and Klamath Ranges up to 7,500 feet, and continues north into the Pacific Northwest, where it joins the great northern rain forests. It is included in many forest associations, growing with redwood, oak, tanoak, pine, and in mixed-evergreen woodland. The best tea is made from the spring-gathered new needles, from March through June. The trees growing in full sun in the moister parts of their range produce Douglas fir sugar during the hot days of July and August.

Conifers

Conifers are needle-leaved trees and shrubs that reproduce through seeds contained in cones. This group includes firs, spruces, cedars, hemlocks, and the largest group, pines. Many conifers produce needles that make excellent teas with high vitamin C content. The vitamin dissolves into but is not destroyed by the hot water used in making tea.

How to gather

Cut the light green new growth off the twigs, or if using mature growth, cut the stem tips off and pull off the individual needles. Scrape the sugar off the tips of the branches into a container, on sunny mornings after frost.

How to use

Use scissors to cut up the needles, pour boiling water over them, and let steep for 5 to 10 minutes, or soak overnight to make a concentrate that can be diluted to taste. Drink hot or let cool for an iced tea with honey and lemon if desired.

Future harvests

Douglas fir has many attributes that enable it to hold its own. Though Douglas fir is an admirable western conifer, I remove its many baby seedlings in our north coast woods, part of the thinning necessary for a woodland restoration project, a slow return to a prehistoric spacing. Also, oaks, gray pines, and other important hardwoods fostered by native peoples for food crops cannot compete with the growth rate of Douglas fir. I use the saplings I pull up to make the tea, which has proved to be a crowd pleaser.

Caution

Avoid tea made from the following conifers: ponderosa pine, *Pinus ponderosa*; Norfolk pine, *Araucana heterophylla*; and Pacific yew, *Taxus baccata*. Do not drink any tea made from conifers if you are pregnant or trying to become pregnant.

evergreen huckleberry

Vaccinium ovatum

black huckleberry, California huckleberry, winter huckleberry, shot huckleberry

`EDIBLE` berries

The dark color of evergreen huckleberries and the high percentage of skin indicate a fruit full of healthful antioxidants.

The evergreen huckleberry is such an attractive shrub, from new growth to flower and fruit, that many try to cultivate it, with mixed results. It usually lives in openings in coastal forests, thriving best under Bishop pines, redwoods, Douglas firs, and coast live oaks. In these locales, the berries ripen even in shade or fog. A friend who has harvested and eaten so many huckleberries in his life that he describes himself as being "half huckleberry" is one of the healthiest people I know. His harvesting methods are so efficient that he gifts us with jars of frozen huckleberries deep into the berryless winter. Dried huckleberry raisins are also a delicacy.

How to identify

Evergreen huckleberry grows 5 to 8 feet tall and wide. It has thick, lance-shaped evergreen leaves about 1 ½ inches long.

The glossy green, toothed leaves of evergreen huckleberry set off its highly appreciated deep blue-black berries.

New leaves are a striking pink-orange color, adding to the beauty of this shrub. Pinkish white bell-shaped flowers occur in the leaf axils, becoming small, smooth, gleaming blue-black berries about the size of a garden pea. Some berries have a whitish bloom.

Where and when to gather
Evergreen huckleberry grows along the coast from northern California to central California and south to the Channel Islands. It also occupies a place of honor in maritime chaparral, a rare form of coastal chaparral where a thin layer of good soil, some moisture, and occasional fog are found. Beginning in July, the green berries turn blue-black and juicy, and the harvest begins. By October, the bushes are usually cleaned out, but you can sometimes find a miraculously unpicked shrub here and there, worth searching for.

How to gather
Particularly plump berries can be gathered one by one with the fingers, savoring the juicy ripeness of each small berry. To speed things up, rake berries into a bowl with your fingers, or use a berry rake. Expect to include some leaves, unripe berries, twiglets, and small insects in your take; then just remove these later by shaking the harvest in a large bowl. Berries will sink to the bottom, and most debris will rise to the top, where you can scoop it off.

How to use
Retaining their shape in pancakes, muffins, pies, and breads, evergreen huckleberries are a treat in baked goods. Eat raw or cooked. They also dry easily, seeming to be almost mold-resistant, turning into superlative raisins that have lasted as long as ten years, even when casually stored in a seed-collecting envelope. They freeze well and make coveted juices, jams, and jellies. Commercial imitations of the jams and jellies are common; the real thing is rare and precious.

Future harvests
Because of their relatively small size, huckleberries are a gathering challenge. Be careful to leave green berries on the shrub to ripen after you leave. These plants are not the easiest to propagate from their tiny seed, so scattering ripe berries or even cleaned seed rarely leads to new shrubs. They are crown sprouters, like the redwoods they live under, sending up new stalks from cut or burned stumps. In wild huckleberry patches, protect them by keeping weeds out, and watch out for the invasion of the weedy thornless blackberries, Himalayan blackberry, or Scotch broom. This kind of attention is what evergreen huckleberries need.

farewell to spring

Clarkia amoena

clarkia, herald of summer, summer's darling, godetia, satin flower, atlas flower

`EDIBLE` seeds

Not only have the flowers of farewell to spring pleased generations of wildflower lovers, but history indicates that the seeds of different species of the plant have been a favorite seed food of many native peoples.

This graceful annual wildflower appears after the main luxuriant spring bloom of California's native annuals begins to set seed. As the bright blooms of early spring disappear from the hills, and the annual weedy grasses succumb to the drought and rising temperatures of a California summer, all kinds of clarkias appear. The thirty-one colorful California *Clarkia* species are set off by the dry plants around them, signaling the onset of California's deep, dry summer.

How to identify

Farewell to spring grows from 8 inches to 3 feet tall, depending on soil type and moisture availability. It has upright or spreading stems with dull gray-green linear leaves that alternate on the stem. Different *Clarkia* species have specific patterns of usually mid to dark pink or red marks or spots on their four cup-shaped petals that help us to distinguish them. Farewell to spring is one of the largest and longest blooming *Clarkia* species. A deep magenta

Farewell to spring, a summer-blooming wildflower, has edible seeds.

This mass of farewell to spring blooms in July on the north-central coast.

marking of varying size appears halfway up the pale pink to deep wine–colored petals. The seed capsules are light tan, curved, narrow pods that curl outward as they open from the top to slowly release the ripe seeds.

Where and when to gather
Farewell to spring is found in the Coast Ranges from northern Marin County to Washington state, at 1,500 to 4,500 feet. It grows in full sun to part shade in a wide range of soils. Blooming from May to July, it sets seed from July to August.

How to gather
Gather seed stalks before the seed capsules have completely uncurled and released the seeds. Cut the flower stalks with the drying seed capsules at the base of the plant. Soak the entire plant in water for two hours, and then dry it in the sun. This process will help the seed capsules to split open, releasing the seeds. Otherwise, they don't readily release the seed. This ingenious method of dealing with this particular species' recalcitrant seed dispersal was practiced by the Sierra Miwok.

How to use
Once the seed is cleaned, it can be toasted and ground to make mush, or mixed with wheat flour to be used in baked goods. Some tribes formed it into large loaves, weighing up to ten pounds.

Future harvests
Invasive species are a problem for this and all annual wildflowers. If you know of good native stands of farewell to spring, take it upon yourself to keep them weeded, and only collect seed sparingly. If you wait to gather seeds until the capsules begin to open, some of the seed will already have been dispersed on the ground, ensuring future harvests. Most *Clarkia* species are vigorous reseeders when given a chance, particularly in the environment where they belong.

fawn lily

Erythronium californicum

bear tooth, dogtooth violet

`EDIBLE` corm

The bulbs of this native species, and others of the genus *Erythronium*, are delicious without cooking, milky and sweet.

The first sighting of a colony of these exquisite woodland wildflowers will be long remembered. The taste of their deeply buried corms, to those fortunate enough to experience it, is similarly memorable. These plants are not common enough any-more for the bulbs to be freely eaten, yet when they thrive, they spread so plenti-fully that the precious experience of a tiny harvest may, in favorable circumstances, be justifiable. And the first taste will inspire protection.

How to identify

The flower faces downward. Five long, tapering petals of pure white rise on a stem of only 4 to 6 inches. Two large, oval, mot-tled leaves rise from the base of each plant.

Under its mottled leaves, a fawn lily flower nods, facing downward.

A yellow ring around the white petals is characteristic of fawn lily.

This mottling, resembling the coloring of a fawn, resulted in the name. The bulbs are narrow and 1 to 2 inches long.

Where and when to gather

Fawn lily is found in open woods from northern California to Vancouver, B.C. It blooms from March to May. The corms may be sampled in June, when the seed has ripened.

How to gather

Dig carefully to find the narrow corm without breaking it.

How to use

Eat raw, boil, or roast, or boil and then roast.

Future harvests

This root food should be considered for eating only in a patch that you are familiar with, or that you have planted and tended.

fennel

Foeniculum vulgare

sweet fennel, large fennel, wild fennel, finocchio, anise

`EDIBLE` stalks, seeds, leaves, pollen

Many parts of wild fennel are edible, with a taste like licorice, an aroma reminiscent of anise, tarragon, and chervil, and a reputation for healthful qualities.

Fennel, a garden vegetable gone wild, is a scourge in California, especially along the coast. Anyone who loves the wildflowers, grasses, and flora of California will be alarmed to see the miles of fennel now moving along our roadways, from south to north. Once established, this plant is difficult to remove, so bring on the foragers.

I have been able to soften my heart toward fennel by learning to use its pollen. Captured from the flowers before they set seed, it has a warm, enticing smell that carries through in baked goods. The new growth tips of the finely divided leaves are as sweet and flavorful raw as a licorice stick, and much healthier. The stalks when young can be eaten like celery.

How to identify

Fennel is an easily recognized upright, nonwoody biennial, with finely divided, feathery soft leaves of a rich green color.

The delicate-looking, golden fennel flowers contain heady anise-flavored pollen.

Growing 3 to 6 feet tall, the stems rise from swollen petioles (leaf stems) that clasp the main stalk to form an edible structure that is commonly referred to incorrectly as the bulb. The yellow flowers appear in the second year in delicate heads 5 to 8 inches across.

Where and when to gather

Fennel is everywhere in California but is most often seen along the coast. There, fennel blooms, sets seed, germinates, and grows all year long. Harvest the pollen in September through January and the seeds in October through January. The leaves are best sampled during the first year of growth. Harvest seed from midsummer through fall. Wild fennel's bulblike root structure is tough, woody, and unpalatable, so don't bother to dig it.

How to gather

Cut the fresh young fennel tips in early spring. Pull or clip the flowers off the stem while pale yellow and just before the seeds are beginning to ripen. Dry in a paper bag. Rub the flowers against a screen to separate the pollen from the rest of the flower. Use fresh or when dried. The stalks should be cut before the plant blooms. Snip flower clusters into a paper bag to collect the seeds in the bottom.

How to use

The new growth of a first-year fennel plant makes an exquisite trailside nibble. Help yourself, then pull the whole plant up by the roots if the soil is still moist enough. The pollen can be used in baking, for a sweet anise flavor. Try muffins, cookies, and particularly, a fennel–olive oil cake. Grind dried pollen to make a fragrant powder that is easily incorporated into many dishes. The thickened stalks can be used like celery, either raw or cooked. The leaves are used as seasoning, in sauces and stews. Serve the seeds as an after-dinner condiment. Candied or plain fennel seeds are frequently offered in Indian restaurants.

Future harvests

I remove fennel even when I don't want to use it, to protect the species that are easily swamped by fennel's aggressive ways. Harvesting its pollen is a good way to lessen the spread. If fennel isn't an invasive problem where you live, it just hasn't gotten there yet. Use and use and use some more of the delicious wild fennel. If you can't dig it out, at least cut the flowers to eliminate seed spread.

foothills palo verde

Parkinsonia microphylla, formerly *Cercidium microphyllum*
yellow palo verde, littleleaf palo verde

`EDIBLE` flowers, fruit, seeds

The young green seeds of foothill palo verde are as sweet and tasty as English peas though considerably easier to grow in the desert.

A deciduous multitrunked large shrub or small tree, foothills palo verde is widespread in desert areas in Arizona but rare in California. Of the two palo verdes in our state, the seed of this species is considered tastier; the young peas of the related blue palo verde, which grows in arroyos and floodplains, can be bitter.

Slow growing, this tree can live for several hundred years. Wherever locals have used it in landscaping, it is a delight, graceful and lacy, open but still providing shade. It has some thorns and reputed medicinal properties. The flowers of foothill palo verde are edible. The immature green seeds are delicious either raw or cooked. The plant requires no water, staking, fertilizing, or protecting from predators.

How to identify

The flowers of the foothills palo verde are pale yellow and white, paler than the bright golden flowers of the blue palo verde. They are ½ inch wide and have five petals each. The top petal is white, and the other four petals are yellow. The leaves are bipinnately compound (finely divided so they have a feathery appearance), with

The seed capsules of foothills palo verde constrict around each juicy edible pea.

five to seven pairs of tiny, oval leaflets. The seedpods constrict between each seed. There is a spine at the end of each yellow-green-barked branch.

Fallen branches under the trees reflect a shedding of limbs and leaves during times of drought, which leaves scars on the photosynthesizing bark of the trunk. When leaves drop early from extreme heat, the bark takes over their job, while the debris creates a fertile nursery for other desert plants.

Where and when to gather

A few populations occur in southeastern California near the Colorado River in the Whipple Mountains. The species is able to handle even more arid conditions than the blue palo verde, and is found on slopes. It flowers in late April and May, a few weeks after the blue palo verde, when the desert's summer heat is beginning. It forms its delectable "peas" in early summer, late May and June. The seeds ripen and dry in June and July, so gather green peas before that.

How to gather

Pluck flowers from the tree. Pluck pods from the tree and remove the immature green seeds, tasting them first to make sure they're still tender and sweet but not chalky. Gather mature seedpods from the tree or shake them off the tree onto a tarp. Freeze two days to kill possible insect infestation.

How to use

The "peas" can be eaten raw or lightly cooked when young or cooked longer when slightly older but still green. They can be blanched and frozen for later use. The dried seeds can be sprouted and eaten raw after squeezing the sprout free of the seed coat. Unsprouted seeds can be cooked after soaking until the seeds pop, and then ground for pinole (see page 62).

Future harvests

Invasive species like buffelgrass can use up available moisture that the young seedlings of foothills palo verde need for early growth. Preventing the spread of such grasses will help with future harvests.

Caution

Process pods from the tree immediately to avoid mold. Don't gather pods that have fallen onto the ground.

The yellow flowers turn this desert tree into a mass of gold in spring.

giant blazing star

Mentzelia laevicaulis

star flower, smoothstem blazing star

`EDIBLE` seeds

Once giant blazing star fades at the end of its season, the treasured seed capsules become visible.

A showy perennial wildflower, giant blazing star presents its extravagant beauty to travelers throughout the drier parts of northern California. It has large and unmistakable shining yellow flowers that open in late afternoon. In full bloom, the plant is stunning, but a couple of months later, while the seeds ripen, it becomes a dried-up shadow of its former self, waiting to fill out and bloom again with the next rainy season. When the seeds are roasted, ground, and cooked into a mush, the taste is surprisingly similarity to peanut butter.

The seeds of other *Mentzelia* species also have a long history of being eaten in California, including the related annual, bushy blazing star, *M. albicaulis*, and Nevada stickleaf, *M. dispersa*.

How to identify

Giant blazing star is an upright perennial growing from 1 to 3 feet tall, depending on soil and moisture availability. It has erect, white, smooth, hollow stems. The bright yellow flowers, with sharply pointed petals, are 3 to 4 inches wide. A stunning

The large bright yellow flowers of giant blazing star have sharply pointed petals.

The showy flower of giant blazing star is a generous provider of edible seeds.

feature of the flowers is the numerous yellow stamens rising from the cupped, elongated golden petals and the yellow sepals between the petals. The triangular, elongated leaves have rough or barbed hairs that make them stick to clothing and to each other. The lower leaves are lobed.

Where and when to gather

Giant blazing star is generally found in Trinity, Humboldt, Modoc, and Shasta Counties, but makes appearances throughout the California Floristic Province in sunny, dry areas below 8,500 feet, excluding the Sonoran Desert and the Central Valley. It is found on roadsides, on steep roadcuts, on dry streambeds, and on disturbed soil. The plant flowers from June through October, depending on locality and elevation. Ripe seed can be gathered from August through September.

How to gather

Many parts of the plant are sticky, so be careful to keep the collected seeds away from the sticky leaves, seed capsules, and stems. Otherwise, you'll waste time separating them later.

How to use

Roast the seed, grind it, and cook it with water slowly and until it forms a thickened mush or soup. It can be used like peanut butter as a spread, a dip, or as porridge.

Future harvests

Scatter seed into likely sandy or gravelly disturbed areas where little competition from other vegetation is present.

golden chia
Salvia columbariae
chia, California chia, desert chia
`EDIBLE` seeds

Golden chia is a showy, drought-tolerant wildflower producing a wild grain that is delicious, easy to prepare, and documented to have health benefits.

Aficionados of chia purchased from health food stores may not realize that they are actually eating the seed of a Mexican species, *Salvia hispanica*, now usually grown in Australia. Long before chia pets and chia seed smoothies, many California Indian tribes counted the seeds of a related species, golden chia, *Salvia columbariae*, among their staple foods, even sharing them with sixteenth-century English explorer Sir Francis Drake and his men. Traditional stories, such as "Coyote Ate Up All the Chia in Town," attest to the long-held custom of gathering and eating this chia. The almondlike, nutty flavor is similar for the Californian and Mexican species, and can enhance many different dishes, both savory and sweet.

Golden chia responds to a wet year with purple-blue flower stalks up to 2 feet tall and a rich seed harvest.

In a drought year in the Mojave Desert, chia still makes its presence known, growing in widely spaced colonies of smaller plants producing less seed.

Chia shows its membership in the mint family with its purple blooms and square stems.

How to identify

Golden chia, a member of the mint family, has square stems and blue-purple flowers growing in a tier along flower stalks that are up to 3 feet tall. When the flowers dry, they become prickly and brown.

Where and when to gather

Golden chia used to grow in sunny, open spots throughout California, including the deserts, foothills, and rocky slopes near the coast. It is most frequently seen now in southern California, where rocky or sandy hillsides still provide opportunities for this colonizing plant to flourish. Blooming in May and June, golden chia sets seed in June and July.

How to gather

As they ripen, the mature flowers turn brown. When tipped over, they release small, oval, gray-brown seeds in a satisfying stream into your gathering basket, paper bag, or open palm.

How to use

The uses of chia seed are many. Toast them in a pan, and as soon as they begin to pop, jumping out of the pan, remove the pan from the heat and pour the seeds out to cool on a plate. Add the seeds whole or ground to baked goods, especially cookies and muffins. Chia seed cookies are a tradition at our annual open house.

The seeds of golden chia have a nutty flavor.

Add the seeds to other grains, like rice, oatmeal, farro, and bulgur, to enhance their nutritive value, and include in granola recipes. Or toast and grind them to make flour or meal, substituting for one-fourth to one-half of the wheat flour in a recipe. When soaked in liquid, the seeds become mucilaginous, part of the reason they are recommended for digestive health and for those with glucose intolerance. They can be used in drinks mixed with lemon and cinnamon (called *agua de chia*), in smoothies, and to make gelled dishes like aspic.

Future harvests

In the wild, gather only 5 percent for your use. And sow some of the seeds in nearby areas with similar conditions, where the soil is lean, open, and free from weeds.

You may look in vain for golden chia in many places in northern California where it once grew. Chia, a colonizer, likes to be the first plant in open ground, a rarer and rarer commodity in California. So give it a place in the garden. Our yearly harvest of an organically grown golden chia is assured by sowing the seed in the fall in lean, weed-free soil. We gather some of the seed to eat, leaving the rest to germinate the following year on its own.

golden currant

Ribes aureum

clove currant, black currant, golden flowering currant, fragrant golden currant

`EDIBLE` fruit

In 1805, Sacajawea pointed out this attractive western shrub to Meriwether Lewis, who soon became a fan of its delicious fruit.

Two different varieties of golden currant occur in California, which together make it widely available. With its shiny green foliage and early blooming, trumpet-shaped yellow flowers, this deciduous shrub is a pleasure to find in the wild, so much so that it asks to be grown at home and frequently is.

The berries produced by some of our other native currants are a bit flat or even sour in taste, while our thorny gooseberries are a bit too prickly, so it is a blessing to find a native currant whose fruit is both tasty and unarmored. Unlike some other red berries, like the red elderberry or hairy honeysuckle, the red-orange to orange-yellow berries of golden currant, though seedy, are sweet and tart in a pleasing ratio, and taste as good as they look.

The five-petaled yellow flowers of the mountain-grown species of golden currant have an inimitable fragrance.

Golden currant in the spring is a mass of yellow blossoms.

How to identify

These shrubs grow from about 5 to 10 feet tall. Small, spherical, bright-green leaves grow alternately on smooth stems and have three to five toothed lobes. The leaves turn gold and drop in late summer, and return in early spring. The five-petaled rich-yellow flowers of the mountain-dwelling species have a pleasant, inimitable fragrance that is hard to describe—somewhat spicy, somewhat sweet. The yellow, orange, to deep-red or purple berries that follow are up to ½ inch in diameter, glossy and juicy. The flowers of the more coastal varieties have no fragrance.

Where and when to gather

One subspecies of golden currant grows in the mountains and another on the coast, so this shrub can be found throughout the California Floristic Province. *Ribes aureum* subsp. *gracillentum* grows from southern California to just south of the Bay Area, and its yellow petals turn deep red, with no fragrance. It prefers areas where it is protected from the wind. *Ribes aureum* var. *aureum* grows in the mountains and east of the mountains as well as in the interior. Its yellow flowers turn orange as they ripen and have a spicy fragrance. They both bloom early, February through April, and the berries form in June and July.

How to gather

With small scissors, cut the entire cluster of berries off the plant. Trim the remaining flower off the individual berries, and then snip the berries from the stem.

How to use

Unlike Sacajawea, you may decide not to make pemmican with these berries, but eating them raw is a treat. The wonderful taste may make you wonder why this fruit is not better known to Californians. The currants are good right off the bush or mixed with other raw fruits. Cook them into jams or jellies, syrups, pies, and fruit tarts.

Future harvests

Many birds, from hummingbirds to thrashers and robins, and mammals, from bears to bunnies, love these berries, so don't strip the shrubs. The birds will help spread the seed. Monarch butterflies can be seen nectaring at the flowers in early spring. Consider planting this shrub in your garden as an ornamental with benefits. Spreading from an underground root system, golden currant responds well to pruning.

golden prettyface brodiaea
Triteleia ixioides

golden triteleia, golden brodiaea, golden triplet-lily, prettyface,
prettyface brodiaea

`EDIBLE` corms

Golden prettyface brodiaea, one of the few yellow-flowered
brodiaeas, combines a striking appearance with a tasty root. It was
traditionally cooked and eaten like other native bulbs.

Golden prettyface brodiaea ranges from the Sierra Nevada to the coast. It is often surrounded by a varied multitude of annual wildflower species, like bird's eye gilia, Chinese houses, and tidy tips. Another example of California's floral beauty going hand-in-hand with wild nourishment,

golden prettyface brodiaea is prolific and responds well to proper harvesting.

How to identify

The flowers of golden prettyface brodiaea can be a unique apricot-yellow, or yellow, or pale yellow, with striking black-purple

Numerous yellow blossoms with purple veins indicate the presence of these edible corms.

Golden prettyface brodiaea, a striking native plant with edible corms, is found from the mountains to the sea.

or dark green veins on the outside of each petal. The flower-bearing stalk is 6 to 18 inches high, leafless, and rough. The flower clusters may include up to thirty-five flowers, each just under 1 inch in diameter.

Where and when to gather

Golden prettyface brodiaea grows in the higher foothills of the Sierra Nevada from Tuolumne County to Kern County at 1,200 to 5,000 feet. It can also be found in Monterey, San Benito, and Tehama Counties and throughout the California Floristic Province. It blooms in April and May, and the corms can be gathered in August and September.

How to gather

When you see the plant in flower, make note of the location. Dig near the dried seed stalk, carefully lift the mother corm, then remove the cormlets from the corm's sides and replant them, keeping the mother corm for your modest harvest. The corms are ¾ to 1½ inches in diameter (see Indian Potatoes, page 54).

How to use

Indian potatoes all taste pretty much the same, like potatoes only sweeter and with more flavor, especially when cooked long enough to begin to caramelize. The corms can be peeled and eaten raw, boiled, steamed, or baked.

Future harvests

Grow first in your own garden to ensure the correctness and efficacy of your gathering methods. Harvest the mother corms sparingly, and replant the cormlets carefully in the loosened soil.

goldfields

Lasthenia californica

California goldfields, valley goldfields

`EDIBLE` seeds

For the native peoples of the California desert, a good goldfield bloom year promised a feast, for the seeds of this annual wildflower were a favored traditional seed food.

In springtime in the western Mojave Desert and the Central Valley, the small annual flower called goldfields becomes responsible for creating a vast acreage of heavenly yellow. Very similar to it in appearance is another wildflower also called goldfields, *Lasthenia glabrata*. Though the flowers aren't notably fragrant individually, or particularly showy, when blooming en masse, both species produce a delicate perfume adding to a scene of transcendent beauty.

Easy to identify and prolific, with no toxic look-alikes, the seed of both goldfields makes a good pinole option for the adventurous forager.

How to identify

The daisylike structure of this flower is carried on a reddish, wiry stem. Its opposite leaves are linear and not very conspicuous once the flower is in full bloom, from March to the end of April. They grow from

Goldfields blossoms viewed individually are modest, small, daisylike flowers.

Goldfields in a good wildflower year, covering many acres in California in the spring, are a true California phenomenon.

4 to 15 inches tall, depending on moisture and the fertility of the soil. Both ray and disk flowers are yellow and are ½ to 1 inch in diameter. The dull gray seed of goldfields has been compared to iron filings by David Prescott Barrows, who recorded a vivid picture of its daily preparation by the Cahuilla people of southern California.

Where and when to gather

Goldfields grows in the California Floristic Province and in the Mojave Desert. It blooms from March through May, and its seed ripens from April to June.

How to gather

Pinch the drying seed head between your fingers, give a light tug, and deposit it in a bowl or a bag. Or use a badminton racquet to pop the ripe seeds into a gathering basket held close to the ground. Rub the seed head between your hands and then winnow (see Pinole: California's Seed Foods, page 62).

How to use

Toast the seeds lightly until they dry and become brittle. Grind and add to flour to be used in baking. Or add salt to the toasted seeds and use as a garnish or for breading.

The seeds can be preserved in a cool, dry place for up to five years.

Future harvests

Sloppy collecting allows plenty of seed to fall to the ground for next year's fields of gold. Weedy species are among the biggest threats to this plant, and to other annual California wildflowers. Vineyards and other kinds of development continue to encroach on California's unique and irreplaceable wildflower fields.

gray pine
Pinus sabiniana

digger pine, foothill pine, blue pine, bull pine, nut pine, ghost pine

`EDIBLE` nuts

From the rockiest, driest, most unpromising Californian soil, gray pines produce tasty, healthful nuts, containing a remarkable 25 percent protein and the highest quality fats and linoleic acid.

Our native nut pines produce nuts with a savor that outcompetes imports. They taste like Italian stone pine nuts, only with a subtle difference—a more intensely nutty flavor. In the landscape, the gray pine tree is distinctive for its long silver-green needles and its spare, frequently crooked growth habit. A unique decision in the history of California taxonomy officially eliminated the common name of "digger pine" previously given to this tree. It was thought to be a derogatory reference to native peoples' practice of digging edible wild roots, a traditional skill that is now greatly admired by foragers and others.

How to identify

The gray pine has sturdy, large, golden-brown cones with sharply pointed cone scales that must be outmaneuvered during the harvest of its nuts. These forbidding scales enclose large, thick-shelled nuts over 1 inch long, the delicate wing barely visible within their resting place.

Gray pine has a delicate, spindly, sometimes almost ghostly appearance. The pale silvery needles in bundles of three are the longest of any of the pines, up to 1 foot long. While many pines are stately in appearance and welcome providers of shade, gray pine grows tall and slender,

Gray pine has sturdy golden-brown cones that range from the size of an orange to that of a football.

from 35 to 50 feet high, rarely 80 feet tall, and from 10 to 40 feet across. Forked dark trunks make a striking contrast against the light-colored foliage.

Where and when to gather

The gray pine grows only within the borders of California, frequenting dry, rocky slopes where rainfall is sparse. It can be found circling the Central Valley, in the inner Coast Ranges, south to Los Angeles County and north to Mendocino County and the Klamath Mountains. It grows surprisingly close to the coast at Big Sur.

Gather cones in early summer to midsummer, from June to July, in the hotter, drier regions, and in August in the northern parts of the state. The cones can be found with nuts intact as late as September and October.

How to gather

Cones can be knocked off the tree with sticks or gathered from the ground. Note how the ground slopes and follow it down to a flat place where the cones will come to rest. Gather into canvas bags or cardboard boxes. Heavy gloves make the task easier.

How to use

Gray pine nuts have a thick, hard shell and a small wing. Sometimes the nuts fall out easily from the cone; other times they need help. Roast the entire cone in a fire, or drive on bumpy country roads with the box of cones bouncing around in the trunk. Or wear safety glasses and smash the cone into four pieces with a hatchet or hammer. A nutcracker with pressure applied at both pointed ends will split the sturdy nutshell

Gray pine stands out against a landscape of chaparral plants.

cleanly, exposing the nutmeat within. Roast or toast the long, narrow nutmeats with oil until light brown. Eat plain, add salt, grind into pesto, or use in the same ways you would other nuts in baking and cooking. Try not to eat them all yourself.

Gray pine nuts store remarkably well, retaining the ability to germinate for up to twenty years. To preserve their freshness, store them unshelled in a cool, dry place in a mason jar. They can also be refrigerated, unshelled, for up to three years.

Future harvests

Gray pine is frequently outcompeted by Douglas fir and other taller woodland species, so while collecting the cones from within gray pine groves, remove the saplings of other species that may overtop gray pine. And share the harvest with the tree planters—the gray squirrels, pinyon jays, scrub jays, and others.

hairy bittercress

Cardamine hirsuta

sneezewood, popping cress, cardamine, touch-me-not, lamb's cress, spring cress, shotweed

EDIBLE leaves, stems

Adding hairy bittercress to a mixed green salad will provide a delicious peppery flavor similar to that of arugula.

This vigorous green from Europe and Asia, whose many common names attest to its long association with humankind, might also be called peppercress, for the enjoyable pungency of its foliage. Hairy bittercress has an illustrious history, being one of the nine herbs mentioned in a tenth-century Anglo-Saxon text. Its peppery quality does disappear with cooking, but in a green salad, bittercress's intense flavor is a tasty element.

Bittercress appears on the California landscape with the rains, where it seems to have been spread by way of nursery plants. Its movement in a garden is little short of breathtaking, requiring ingenuity to think of ways to use up its springtime abundance. It disappears totally in the summer,

A weed that gardeners find challenging, hairy bittercress is also a delicious wild green.

leaving so little evidence of its presence that you wonder if it was all a dream.

How to identify

This deep green herb grows close to the ground, usually somewhat under 1 foot tall, with distinctive round leaflets alternating on stems up to 9 inches long at the base, and becoming smaller as they go up the stem. Each leaflet has a hairy leaf stem. Tiny white flowers with four petals each are borne in clusters at the ends of the flowering stems. It has the distinctive seedpod (called a silique) of many mustard family plants, which is a long, narrow capsule containing many seeds.

Where and when to gather

Hairy bittercress likes the cool growing conditions present in many parts of California in the winter. Gather as soon as it appears in the late fall and early winter, from November through March.

How to gather

Pull up by the roots before it flowers, to avoid spreading seed.

How to use

Use as any green, in salads or boiled or steamed. It can pep up many dishes, such as quiches, vegetable lasagnas, and pastas. It's a useful addition to sandwiches and makes a zingy soup.

Future harvests

This plant causes considerable concern among vegetable gardeners. It can spread easily, so harvest before the seeds form. The seeds ripen quickly and spring open with a touch.

harvest brodiaea

Brodiaea elegans subsp. *elegans*

Indian potato, elegant brodiaea, elegant cluster-lily, harvest cluster-lily

EDIBLE corms

The taste of harvest brodiaea's underground corms, when boiled or roasted, is remarkably similar to that of potatoes, only better.

For a plant that is as beautiful as it is delicious, try harvest brodiaea. Its open-throated colorful blossoms are flung across the grassy hillsides and meadows of many parts of California, marking the arrival of early summer. Though harvest brodiaea belongs to the lily family and is not botanically related to potatoes, the bulbs taste like potatoes when cooked. They have a faint sweet aftertaste that is at least as compelling as potato chips, and it is just as difficult to eat only one.

How to identify

This perennial native bulb may look familiar, like a smaller, daintier agapanthus lily, to which it is related. As the grasses on California hillsides begin to go dormant in May and June, look for harvest brodiaea's umbrellas of deep blue–purple flowers and grasslike, fleshy leaves growing 1 foot tall. In the center of the flower are five to six white or pale purple sterile stamens known as staminodes; these are flat, with pointed or toothed tips, between $1/5$ and $2/5$

Clusters of elegant deep purple flowers indicate the location of delicious harvest brodiaea corms.

Tiny cormlets cling to the mother corm of harvest brodiaea.

How to gather and use

Indian potatoes are an important part of the traditional indigenous diet. Specific gathering techniques were practiced to ensure the sustainability of this harvest, which the modern forager can easily follow. (See Indian Potatoes, page 54, for a discussion of how to harvest and prepare them.)

Future harvests

The seeds are important for future crops, so don't pick the flowers. When digging the corms, err on the side of caution by digging farther down than you think is necessary, usually to 6 inches deep. This will help avoid inadvertently destroying the mother corm while harvesting, which was thought to be bad luck by some tribes, and is certainly a disheartening and wasteful experience. After replanting the cormlets, when the fall and winter rains come, the cormlets will first send up stalks and then roots. Frequently they flower and their corms will be ready to harvest the next year.

of an inch long. Next to these are the fertile stamens topped with large pollen-bearing anthers. The corms are about 1 inch long.

Where and when to gather

Harvest brodiaea can be found in the California Floristic Province, in the Klamath and North Coast Ranges, and in the northern Sierra Nevada to southwestern Oregon. This species will tolerate heavy soils, both summer drought and occasional moisture, and sun to part shade. In early summer to midsummer, harvest brodiaea can be found blooming throughout the state, even in the mountains up to 7,000 feet, but not the deserts. Look for the plant later in the wildflower season, blooming from June to July. You will spot the gorgeous flowers on sunny, grassy hillsides, in lightly grazed pastures, in sunny woodland clearings, and on banks along roads. The seed stalks serve to mark the location of the underground corms in the late summer, when the narrow leaves have dried up and disappeared. Gather from July to September.

Growing harvest brodiaea in your garden, either in the ground, or, in the presence of gophers, in large containers or wooden boxes at least 1 foot deep, is a good way to learn the rhythm of harvesting and replanting without harming any native stands. Water lightly and infrequently in the summer, stopping when flowers begin to set seed. Once your brodiaea boxes have proven to be sustainable through time, you've accumulated some of the necessary experience to gather from the wild.

Himalayan blackberry

Rubus armeniacus
bramble
`EDIBLE` berries, leaves

Himalayan blackberry has large black berries of an irresistible sweetness and juiciness that everyone loves, while disliking its nasty thorns and invincible conquest of territory.

Actually arriving here from Europe, probably as a garden plant, the so-called Himalayan blackberry does now actually grow in the Himalayas, as well as in many other parts of the world. Wherever it finds itself, the phrase "impenetrable thicket" is used, to describe the growth habit of this plant. Scourge of the countryside, destroyer of ecosystems, thorny slasher of down parkas and soft skin, ruination of white clothing, this invasive plant, its delicious berries notwithstanding, should be destroyed whenever you have the chance.

But meanwhile, avail yourself of its tangy, strongly flavored, sweet berries whenever possible. Make jam, make jelly, make pies. The less the birds, inveterate seed spreaders, eat, the better. Never was a species at once so good and so bad.

How to identify

This thorny rambler has large, white, five-petaled flowers, three to five leaflets per leaf, and soft, black berries that everybody recognizes. It has large thorns and white undersides to the leaflets. It spreads

Himalayan blackberry has large berries that are juicy and sweet.

Himalayan blackberry also has large thorns, to be avoided.

through its rambling canes that root as they go, and through the seeds that are dropped by birds.

Where and when to gather

This species has spread over the entire United States. It disrupts forest understories, riparian habitat, coastal scrub, it simplifies and destroys many ecosystems, and it is a true foe of biodiversity, yet it exemplifies ingenious survival. The berries ripen in August and September throughout California.

How to gather

Protect yourself from thorns with gloves and long-sleeved, heavy clothing, and pick with both hands into a berry pail tied to your belt. Don't bother with berries with any red on them, for they will be powerfully sour.

How to use

Pick one perfectly black, perfectly ripe berry, and the answer will be apparent. Eat raw, eat now. The ones that make it back home are candidates for berry crisp or crumble, berry pie, fruit tarts, berry ice cream or sorbet, berry jam or jelly, and wine. The berries can be frozen or dried for later use.

Future harvests

These invaders can grow 20 feet in one season, so fight them with all the power at your command, which also means eating as many berries as possible. If attempting to actually remove Himalayan blackberry, simply cutting to the ground will be useless. These plants must be removed by the root, or don't bother. Or cut to the ground and then sheet-mulch with impermeable substances like cardboard or canvas tarps, to be removed when the roots of the blackberry plants have died.

holly leaf cherry

Prunus illicifolia

islay, California laurel cherry, hollyleaf, mountain evergreen cherry

EDIBLE fruit, seeds

The dark red to black cherries of holly leaf cherry are sweet and flavorful.

A grove of the beautiful little trees known as "islay" in a cool canyon or near a creek in the Coast Ranges of central California is a pleasant place to be in spring, when the fragrant white blooms draw the hum and buzz of many visiting bees. The dark red to black cherries that follow are an additional treat. Though not meaty, the thin juicy coating of skin and flesh is pleasant.

The Indians were more interested in the kernel inside the stone enclosed by the thin fruit, which they pounded in a mortar, leached with water, and made into a well-loved gruel that tastes like beans. During the Spanish Mission era in California, Indians living at the missions were sometimes given time off to allow for harvesting of this interesting and nourishing food, which today is much less well-known than acorns.

Many a California canyon or creek is named after this white-blossoming shrub or small tree with the nickname islay.

The fruit of holly leaf cherry can be soaked to make a refreshing beverage. These cherries will be dark purple when ripe.

How to identify

This small, evergreen tree or large shrub, usually around 15 to 20 feet tall, is easy to recognize with its fragrant white cherry blossoms in spring. Shiny, spiny, evergreen leaves similar to holly leaves are 1 to 2 ½ inches long and 1 to 1 ½ inches wide.

Where and when to gather

Occurring from just north of San Francisco Bay and south through the Coast Ranges down to Baja, holly leaf cherry can be found in canyons, by streams, and also competing with other shrubs in the chaparral of coastal California. An island form, *Prunus illicifolia* var. *lyonii*, without the spines on the leaves and with larger fruit, is found in the Channel Islands. Gather the ripe cherries in July through early September.

How to gather

Pluck the cherries from the tree by hand when dark purple to black.

How to use

The thin flesh is best for snacking on raw, for making fruit leather, or for soaking the pulp to make fruit juice. After that, the pale stone inside should be soaked in hot water or boiled, then spread out to dry in the sun for a few days. The pit is then cracked open, and the kernel within can be stored indefinitely. Like all cherry pits, these kernels contain hydrocyanic acid, which is toxic and must be removed. Accordingly, the kernels are pounded, and the acid is leached out with running water until they are no longer bitter.

Ethnobotanist Jan Timbrook describes another method involving soaking the kernels in cold water: Bring them almost to a boil, and pour the water off, performing this task three times to leach out all bitterness. And if you're still interested—and given how popular this dish was with California's native peoples, your curiosity may well be aroused—boil the pounded and leached kernels in water for two hours. Ash was sometimes added to remove any further bitterness. Once the kernels have softened, mash again and form into small balls. Roll them in pinole flour (see page 62) and leave to dry. This is the traditional method. For modern times, add oil and garlic to make a hummus. These islay balls can be preserved for a week.

Future harvests

Holly leaf cherry is a useful hedge component, street tree, and a frequent addition to native plant gardens. Rarely are they planted in groves to mimic their natural occurrence. Islay orchards could be a useful landscape design element.

Caution

Hydrocyanic acid is considerably more dangerous than the tannic acid found in acorns. This may be the reason that the kernel preparation procedures have fallen into disuse. Process with care.

honey mesquite

Prosopis glandulosa var. *torreyana*

western honey mesquite, mesquite, algaroba

EDIBLE pods

Every part of honey mesquite was used by desert native peoples, from pods to thorns, bark, gum, roots, twigs, and leaves.

Honey mesquite is a necessity of life for large numbers of Californian desert wildlife, from mule deer to skunks, coyotes, and doves. Though cooks who use mesquite flour are not as numerous as they once were, every Indian household in the desert traditionally ground the tough, leathery pods with the seeds in them into flour. The seeds were removed and sometimes discarded as they were freed from the pod in the grinding process. Many devoted mesquite users still enjoy this naturally sweet, nutritious food. It has a rich molasses taste that makes superb baked goods. The loss of mesquite flour from indigenous diets is thought to be one of the factors responsible for the increase in diabetes among desert tribes. A current revival of interest in mesquite flour has led to the recent enjoyable availability of mesquite tortillas.

How to identify

Honey mesquite is a deciduous large shrub or small tree growing from 10 to 20 feet tall with a rounded, irregular shape. It produces long, yellow, flower spikes that become 8-inch-long beanlike pods. Drooping branches have 3-inch-long paired spines. The leaves are alternate, deep green, and bipinnately compound (doubly or twice divided), with simple leaflets less than 2 inches long that produce a feathery, lacy look. If cut down, honey mesquite will sprout from the base and become a multi-trunked shrub or tree.

Where and when to gather

Found in southeastern California, in the Mojave Desert and the San Joaquin Valley, as well as in Arizona and Baja, honey mesquite is adaptable to different desert situations with availability of underground water. The pods are ripe when they have turned a tan color and have begun to drop from the tree. Pods ripen from June to August, depending on locale.

How to gather

Rake the pods into a pile and remove the debris. Let them dry in the sun for a couple of days. Some prefer to pick the pods directly from the tree, but watch out for the thorns. Sweetness of the seed varies from tree to tree, so sample before gathering.

Honey mesquite will fruit even during drought years, providing a reliable source of food.

How to use

Special hammer-mills offer a "you collect it, we'll grind it" service, but if you'd like to do it yourself, dry the pods in the sun and grind in a food blender, sifting out for your use the fine flour that results first. The seeds and the outer part of the pod, more difficult to grind, should be left behind if you are processing the pods yourself. As a rule of thumb, use a proportion of 25 percent mesquite flour to 75 percent wheat flour in baking. Mesquite flour is also used as a seasoning, and in drinks. The flowers can be used to make tea. The uses of mesquite as firewood for adding a tasty smoky flavor in cooking are well known.

Future harvests

Overgrazing led to the multiplication of mesquite in many arid rangelands, where it is now considered a weed to be attacked with aerial spraying and heavy machinery. Honey mesquite needs to be recognized as the miracle plant that it is. Pruning can help productivity, as well as creating comfortable openings in the scrub, for the honey mesquite is said to produce remarkably pleasant shade, an invaluable commodity in the desert.

Indian ricegrass

Stipa hymenoides, formerly *Achnatherum hymenoides*,
formerly *Oryzopsis hymenoides*
sand grass, Indian millet, Indian mountain-rice grass, silky mountain grass, wye

EDIBLE seeds

Indian ricegrass is tough enough to handle harsh, sandy, dry conditions, and its seed makes a tasty desert popcorn or breakfast mush.

A perennial bunchgrass found in the deserts of California and in much of the semiarid west, Indian ricegrass was called the Queen of the Desert in a poem by early ethnobotanist Edith Van Allen Murphey, who encouraged its replanting in the early 1900s. Since the seed is relatively large for a grass, it contributed significantly to the diets of indigenous desert dwellers and was probably the most important grass seed food in the Southwest. The ease with which the seed can be harvested and cleaned, its early ripening at a time when not many seed foods are available, its relatively large grain, and its delicate savor were factors in its popularity.

How to identify

Ornamental flowers in clusters of unusual grace and delicacy make this hardy plant one of the easier grasses to identify. It is one of the most common bunchgrasses in the desert. The thin, upright grass blades are rolled, with a distinctive curve from base to top. The plant, including the flowers, can grow up to 2 feet tall in good conditions, but is usually closer to 1 foot tall.

The flowers grow in an open cluster with curving, very thin stems producing a light, airy appearance. Two bell-shaped leaves (bracts) encase each single flower, and you must open these to release the ripe seed. The small, round to oval, dark seeds are hard and pointed at the tips.

Where and when to gather

This once-abundant plant of desert and Great Basin grassland can still be found growing in light, sandy soils from the Colorado and Mojave deserts, except in the higher mountains and driest areas. It also grows north along the east side of the Sierra Nevada. A cool-season grass, it starts growing with the fall and winter rains, and it flowers and sets seed in late May or June.

How to gather

The seeds of Indian ricegrass fall easily (shatter) from the plant if shaken, and need to be harvested promptly upon maturity or the wind will blow them away. This characteristic also makes it one of the easier native grass seeds to gather, since it

This tough desert bunchgrass has a delicate, lacy appearance.

falls right into your basket or bag if your collection is timely.

How to use

Toast, grind, and cook in water for making mush, which is light gray with the texture of Cream of Wheat but more flavorful. A range of culinary uses includes dumplings, soup, bread, and tortillas. Use it in baked goods, mixed with wheat flour. It can also be used as breading and mixed with other flours, like cornmeal. Used like gomasio (see page 62), it is delicious toasted in oil, ground with salt, and used to top rice and other cooked grains. It is easy to digest, high in protein, and nutritious.

Future harvests

Indian ricegrass has major habitat value for a wide range of wildlife and domestic stock. The range of Indian ricegrass has seriously diminished as a result of over-grazing, development, competition from weedy grasses, and drought. Success in scattering seed in likely areas near your gathering site requires that many factors cooperate. Find open, sandy areas free of competition and sow seeds in the fall. This fascinating grass germinates best when the seed has been stored for four to six years, making this a long-term project.

Kellogg's yampa

Perideridia kelloggii

yampa, yampah, wild celery, wild caraway, white anise, peppergrass, wild anise

EDIBLE leaves, shoots, tuberous roots, seeds

Kellogg's yampa is a perennial wildflower with a number of easily prepared and enjoyed edible parts. Highly valued by the native peoples of California, its roots were dug by the bucketfuls from fields where they grew thick as grass.

The different forms of edible root that Kellogg's yampa produces are all sweet, from the twisted enlarged crown rootlets to the elongated or pearl-like swellings all along the wiry stems. The leaves are a tender and mild green when young, followed by the flower shoots, which resemble a mild asparagus. Even the seeds of this multifaceted plant provide an anise-flavored seasoning. Try any of these parts, and you'll understand why some villages used to set up near yampa fields, harvest, and then proceed on to another yampa meadow, to do the same thing over again.

How to identify

Kellogg's yampa is a perennial herb 2 to 4 feet in height, depending on available moisture. Its slender, erect stems grow from a cluster of long, narrow, fibrous roots at the crown, each up to 3 inches long. Leaves growing from the base of the

The young, narrow leaves of Kellogg's yampa make a delicious potherb raw or cooked.

Before the buds of the lacy white flowers of Kellogg's yampa open, the flower stalks can be harvested and cooked like asparagus.

plant are divided into three narrow leaflets. Before the flower stalks arise, it has a dainty appearance, with its crown of graceful, curving, slender leaflets. The flower is a compound umbrella of spherical clusters of small white flowers. These yield ribbed, oblong fruits, each about ¼ inch long.

Where and when to gather

Kellogg's yampa is endemic to California, where it is known from the north and central coasts, the San Francisco Bay Area to Sonoma County, and the foothills of the Sierra Nevada. It grows in grassland habitat, sometimes on serpentine soils, and is found in moist mountain meadows and wet lowland grasslands.

The plant goes dormant in the late summer. New leaves appear as early as November and can be gathered, depending on rainfall, from late winter until early spring, The young flower stalks (shoots) appear in March through June. Harvest the roots when the leaves have died, and before the flowers form, in spring to midsummer, April through July. Dig the roots after a good spring rain, so the soil will still be moist for easy digging and the edible sugars will still be stored in the roots. The seeds ripen July through September.

How to gather

Snip the leaves with scissors. Cut the flower stalks with pruners or a knife, taking only one or two flower stalks from each plant. To gather the roots, loosen the soil around the plant with a hand pick. Pry up the roots and untwist the swollen root parts, replacing the smaller pieces back in the soil. Contained in the fibrous root mass

The sweet tuberous roots of yampa were a traditional root food.

are the pea to peanut-sized edible root-lets. Cut the seed stalks and place them in a paper bag to catch the seeds as they drop to the bottom.

How to use

The slender young leaves can be eaten raw, or boiled, steamed, or baked. They will plump up when boiled, becoming sweet and mild. Cut the flower shoots and steam, boil, or bake. Untangling and discovering the different kinds of edible roots provided by this plant is fascinating work They will shrivel up after being gathered, and will soften when chewed, releasing a uniquely pleasant flavor. They can also be boiled, baked, or steamed. The seeds are used as seasoning and for pinole (see page 62).

Future harvests

Replant a few of the untwisted tubers and swollen rootlets in the loosened soil. Har-vested seed can be scattered nearby in soil loosened by your root removal. Kel-logg's yampa is one of many species of *Perideridia*, which are similar in appear-ance. Most are edible. Weedy species and the conversion of yampa fields to develop-ment are the greatest threat to the survival of the twelve different species of yampa in California, which richly reward our atten-tion and care.

Caution

The dainty white flowers of Kellogg's yampa bear a minor resemblance to another member of the carrot family that is poisonous, the poison hemlock. However, the leaves, growth habit, and certainly the roots of yampa are easily distinguished from poison hemlock. Poison hemlock is an annual with a minimal root system that is nothing like the sturdy roots of yampa. Poison hemlock has fernlike or parsleylike dissected leaves that begin going dormant quite early, unlike the leaves of yampa, which resemble gently curving, flattened potato sticks. Once you get used to these two species, their differences are obvious. Have an expert validate your identification.

lady fern

Athyrium filix-femina var. *cyclosorum*
western lady fern

`EDIBLE` shoots

The curled-up fiddleheads of lady fern are a widely enjoyed woodland delicacy, with a taste and texture similar to those of asparagus.

Easy to find, gather, cook, and enjoy, the uncurling shoots of lady ferns are a welcome sign of spring. The young shoots before they stretch out into leaves are known as fiddleheads because of their resemblance to the scrolled end of a violin. Lightly steamed, they almost melt in your mouth. Lady fern is one of the two ferns native to California whose fiddleheads are edible, the other being bracken fern.

How to identify

The basic visual component of many a northern California woodland understory, the graceful, feathery lady fern can be a bit challenging to identify because it looks so generically "ferny." One helpful characteristic is that the fronds are wider in the middle, narrowing at both the tip and base of the leaf.

The fronds of lady fern are wider in the middle, narrowing at both the tip and the base of the leaf.

New lady fern fiddleheads continue to grow up through the unfurled fronds until June.

Lady fern fiddleheads should be cut for eating while still tightly furled.

Where and when to gather

Found in seasonally flooded swales and moist woods, meadows, roadside ditches, coastal swamps, lakeshores, marshes, and riverbanks, lady fern is one of the most common native ferns, second only to bracken fern. You will see it with other wetland plants, like sedges and willows, as well as with woodland plants, like redwood alder, oak, and California bay laurel. Harvest lady fern fiddleheads from early to late spring, March through May, before the fronds have unfurled.

How to gather

Look down into the dormant crown of the lady fern, and you will find the curled up fronds nestled in a cluster at the base. Be ready to harvest them as they slowly lengthen and rise up, before the tip unfurls. A young lady fern specimen may produce fiddleheads only 3 inches long, while older, larger, well-established plants send up robust fronds up to 1 foot long. Use a sharp knife or pruners to cut the fiddle-heads cleanly at the base.

How to use

Wash off the brown, flaky coating. Eat only the part of the stem that will still snap in two. Small fronds can be sautéed quickly in oil or butter. Larger fronds should be steamed or boiled. Like asparagus, the lower stalk will take longer to cook than the tender curled tip. The fronds are delicious in stir-fries and with pasta, or just by themselves.

Future harvests

To ensure the future health of the plant, remove no more than one-fifth of the fronds in one gathering season. Harvest only two or three fiddleheads from each plant, and don't return to those plants until two years later. Overharvesting has been found to seriously injure or kill lady ferns.

lambsquarters

Chenopodium album

wild spinach, fat hen, goosefoot, pigweed

EDIBLE leaves, leafy stems, buds, seeds

In many parts of the world, lambsquarters is admired and welcomed as a delicious green. Many species in the genus *Chenopodium* are edible. Particularly well-known is the protein-rich grain from the Andes called quinoa, *Chenopodium quinoa*.

David Douglas, an early naturalist exploring the west from 1825 to 1834, was surprised that the native peoples were suspicious of this green, which then was newly arrived on our shores. These days, it's one of the more well-known wild greens. Lambsquarters belongs to the illustrious goosefoot genus, so named because of the webbed goosefoot shape of the leaves. It has an impressive nutritional profile, with high amounts of protein, iron, manganese, potassium, vitamins, and carotinoids. It's easy to identify, easy to gather and cook, spreads generously, and stays sweet and tender for a relatively long time, spring into summer.

How to identify

This annual herb grows from 1 to 5 feet tall, depending on soil and moisture conditions. Its spadelike leaves are covered with a waxy powder, which is most noticeable

Lambsquarters is a favored edible plant worldwide.

Lambsquarters is found throughout California up to 5,900 feet.

How to gather

Snap off the top 3 to 5 inches of leafy stems to encourage the plant to become bushy and produce more growing tips for future harvesting. Any part that you can snap off cleanly will be good to eat. If it bends instead of snapping off, harvest more toward the top of the stem, or gather only the leaves. Put leaves and stems into a bowl of cold water until ready to use, and rinse thoroughly.

How to use

In earlier times, the main part of lambsquarters used was the small black seeds; charred remains of the seeds have been found in numerous archaeological sites. You can still process the seeds as pinole, though the leaves are now the most frequently eaten part of lambsquarters. It can be prepared and eaten as you would spinach, in omelets, in vegetable lasagnas, or raw in a salad when young. To use as a potherb, boil for about fifteen minutes. Like spinach, it makes a great soup.

on new growth. The leaves become gently toothed as they reach maturity. The plant starts out with one stem growing upright and branches out with maturity and pruning. The bud clusters adhere closely to the flower stalk, and the flowers are greenish white.

Where and when to gather

Lambsquarters grows everywhere in California, including in the deserts, where it is edible for a shorter time. It germinates with the fall rains and grows through the winter. In the California desert, it may also germinate and grow with the monsoon season, in July and August. Begin harvesting the leaves as soon as the plant is about 1 foot tall, from December through March or April. Harvest young bud clusters while still tender and green, throughout the rainy season and into March and April. The seeds ripen May to July.

Future harvests

Plants growing in the wild near vulnerable native species should be pulled up from the root and not allowed to set seed. But those found in vacant lots or in your vegetable garden can be mulched and pruned for long-term continual harvesting. Remove the plant as soon as it begins to flower. Lambsquarters produces millions of seeds, which grow readily and need no help.

lemonade berry

Rhus integrifolia
coast sumac, lemonade sumac
`EDIBLE` coating of fruit

The small flowers of lemonade berry become small, hard fruits called drupes, which when ripe have a waxy seed coating that almost magically turns water into lemonade.

Widely used in landscaping, this native shrub is a handsome member of the southern coastal scrub plant community. Children in particular are drawn to the ease of collecting the fruits of from this appealing shrub, because their little fingers will meet with no painful thorns. This plant could provide lemonade stands with a new twist.

How to identify

This drought-tolerant evergreen shrub grows about 15 feet tall and 8 feet wide.

Thick leathery leaves about 1 inch long have toothed margins. Unlike its close relative sugar bush, its leaves do not bend at the midrib but remain flat. Small flowers of pale pink or white grow in tight clusters that turn into small red fruits with a sticky covering that tastes lemony.

Where and when to gather

Lemonade berry is found in southern California near the coast on north-facing bluffs and in canyons in coastal scrub and

This shrub of southern coastal chaparral bears a thirst-quenching fruit for the hiker.

The ripening fruit of lemonade berry has a unique, lemony waxen coating that can be used to make lemonade.

chaparral. The five-petaled pale pink flowers bloom from February through May. The fruit ripens at the end of May and remains on the plant through July.

How to gather

Pluck the fruits from the shrub and place in a nonsticky glass or ceramic container. Or drop directly into your water bottle.

How to use

The ripe fruit is soaked and stirred or shaken in water. Like the manzanita berry, you can also put them in your mouth and suck on them. The seeds traditionally were also ground and roasted.

Future harvests

Currently lemonade berry is not threatened. Its utility in landscaping also ensures lemonade berry a place with us. You don't need many of its fruits because they pack a powerful punch, so share some with the birds.

Caution

Lemonade berry is in the cashew, or sumac, family. If you are allergic to plants in the cashew family, such as cashews, you might be allergic to these fruits.

madrone

Arbutus menziesii

Pacific madrone, madrono, tree arbutus, strawberry-tree

EDIBLE bark, berries

Made into a tea, the curling red bark of madrone has an indescribable many-layered taste, with woodsy overtones of fruit and cinnamon.

One of the most striking trees on the West Coast, madrone is hard to miss, with its large, thick, tropical-looking leaves, delicate but showy white flowers, red berries, and fascinating reddish orange bark that sheds in pieces. Though madrone has delicious-looking red-orange berries, they are not compelling in their taste. The unique bark, made into tea or stock, may contribute the most to our culinary possibilities. It calls to the creative cook: "Use me."

How to identify

Madrone is a sun-loving tree that sends its trunk and limbs in search of the sky. The white urn-shaped flowers in spring, on tiny stalks attached to spikelets, are followed by scarlet-sienna berries. The

The red-orange shredding bark of the madrone tree makes a splendid tea.

Madrones have sculptural trunks and branches.

most compelling identifying feature is the bark, with its dark gray, rough, checkered outer bark that peels off to reveal, on older trunks, rich dark red, smooth inner skin, and on younger trees, a lighter bark that is orange or light green. The evergreen leaves are 3 to 5 inches long, and 3 inches wide, with an upper surface that is bright green and glossy, and a whitish, leathery underside. Madrones can grow to 40 feet in height and 2 feet in diameter.

Where and when to gather

You will find madrone trees growing with Douglas fir, tanoak, and other oak trees, in a forested belt east of the redwoods, up to 3,000 feet. They grow in both the inner and outer Coast Ranges from northern to southern California, in the foothills of the Sierra Nevada, and in the Transverse Ranges. In June, July, and August, harvest the red bark as it dries and peels off in long, shaggy curls.

How to gather

The bumpy-skinned berries, which look like globular carnelians, are fairly bland. The beautiful flowers, though edible, are best left on the tree. Instead, harvest the red bark as it peels off. The bark can be stored in a cool, dry place for up to a year.

How to use

Make a tea with the bark by pouring boiling water over the dry curls and simmering until the water is dark red. Use the infusion in cooking grains and as a flavoring in making custards, ice cream, stews, or in any situation where a flavorful, colorful broth is needed.

Future harvests

Madrones, though subject to various diseases, are still doing well in their native ranges. Harvest small amounts of curling bark from a number of different trees.

manzanita

Arctostaphylos species

little apple

`EDIBLE` berries, seeds

Manzanita's ripe fruit, the "little apples," are appreciated for the surprisingly sweet cider that can be made from their brittle, dry red or red-orange skin.

Manzanita is among the most beautiful California shrubs, varying from a low-growing ground cover to a large shrub, and ranging from the coast to the foothills of the Sierra Nevada. The many species are evergreen, with smooth, red to mahogany to chocolate-colored bark, and are often sleekly sculptural, with intriguing crooked stems. Though the seeds were once ground to make pinole, today it is the berries that are most widely used. When chewed, the taste is first merely sawdustlike, then suddenly an intense flavor burst emerges. This sweetness is a welcome surprise on a hot hiking trail, and one that can be prolonged and shared when the fruit is made into manzanita cider.

Over forty different species of manzanita are found throughout California, all with edible berries.

The bell-shaped flowers of manzanita come in shades of pink and white.

How to identify

Manzanitas grow throughout California in full sun to part-shade. Though identification as to species can be confusing, they all bear similar fruit. They have in common the bell-shaped, waxy, white to pink flowers, the deep orange to mahogany-red fruit shaped like little apples, the simple and alternate leathery evergreen leaves ranging from deep green to silvery-blue-green, and the smooth, frequently deep red bark.

Where and when to gather

Manzanitas can be found from Oregon to San Diego, in the California Floristic Province. They inhabit different locales, including chaparral, foothill woodland, maritime chaparral, closed-cone pine forest, Joshua tree woodland, and serpentine soil areas, with each species growing in its chosen habitat. They bloom from January through April, depending on species. Likewise, their berries ripen from early summer through fall, depending on location and species, and some can persist through the winter.

Manzanita berries make a refreshing drink, both tart and sweet.

How to gather

Place a sheet under the bush and shake or knock the berries off, or gather the berries individually.

How to use

Manzanita cider is made by crushing the berries, placing them in a colander set over a bowl, and pouring warm water through them, which is collected in the bowl. Some like to boil the crushed berries in water, which can be used to make jelly or a beverage. Most species' berries are sweet enough that the cider doesn't require additional sweetening. Also eaten by native peoples was a dish made of crushed seeds that were then toasted.

Future harvests

Except for those species that are adapted to shade, manzanitas require full sun. It is not uncommon to see half-dead manzanitas struggling in the recently arrived shade of fast-growing conifers such as Douglas fir. Where appropriate, pull out young conifer saplings to maintain a balance of chaparral and woodland.

meadow barley

Hordeum brachyantherum subsp. *californicum*
California barley, wild barley

EDIBLE seeds

The seed of meadow barley has a delicately wild taste, is easy to clean, and is a pleasure to harvest and eat.

A soft-looking grass with a compact row of seeds at the end of the flower stalk, meadow barley's flower head gracefully droops as the seeds ripen. It may look familiar to a barley grower, being related to that domesticated crop. Meadow barley tolerates wetter areas, like clay banks near streams and wet marshes, and seasonal flooding as well, but it is also adaptable to drier areas. Fast growing and tough, it is frequently used as a nurse crop for slower growing species in erosion control and revegetation projects.

How to identify
Meadow barley is considered a short-lived perennial, producing compact, narrow, shiny flower heads 3 to 4 inches long and purplish when young. The stems grow 1 to 3 feet long, depending on soil moisture.

Where and when to gather
Meadow barley grows from Alaska to northern Mexico, in wet meadows and grasslands with extra moisture. Interestingly enough, it also grows in Russia and Newfoundland. It is found in riparian zones, forest clearings, grasslands, or roadsides, usually in full sun. Meadow barley flowers from May through July, and sets seed from June through August.

How to gather
Either cut the stalks and thresh them in the traditional manner, or slide your fingers up the stalks to remove the seeds.

How to use
Meadow barley can be used as a cereal, in soups, and as a grain like its domesticated counterpart (see California's Native Bunchgrasses, page 68).

Future harvests
Drop a bit of seed in moist disturbed areas.

Meadow barley's arching reddish seed head is seen above a grassy meadow.

The seeds of this fast-growing, widespread bunchgrass are used to make porridge.

meadowfoam

Limnanthes douglasii

Douglas meadowfoam, fried egg plant, poached egg plant

`EDIBLE` seeds

Shortly after blooming, meadowfoam sets seed that is easy to collect, relatively large, and delicious when toasted.

While flowering, meadowfoam's blooms turn seasonally wet fields to creamy expanses that lift the spirits with their sheer prettiness. After that floral display, this annual wildflower ripens a relatively large seed that deserves a place in the pinole panoply. Though demonstrating a fragile beauty, meadowfoam is an unusually strong reseeder, with an impressive ability to maintain its hold on even weedy land, both returning every year and increasing territory. Its animal allies serve effectively to disperse the seed, a heartening phenomenon. It is an obligate host plant for a certain bee species, meaning that that particular bee cannot live, and will not emerge from the larval stage, without the bloom of meadowfoam.

How to identify

This charming, bell-shaped flower, growing 6 to 14 inches high, has yellow petals with crisp white tips and substantial, almost succulent leaves. It blooms on

Meadowfoam, an annual wildflower, grows in seasonally moist fields and is necessary to the life cycle of a native solitary bee species.

The beautiful flowers of meadowfoam produce edible seeds.

slender stalks in the upper leaf axils. It has five subspecies, including a protected form with all-yellow petals growing on Point Reyes in northern California. Meadowfoam flower petals have a translucence that creates a shimmering effect at a distance. Its basal leaves are 3 to 5 inches long, pinnate (divided, featherlike), alternating, and low to the ground. Each flower produces three to five smooth, light beige nutlets.

Where and when to gather

This moisture-loving wildflower is found from southern Oregon to southern California in wet, grassy habitat and sometimes in the woods. It blooms from March through April, and its seeds ripen about a month later, in late April and May.

How to gather

Pull plants when seed is ripening, leaving roots behind, and store in paper bags to finish ripening. Seed will fall to the bottom of the bag. Keep as much dirt out of the bag as possible (see Pinole: California's Seed Foods, page 62).

How to use

Toast the seeds in light oil and serve as you would popcorn. Or toast, grind, and use them in baked goods or as a topping for grains. The seeds can also be made into mush.

Future harvests

If you take only a small share of seed and plant some of the seed in likely places, meadowfoam and its allies will do the rest. Though it likes moist places, it doesn't require a wetland to sustain itself, just a good year of fall and winter rain. I used to see them in every mud puddle in the spring.

milkmaids

Cardamine californica

California toothwort, bittercress, radish root

EDIBLE leaves, flowers, roots

The blossoms of milkmaids are edible, as are the roots, but the peppery leaves of this member of the mustard family are truly outstanding.

One of the earliest harbingers of spring, milkmaids begins its bloom time in February, and is readily recognized at woodland edges or openings for its pretty white or pale pink flowers. It's a spring wake-up call to put one of the plant's pungent greens in your mouth. The leaves have a clean, strong bite and a delicate texture that makes them a perfect combination with more bland greens. Sampling the leaves while enjoying the beauty of the flowers indicates that you are in the right place at the right time.

This perennial wildflower has tender spicy leaves and delicate white blossoms in late winter.

How to identify

About 8 to 16 inches high, this herbaceous perennial plant is noticeable for its white or pink flowers on a spike, each with four white petals in the classic, cross-shaped mustard family style. The leaves are variable, sometimes toothed on the stem, and heart-shaped to round along the ground. Milkmaids spreads through underground rhizomes that thread their way through the forest duff, encountering other woodland carpet formers as it goes.

Where and when to gather

In forest openings and edges, milkmaids grows in most parts of the California Floristic Province. You'll find it in many shady plant communities, from redwood forest to mixed evergreen forest, coastal prairie, and oak woodland, from sea level to 6,000 feet. Clipping leaves before the plants bloom in January and February provides the best taste, though they are still edible when the flowers bloom. You'll need to be alert

Milkmaids is found at the edge of shady woodlands.

to catch these slender plants before they bloom, so make a note of where they are the year before and what their leaves look like, and head out to find them on a nice day in January.

How to gather

Clip no more than two or three leaves from each slender plant. Handle the leaves carefully since they are thin and fragile. Plunge briefly into cold water as soon after harvesting as possible.

How to use

Eat raw as a trailside nibble, in a chopped salad to add spark, or lightly steamed. They are also good with deviled eggs and in sandwiches, as a topping for pizzas, and to garnish pasta.

Future harvests

This delicate flower requires a delicate touch in harvesting. Leave most of the leaves on each plant, to ensure its healthy progression through its life cycle. Treat it as seasoning rather than as the salad green itself. Be sure to leave plenty of flowers for reseeding, though milkmaids reproduces more effectively through its underground traveling root system than through its relatively scanty seed production. A milkmaids meadow is a fragile place; walk carefully through it.

miner's lettuce

Claytonia perfoliata

Indian lettuce, winter purslane

EDIBLE leaves, stems, flowers, seeds

A California child's first trailside food, the mild, succulent leaves of this easily recognized shade-loving annual have a long tradition of being appreciated in the Golden State.

Miner's lettuce is one wild green that is a welcome sight to most California hikers. Tender and juicy, it is a pleasant addition to a sandwich, salad, or snack, Though the plant can be found in many situations, some spots produce better crops than others. The duration of the quality of miner's lettuce leaves in a given site is related to how moist and shady the site is. In sunnier, drier locations, miner's lettuce will quickly start to flower and go to seed. In moister situations, you may harvest miner's lettuce for months. Salads featuring miner's lettuce are being seen more frequently in restaurants.

How to identify

Miner's lettuce has a pair of leaves united together around the stem, looking like one round leaf (perfoliate). The leaves are a unique feature of this sturdy annual. Tiny white flowers rise in a series above the leaves on a long flower stalk, whose length, from 1 to 4 inches, depends on the moisture and shade of the growing site. These factors also impact the number and size of the seeds.

Where and when to gather

Miner's lettuce has a broad distribution throughout the California Floristic Province. On the coast, in humusy forest soil in part-shade, rain in late spring will keep it delicious from December through April. Hotter, drier inland areas will have much shorter harvest times and much smaller leaves and flower stalks.

How to gather

You can prolong harvest by plucking off the seed stalks, which retards the development of a slight bitter taste in the leaves. Careful picking to keep the succulent leaves from being crushed is worth the harvester's time. As soon as the flowers begin to form, the leaves lose some of their mildness and assume a very faint though not unpleasant bitterness.

Though many flowering plants have seed capsules that turn dry, hard, and brown when the seed is ripe, miner's lettuce, along with red maids, is an exception. Pierce the still green calyces enclosing the seed, beginning at the bottom of the flower stalk, to see if the tiny, shiny, black seed inside is ripe. If so, pull up the whole plant

Miner's lettuce usually grows in large masses in partly shaded areas under oak trees and in the woods.

and store it in a paper bag, until the seed falls to the bottom. Or put the seed stalks in a paper bag, and allow them to dehisce. After a couple of weeks, remove the drying leaves and pour the seeds into a bowl.

How to use

As well as a trailside nibble, miner's lettuce is often used in salads. Its appealing leaf shape can be used to fit perfectly on round crackers or slices of bread. Or cook the leaves with wild onions to make a cream soup.

The seeds lose acridity when heated briefly. Toast on low heat, since they are easily charred, and use to top a dressed leafy salad containing miner's lettuce greens.

One lesser known edible component occurs when this plant is found growing on a site with sufficient humus and moisture to grow large and sturdy. The leaf stems (petioles) become pink and sweet, about $\frac{1}{4}$ inch in diameter and up to 8 inches long, with a celerylike texture and a surprising sweetness. They are delicious raw, and are sturdy enough to serve with a dip.

Future harvests

Miner's lettuce is amazing for its ability to turn up in window boxes two stories up, in greenhouse soils supposed to be weed-free, and in places far from its original site. It may be that the tiny white elaiosome (a white structure on the black seed) at its tip is responsible for encouraging large-jawed native ants to pick it up and carry it around. If you are intentionally spreading the seed, be careful to sow it away from any less vigorous native species.

Mormon tea

Ephedra californica

California ephedra, desert tea, joint-fir

`EDIBLE` leaves, stems

You might be surprised that Mormon tea, a plant so insignificant in appearance, could produce such a well-loved and useful tea from its seemingly leaf-deprived twigs.

Mormon tea is a well-known staple of desert cupboards in California and throughout the Southwest. Its refreshing qualities and medicinal properties make it a popular tea. The seeds were also traditionally used for pinole. California's Mormon tea looks as tough as it actually is. To survive scanty rain and soils that don't hold moisture, it has green scales on the stems instead of leaves that are used to photosynthesize. Both of these plant parts are used for the tea. Unlike the Eurasian ephedras, our native shrubs don't contain significant amounts of the now illegal substance ephedrine.

Mormon tea can be harvested near Gorman in southern California.

How to identify

This unusual native shrub grows between 3 and 5 feet tall and equally wide. It has numerous yellow-green to gray-green twiglets emerging in all directions and barely detectable tiny leaves in threes. Southwestern species of Mormon tea look similar to each other and can be used in the same way. They are all gymnosperms, meaning that their seeds are contained within cones, like pines and firs. The leaves at the nodes are barely evident, drying up during drought and disappearing.

Where and when to gather

Mormon tea is found in desert scrub, chaparral, and dry grasslands in the Elkhorn Plain and in parts of the Temblor and Caliente Ranges, in the southern Sierra Nevada foothills, Tehachapi Mountains, western San Joaquin Valley, south Coast Ranges, and in southwestern California. It can be gathered throughout the year. It flowers in spring, from April through May, but ripens seed only occasionally, during heavy rainfall years.

How to gather

Cut young green-gray stems from the plant with a knife or pruning shears.

How to use

Use the clipped twigs fresh or store them. Pour boiling water over the twigs and let steep for 20 minutes. Use one cup of twigs for six cups of water. For pinole, toast the seed, then grind or eat whole.

Future harvests

Mormon tea is strong, so use sparingly, like you would all desert plants. Carefully done, harvesting can serve as pruning, helping the plant stay healthy.

mountain mule's ears

Wyethia mollis

woolly mule's ears, Indian wheat

EDIBLE shoots, seeds

This deep-rooted, easily recognized perennial in the sunflower family provides us with a double crop: edible shoots in the spring and seeds for pinole-making in the fall.

In California's eastern Sierra Nevada and in Lassen County, you may come across acres of meadows inhabited almost entirely by mountain mule's ears, which, if you were wise to this species' food uses, would be akin to finding an upland agricultural field, but one requiring no plowing, planting, or watering. Its lowland cousins, like narrowleaf mule's ears, *Wyethia*

angustifolia, occur in smaller patches, rarely providing such a munificent opportunity for collecting. It is another one of the native seed producers that were once called Indian wheat.

How to identify

Mountain mule's ears' silvery, fuzzy leaves are the most strikingly reminiscent of

This hardy perennial of the eastern Sierra Nevada and other mountain regions yields a quantity of sunflowerlike seeds.

actual mule's ears of any of the species in the genus. Like us, it may lose its hairs with age. Arising directly from the base, leaves are from 1 to 3 feet tall, have long pedicels, and die back in winter. The flowers rise 10 to 16 inches high, resemble small sunflowers, and are a bit less than 2 inches wide, with yellow centers.

Where and when to gather

Mountain mule's ears is found in high mountain meadows at 8,000 to 10,000 feet. It likes dry, rocky slopes or gravelly openings. The shoots can be gathered in April through June before the flowers appear. The flowers, which bloom in July and August, set seed about a month after that, in September and October. The seed is ripe when it progresses from light green to light brown.

How to gather

Cut young shoots at the base before buds appear. Gather ripe seeds by snipping the seed heads with a knife or with scissors. The mountains can be munificent, ripening seed in just the few months of temperate weather allotted to them.

How to use

Remove the dark mahogany-colored sheath covering the shoots of the young flower stalks before eating them, either raw, boiled, or steamed. Rub the seed heads so the seeds fall to the bottom of a bag or bowl. Winnow and toast the flat, black seeds. Salt and eat, or grind and use as a topping for vegetables or grains.

The flower stalks can be harvested and cooked like asparagus.

Future harvests

Harvest circumspectly, gathering only enough for a couple of meals. Our Sierra Nevada meadows are experiencing diverse pressures these days, so err on the side of too little.

mountain pennyroyal

Monardella odoratissima subsp. *pallida*

western pennyroyal, western mountain balm, mountain mint

EDIBLE leaves, stalks, flowers

Mountain pennyroyal provides one of the most enjoyable wild teas, and since pennyroyal tea is delicious even when made with cold water, it's a practical beverage on the trail.

Found only in mid-level to high elevations in the mountains of California and other parts of the west, mountain pennyroyal is a pretty perennial in the mint family. Backpackers need use only a sprig or two of its showy white to lavender flowers and green leaves for a perfect cup of mountain tea. Growing in sun or part-shade, in rocky boulders and cliffs or in moist flat areas, mountain pennyroyal graces alpine and sub-alpine meadows with its vivid puffs of flower color. Its strong taste and subtle fragrance will enhance and evoke field memories of exhilarating hiking adventures in high places.

How to identify

Like most members of the mint family, mountain pennyroyal has square stems and oval to lance-shaped leaves that are green

Mountain pennyroyal graces an alpine meadow in August.

A few stems of mountain pennyroyal make a fine mountain tea.

on both sides. It has opposite leaves and sends out many small stems from the central root. The plant grows about 2 feet tall and equally wide. Its showy flowers vary in color, from white, pink, lilac, to purple.

Where and when to gather

Mountain pennyroyal can handle the tough conditions of the Sierra Nevada and is found from 3,000 to 11,000 feet. A different subspecies, the purple-flowered *Monardella odoratissima* subsp. *odoratissima*, grows in far northeastern California. You will find both on rocky ridges and gravelly flats, in full sun or a bit of shade. Mountain pennyroyal flowers in midsummer and can be harvested both before and during flowering.

How to gather

Cut stems, leaves, and flowers with a knife, taking a small quantity from several plants rather than harvesting all from a single plant.

How to use

For tea, steep leaves, flowers, and stems about ten minutes in hot, not boiling, water, or one hour or more in cold water. The infusion can be left in the sun to make sun tea. Honey enhances the taste. The leaves are also used to make jellies and syrups.

Future harvests

Harvest small amounts of the leaves of this California perennial mint species, gathering small quantities from a number of plants, so that it is hard to tell you've been there.

Caution

Avoid if pregnant.

mountain sorrel

Oxyria digyna

alpine sorrel, alpine mountainsorrel, wood sorrel

EDIBLE leaves, stems

Mountain sorrel is a reassuring sight at high altitudes, promising a succulent, restorative snack with a significant amount of vitamin C.

Though not related to miner's lettuce, mountain sorrel can't help but be compared to it. It is delicious, with tasty and tender, pleasantly sour leaves that you might even prefer to miner's lettuce. Mountain sorrel seeks the sheltered, shady, moist cracks and crevices of north-facing slopes up to and including alpine zones. This specialized species may even greet you in the tundra.

How to identify

This perennial herb grows to 1½ feet tall and 1 foot wide, with rounded kidney-shaped leaves on long leaf stalks (petioles) similar to miner's lettuce, but with a thicker, more substantial leaf with wavy edges. The leaf stalks grow outward from the central rosette, while the small red and greenish flowers emerge on upright stalks, in striking contrast to the basal leaves. The

Mountain sorrel seeks out cool places under rocks for its roots to grow.

seeds are small, flat disks forming in the center of the flowers, with deep red wings when ripe that make the whole seed stalk look deep red. The leaves also may acquire a reddish tinge by the end of the summer.

Where and when to gather

You will find mountain sorrel growing in most of the mountains in California, including the Klamath Ranges, Cascade Range, Sierra Nevada, San Bernardino Mountains, San Jacinto Mountains, Warner Mountains, and on the east side of the Sierra Nevada. The plant likes moist soils with good drainage and is often found in rocky crevices and dry creek beds. It flowers from July to August, and the leaves are still good for harvest during and after flowering, especially with protection from sun and with sufficient moisture.

The rounded leaves of mountain sorrel are good eaten raw or cooked.

How to gather

Cut leaves off gently, only a few from each plant.

How to use

Use mountain sorrel as a trailside snack, or enhance a sandwich with a leaf or two. It is excellent cooked like spinach, becoming less acid when steamed or boiled. It can be added to stews and soups.

Future harvests

Be careful not to harm the roots of this perennial plant when you gather, and gather leaves and stems only where plants are numerous.

narrowleaf mule's ears

Wyethia angustifolia

Indian wheat, California compassplant, Coast Range mule's ear

EDIBLE shoots, seeds

Narrowleaf mule's ears, a sturdy perennial with cheerful yellow flowers, has edible green shoots and seeds that look and taste like sunflower seeds.

Narrowleaf mule's ears is a tough wildflower often found growing with annual wildflowers in meadows, adding its cheerful yellow sunflowerlike blossoms to the beauty of the California spring and early summer. One of ten species in this genus found all over the west, the shoot of this plant's flower stalk is an enjoyable vegetable, to be gathered and eaten like asparagus before the flower forms. The wildflower seeds have a taste similar to sunflower seeds and can be eaten raw or as pinole, earning it the name Indian wheat.

How to identify

The long mule-ear-shaped or tongue-shaped leaves of this stocky perennial grow up to 2 feet long, partially hiding the flower stalks, which are about 1 foot long. The plant grows from a tough taproot and

The shoots of narrowleaf mule's ears can be harvested as a delicious vegetable.

thickened base, from which the bright green leaves arise. The flower cluster produces one or more large flower heads, 3 to 5 inches wide, at the top of the stem. Each seed is about ½ inch long.

Where and when to gather

Common on low hills in the north and central Coast Ranges, narrowleaf mule's ears is found in small masses in grasslands and coastal scrub. It only grows in California, where it blooms in late spring and early summer, so harvest the tender shoots of the flower stalks in May and June before the flowers form. When the grasses of summer are dry, the ripened seeds on 1- to 2-feet-long stalks are easy to spot, with their brown, bristly seed heads held above or within the sturdy leaves. Gather seeds in midsummer to late summer, from June through August.

How to gather

Cut the flower stalk off at the base before the plant flowers. Twist the seed heads off at the top of the stem when dry and bristly, rub them through your hands to detach the seeds, and let the seeds fall into a bag, where they will rest at the bottom. When fully ripe, the seeds will easily detach.

How to use

The green shoots of the flower stalks are chopped into sections and eaten raw or boiled. The seeds are parched and ground into pinole (see page 000). The challenge with cleaning this seed is the chaff (dried bracts) within the seed head that are

The basal leaves of this sturdy perennial have a varnished appearance.

about the same size as the seeds, so strainers won't work. They are lighter than the seed, though, so shaking the bag will allow the seed to settle out, and the chaff can be lifted out or winnowed. Harvest, clean, and toast the seeds with oil in a pan over a small campfire; season with salt and pass them around for a snack. You can grind the seed and add it to baked goods or use as a thickener in soups for a nutritious flavor boost.

Future harvests

Narrowleaf mule's ears is frequently found in colonies managing to survive in the midst of weedy grasslands. Harvest circumspectly, taking a bit of seed and a few flower stalks from each colony, depleting none of them. Dormancy in summer is always the danger time for mule ears, when weedy species can move in and prevent the next rainy season's newly sprouting leaves from finding the sunshine they need.

nasturtium

Tropaeolum majus
garden nasturtium, Indian cress

`EDIBLE` leaves, stems, flowers, immature and ripe seeds

One of the first flowers to become part of the "edible flower" fashion, the nasturtium's spicy, mustardy leaves and large tangy yellow or orange flowers are a frequent sight in creative salads.

Nasturtium is a perennial originally from Peru. High in vitamins A, C, and D, nasturtiums are easily grown from seed. On the coast of California, they have naturalized, and, though still planted as a garden flower, are classified as an invasive weed. Frequently a child's first flower gardening effort, they can become too much of a good thing quickly in a mild climate. The young seeds can also be pickled like capers. Though nasturtium is not for the faint of heart, cooking tames some of the heat of the leaves, which grow hotter in the sun. Harvest from shadier areas if you prefer less zing.

The large leaves and showy flowers of this escaped garden plant are edible, with a peppery zing.

How to identify

Nasturtium has a vinelike growth habit. Large, distinctive round leaves look similar to miner's lettuce leaves, only thicker, larger, a duller green, and with noticeable white veins that meet in the center of the circular leaf. They crawl and sprawl in a rambunctious manner, soon producing five-petaled flowers whose most common colors are orange or yellow. Many showy garden cultivars have been developed in a wide range of colors, and they are also edible.

Where and when to gather

Nasturtiums have escaped from gardens in frost-free parts of California and along the coast. The leaves can be harvested all year long, except in the driest part of the summer. The plant flowers from July to September, and the seeds ripen from August to October.

How to gather

Gather young leaves and flowers, and wash immediately in cold water.

How to use

Nasturtium leaves and flowers can be used in pesto, salads, stir-fries, and with pasta. Stuff the flowers, and eat the immature seeds raw or pickle them. You can snack on the mature seeds. Also try them as a pepper substitute.

Future harvests

Some supposedly "protected" coastal forests have little left but weedy species. The plant palette in a given area may consist of eucalyptus trees from Australia with an understory of cape ivy and nasturtium—nasturtium being the only edible among them. If there is something native left in an area to preserve, keep the nasturtiums away from these species through your harvesting.

Nevada stickleaf

Mentzelia dispersa

Nevada blazing star, Nevada sandseed, bushy blazingstar, scattered blazing star

`EDIBLE` seeds

Nevada stickleaf has gray-black seeds that have served as an important and tasty seed food for many centuries and continue to do so today.

Historical accounts indicate that many *Mentzelia* species were important seed foods throughout California and the west. One of those, Nevada stickleaf, a fire-following annual wildflower, appears by the thousands in sagebrush scrub, usually after fire. Though not as individually showy as its relative, the giant blazing star, the large numbers of plants that germinate after a fire can add up to significant seed harvests. It has a wide distribution throughout the west, from California to Washington state and to the Rocky Mountains. Dishes made from these seeds are nourishing and easy to enjoy.

The seeds make a gravy or mush that resembles the taste and smell of peanut butter. Once toasted and ground, they can also be rolled into small balls.

How to identify

Nevada stickleaf has small, shiny yellow flowers less than 1 inch long, each with an orange spot at the base. The leaves enclosing the flower (bracts) are green. The seed capsules eventually dry to a crumbly, pale capsule holding many smooth, shiny gray-black seeds. Sticky leaves at the base of the plant are sometimes smooth and sometimes finely toothed. The distinctive white stems in masses have a sheen that leads you to them.

Where and when to gather

Nevada stickleaf grows in many parts of California, throughout the California Floristic Province and also in the Great Basin. It is found in sandy and rocky soil in full sun. Harvest when plants have begun to die back and are losing their green color. Depending on location, the seed is harvested from June through early August. The seeds are ripe when they are gray and so hard that your nail can't pierce them.

How to gather

Clip the annual plants and collect in a bag. Let the seed fall out and sink to the bottom of the bag. Shake the bag, and lift off the plant debris, leaving the seed behind. Or, tap the plants in place so that the seed falls onto a tarp, or into a bag, and then winnow it.

How to use

Lightly toast the seeds in a frying pan. Grind into a fine powder, then mix with water and cook slowly, stirring constantly. Use as a gravy, an accompaniment to meat and vegetables, or as a soup, spread, or dip. The dry powder can also be rolled into balls, or sweetened to make "stickleaf truffles."

Future harvests

Nevada stickleaf needs controlled burns to maintain populations, and will disappear a few years after a fire. Consequently, it is seldom found in developed areas where fire is suppressed.

Nevada stickleaf's long, narrow seed capsule contains a quantity of important edible seed, remnants of which have been discovered in ancient food preparation sites throughout the west.

Nootka rose

Rosa nutkana

bristly Nootka rose, wild rose

EDIBLE shoots, leaves, flowers, fruit

Thickets of the Nootka rose provide intensely fragrant flowers, leaves for tea, and very nutritious fruit.

Growing from Alaska down to northern California and east to Colorado, Nootka rose was first documented at Nootka Sound, off Vancouver Island, B.C. It is one of the showiest of California's native roses. It is also one of the most fragrant, with glands that release a heady fragrance from its flowers, leaves, and shoots. It makes an intensely flavored leaf tea. These dense, shrubby, deciduous plants grow with great vigor, forming impenetrable thickets. While mildly flavored, the rose hips are said to be rich in vitamins A, C, D, E, bio-flavinoids, and even fatty acids, which is unusual for fruit.

How to identify

Flowers of the Nootka rose are among the largest of native rose species. Like other wild roses, it has five petals and many

The five single pink petals of this vigorous wild rose are particularly fragrant.

yellow stamens in the center. The deep pink flowers 2 to 3 inches in diameter turn into bright red, round fruits, or rose hips, 1/2 to 3/4 inch long. Leaves are compound with five to nine leaflets. It also has the most vicious prickly thorns of all the native California roses: thick at the base, straight, and dense. The shrub is upright, with stiff, erect branches from 3 to 8 feet tall.

Where and when to gather

Nootka rose is found in open woods and scrub from Alaska to Mendocino County, with some possible scanty appearances south of that. Look for it in the borders between woodland and grasslands, and in sunny and well-drained areas, unlike the wood rose, which prefers the shade.

Gather the new shoots as they emerge in early spring, February through March. Nootka rose blooms from May to July, and ripe hips appear from June to July and can persist into winter if not harvested by birds and animals. Gather leaves for tea in early spring, March through May. Rose hips can be gathered in the fall, and it is commonly thought that they are tastier and richer in vitamin C after the first frost.

How to gather

It's not necessary to wear gloves while gathering the Nootka rose; just be careful. Pluck the petals with your fingers and use quickly. Rose hips should be cut in half to remove the seeds, which, though containing significant amounts of vitamin E, can be irritating to the hands, mouth, and digestive system. Cut young rose leaves and place in paper bags. The bitter white base of the petals should be trimmed off before using.

How to use

The uses of rose petals and rose hips are the same from species to species, except that the Nootka rose hips make such fragrant and exceptional tea; just be sure to remove the seeds with a knife. Boil rose hips for fifteen minutes, or soak in cool water for several hours. Do the same with the leaves. Use petals in soups, salads, sandwiches, desserts, and candies that are relatively bland, so as not to overcome the subtle savor of rose. Pull the rose hips open with your fingernails, scoop out the seeds, and remove the hairs. The seeds can then be ground in a blender and added to smoothies as a nutritional supplement. Use the hips in tea, dried as raisins, in jams, and in soup. The young shoots are peeled and eaten raw or cooked and eaten like asparagus.

Future harvests

California's populations of Nootka rose along the coast, like many other shrubby species, are threatened by Himalayan blackberry.

Caution

The hairs on the seeds inside the rose hips can be irritating to the stomach, so be sure to remove them.

northern California black walnut

Juglans hindsii
Hinds black walnut, Hinds walnut
`EDIBLE` nuts

The handsome deciduous northern California black walnut tree has been discovered mostly at the sites of old Indian villages, suggesting that Indians brought nuts with them to sow when they moved to new resting places.

Though early settlers were not impressed by the size of the nuts produced by the northern California walnut, early on they used it as disease-resistant rootstock for the larger-nutted eastern black walnut and for the English walnut. Eventually, many of the grafts died, leaving the native walnuts to flourish. The lumber from such practices shows the grafting site and is sought after by California woodworkers.

Today's cooks have discovered that the intense flavor of these nuts makes it worthwhile to take the time to crack them and pick out the relatively small nutmeats. It doesn't take many toasted, chopped native black walnuts to distinctively flavor your ice cream or enhance a salad. The tree produces large quantities of nuts and is immune to drought, gophers, and oak root fungus.

How to identify

Early descriptions indicate that old-growth native walnut trees grew up to 6 feet in diameter and could rise clear of branches for 40 feet, with the trees growing 30 to 60 feet high. The leaves are 9 to 12 inches long, consisting of fifteen to nineteen pinnately compound leaflets 2 to 4 inches long. The leaflets are shiny, bright green above, with tiny hairs underneath and in the axils of the veins. The dark brown bark has deep vertical grooves. Male flowers are noticeable as slender, 5-inch-long catkins. The fruit is up to 2 inches in diameter. The husk is first light green and firm, then turns yellow and softens as it ripens. To complicate matters, the northern California black walnut hybridizes readily with the English walnut, possibly producing offspring with the virtues of both parents.

Where and when to gather

The ease of moving the nuts of northern California black walnut around for planting near dwelling places is demonstrated by occurrences of trees near Walnut Creek in Contra Costa County, the banks of the Sacramento River, Walnut Grove, Palo Alto, near Wooden Valley, and east of

The nut of northern California black walnut ripens in April.

Napa. Northern California black walnut likes canyons and valleys and is somewhat rare, though it is now frequently used as a street tree in towns in the inner Coast Ranges and valleys, and in the Sierra Nevada foothills. Gather the nuts in midsummer to early fall. A new use of native black walnuts in salads calls for an early gathering of the still green nut, before the nut has dried in the shell.

How to gather

The walnut husk was used as a fabric dye—an effective and long-lasting one. So dress accordingly, and wear gloves when gathering and preparing. Soak the nuts in water in a galvanized tub to soften and remove the husk; then dry the nuts in their shells. Some aficionados drive their cars over the nuts to crack the rigid shells. Pliers or a table-mounted nutcracker can also be used.

How to use

The early gathered nuts are considered a treat when picked slightly green, roasted, and used in a lettuce salad. Those that have ripened fully and dried can be used like any walnuts, in ice cream, puddings, cookies, cakes, and muffins, only you need less. They can be stored in a cool, dry, dark place for up to a year.

Future harvests

Encourage the planting and preservation of these pleasing and useful trees, as street trees and in larger gardens.

ocotillo

Fouquieria splendens subsp. *splendens*

devil's walking stick, candlewood, slimwood, coachwhip, vine cactus, flaming sword, Jacob's staff

EDIBLE flowers

The blossoms of ocotillo provide a reviving trailside nibble and also make a splendid beverage for hot summer days when soaked in water.

This thorny shrub of the Sonoran Desert is totemic there, based on the number of towns, lodges, campgrounds, and restaurants named after it. With its numerous long, gray, wandlike stems reaching upward from a single base in a graceful mass, ocotillo has a striking silhouette. Its showy red flowers clustered at the stem tips have a tubular structure perfect for attracting hummingbirds. Ocotillo stems are used

The edible flowers of ocotillo often appear before the leaves in spring, from March to June.

to build fences around desert homes. The stems can root in place, making a living natural fence and thorny barrier.

How to identify

Ocotillo grows from 10 to 30 feet tall with spines to 1½ inches long. It is highly responsive to water. It will sprout bright green, thick, leathery, 2-inch-long leaves along the gray stems almost immediately after it rains, and this may happen even four times a year. The leaves drop in the dry season, so ocotillo is leafless most of the time.

Where and when to gather

Ocotillo is found on dry, well-drained, rocky slopes, mesas, alluvial fans, plains, and valleys in desert shrub and desert grassland habitats. In the Sonoran Desert, ocotillo is found from the valley plains to upper *bajadas*, places at the base of mountains where debris, soil, and moisture collect. Ocotillo is found from sea level to 5,000 feet. The flowers often appear before the leaves in spring, from March to June.

How to gather

Snip blossoms, which are easily harvested from the ends of stems, with your fingernail or a knife, being careful to avoid the spines.

How to use

Pour cold water over the blossoms, and soak for several hours in a glass container. Strain and drink.

Future harvests

Seedlings are found under the canopies of mature plants, and survival is dependent on rainfall, so future harvests cannot be affected easily by the casual scattering of seeds. Protecting habitat is the best idea.

Oregon grape

Berberis aquifolium
holly-leaf barberry
EDIBLE flowers, fruit, leaves

Your face may pucker up when you taste Oregon grape's fruit raw, but once the berries are made into jelly, syrup, or wine, your expression will change to one of utter bliss.

Oregon grape has been widely planted in the urban landscape, where it does a good job as a hedge or specimen plant. A surprisingly adaptable shrub, it thrives in a variety of situations, both in the wild and planted in gardens. Little did the landscapers know that the flowers and the berries are an inventive cook's delight, or that the tender young leaves can be added to a salad. The grapes, actually berries, are seriously tart, with an intense and complex flavor, containing hints of many other fruits. To eat jelly made from these berries, picked at their peak ripeness, is a rare experience.

How to identify

The glossy, dark green leaves, frequently used in the floral trade, have spines at the tips reminiscent of holly and are pinnately

The showy flowers of the Oregon grape are fragrant and edible.

The deep-purple fruit of Oregon grape is popular with birds and humans alike.

compound (divided so the leaflets are arranged on two sides of a midvein, like a feather), with from five to nine leaflets for each 10-inch-long leaf. The new leaves are reddish in color, and plants in full sun may retain this color to some degree. They also turn red with winter's chill. The fragrant yellow flowers, up to fifty in a cluster, are followed by blue berries up to ½ inch in diameter with a white bloom.

Where and when to gather

Found in dry, open, and lightly wooded slopes, Oregon grape grows in the California Floristic Province and north into British Columbia. It can also be found occasionally in northern coastal scrub. New leaves appear in February through March, and must be gathered immediately before they develop any leatheriness or the spines turn sharp. The blossoms appear in April through May, followed by berries ripening to deep purple in August through September.

How to gather

Snip leaves, flowers, and fruit at the appropriate times with pruning shears. Make sure the berries are dark blue to purple and fully ripe. Choose the ones growing in the sun at the ends of branches or at the top of the shrub.

How to use

The leaves should be eaten raw in salads as soon as they emerge, while they are soft and spineless. The flowers can be used raw, fried as fritters, added to puddings and custards, or used to decorate cakes. Definitely requiring sweetening, the fruit of Oregon grape makes flavorful jellies, drinks, syrups, fruit soups, wine, and sauces. Be sure to remove the seeds and skin. The berries can be frozen immediately after harvesting, to be processed later.

Future harvests

Share with the birds, and they will spread the seed for you.

Oregon grape is an adaptable shrub found in a variety of situations on the Pacific Coast, providing large quantities of easily gathered fruit.

perennial pickleweed

Salicornia pacifica

sea beans, samphire, samfire, marsh samphire, glasswort, turtleweed, Virginia pickleweed, sea asparagus

`EDIBLE` leaves, stems, seeds

Perennial pickleweed, a unique and abundant succulent perennial found in coastal salt marshes, comes with its own salty taste and appealing crunchiness.

As the name suggests, perennial pickleweed is frequently made into pickles, and perhaps more frequently simply nibbled on raw while exploring California's coastal wetlands. A number of pickleweed species are found in California, all edible, with a similar flavor and texture. They add interest and nutrients, as well as saltiness, to stir-fries and soups.

How to identify

Perennial pickleweed has a distinctive, leafless appearance, with long, succulent, segmented stems from 6 to 20 inches in length and small stemlets or branchlets 4 to 6 inches long arising from the main stems. It has a semiwoody base, which distinguishes it from the annual pickleweeds that have no woody tissue. Scales bear

Perennial pickleweed is one of many edible, crunchy, salty pickleweeds.

tiny, pale yellow flowers. The entire plant turns coastal marshes reddish green in the fall.

Where and when to gather

Perennial pickleweed is found in coastal salt marshes in northwest and coastal California, particularly in the San Francisco Bay estuaries. The pickleweed species that grow in California include *Salicornia bigelovii*, which is found in southern California, *S. subterminalis*, which grows inland in the San Joaquin Valley, and an annual pickleweed, *S. europea*, the least common. Most pickleweeds can be gathered anytime of year, but particularly in the spring before they flower.

How to gather

The stem tips can be snapped off easily.

How to use

Eat raw, either rinsed with fresh water or not, or use in any pickle recipe. The tips can also be used in stir-fries and as a boiled or steamed vegetable. You won't need to add salt, of course.

Future harvests

Commercial harvesting of pickleweed may become a matter of concern, but modest and occasional foraging harvests should not be a problem. Perennial pickleweed is being considered as a source of biofuel, since it can be irrigated with salt water.

Point Reyes checkerbloom

Sidalcea calycosa subsp. *rhizomata*
Point Reyes sidalcea

`EDIBLE` leaves

In its coastal environs, Point Reyes checkerbloom covers the ground thickly. Its edible leaves are mild and delicious, and available along the coast for much of the year.

The stunning, large, pale to deep pink blossoms of Point Reyes checkerbloom, 2 inches across, are as showy as any cultivated flower. Though found along seasonal ponds and seeps in coastal prairies, the species is also adaptable on the coast to drier situations. Its long season of leaf production makes it a prize as a provider of

This showy native perennial provides months of mild, tender greens along the coast.

versatile and easy-to-use greens. I planted it first as an attractive, low-maintenance ground cover and have since come to value it as a reliable food source. Permaculturists take note!

How to identify

Point Reyes checkerbloom has typical mallow family flowers, ranging in color from pale to deep pink. The triangular seeds are wedged tightly together into a circular shape, like segments of a pie. The plant has a noticeably prostrate habit, with handsome, round, scalloped dark green leaves at the base and deeply lobed leaves higher up. Its rhizomatous growth results in a thick carpet, as opposed to the common checkerbloom, which occurs in more discrete clumps and is more upright.

Where and when to gather

Point Reyes checkerbloom has been found along the coast from San Francisco north to Mendocino County. It likes moist pastures and the edges of wetlands, as well as vernal ponds. This plant is listed as rare and endangered probably because its habitat is being lost. Grown in a garden, it is extremely vigorous. Along the coast, from April through August, the leaves have a fairly long period during which they remain sweet enough to be eaten raw with no bitter aftertaste. Both the basal leaves and the flower stalk leaves can be eaten.

How to gather

Cut with a knife, pruners, or scissors. You can pluck the stems from the plant with your fingers as well, and then you can remove the leaves from the stem later.

How to use

The leaves eaten raw are mild and delicious, and can be incorporated into chopped salads or salsas without processing. They are substantial enough to be well worth gathering for a mealtime vegetable. They also can be used in stews, where they act as a mild thickening agent.

Future harvests

Since the plant is considered uncommon in the wild, harvest gingerly from the middle of the patch rather than from the edges, leaving enough so that the plant can readily fill in.

prickly pear

Opuntia species

nopales, paddle cactus, prickly pear cactus

`EDIBLE` stems, fruit

The fleshy stems, or pads, of prickly pear provide a healthful, tasty vegetable frequently compared to asparagus, and the luscious fruit tastes like a combination of watermelon and pear. Both can be used in many ways.

The rubric of prickly pear cactus includes a number of desert species native to western North America and even one imported species. The pads, called *nopales*, and the fruits, called *tunas*, are sometimes available in specialty grocery stores, usually from the thornless commercially grown species. The ruby-red fruit is thought to be high in phytochemicals that help regulate cholesterol and blood glucose levels. Prickly pear has been a lifesaver for more than a few wanderers lost in the desert. It's an exotic wild food plant well worth investigating.

Many species of prickly pear have been domesticated for their fruit and edible stems all over the world.

How to identify

Prickly pear is easily identified by its flat stems, resembling ping-pong paddles, usually with significant thorns in depressions in the pad, and also by the bright pink or maroon 1- to 3-inch-wide flowers. The blossoms are followed by cup-shaped fruits edging the top rims of the pads, in shades of light pink to yellow to deep maroon.

Where and when to gather

Though most common in the desert and in southern California, prickly pears have a surprisingly broad range in California, setting fruit even on the coast as far north as Marin County. The pads can be gathered almost year-round, and the young pads are best. Check them out from September until till May. Fruits are gathered from May to October.

How to gather

Gather using heavy gloves and tongs to pluck the fruit off or to snip the pads off. Sometimes thorns and glochids are removed by brushing them off or by burning them off with matches, over a gas burner on the stove, or even with a propane blowtorch, an exciting procedure. It is best, if possible, to remove the thorns and glochids before collecting the pads and fruit in a container for transporting. Some even perform this task while the *nopales* and *tunas* are still attached to the main plant. You can roll them in the gravel or sand using tongs. Or impale a *tuna* on a stick and rub it in sand, gravel, or dry grass. Visual demonstrations, like those found on YouTube, can be helpful.

How to use

To prepare prickly pear pads, either gouge out each thorn individually with a paring knife, slice off the skin in sections, or slit open the pads and remove the flesh within. Or, trim off the thorny edges of the pad with a butcher knife, removing a piece about 1/4 inch wide around the circumference of the pad. And then with the same knife, scrape the thorns and the skin off the flat surface. Dice into cubes and sauté or boil, rinsing off the sap. Or grill until tender and lightly browned.

The fruits' thorns and glochids should be either singed off over a flame or brushed off with a scouring pad, vegetable brush, or other stiff material. Or, slice off the ends, make a longitudinal slit between them, and peel the thorny skin off to get at the seeds and pulp. Strain out the seeds and discard. The fruit also can be sliced in half and held with tongs or in a gloved hand while the flesh and seeds are scooped out. The seeds can be strained out after the fruit is mashed or blended. Eat raw, make sherbet, jelly or juice, salad dressing, mojitos, and smoothies. Or, mash, strain, and dry as fruit leather.

Future harvests

Edible prickly pear species range from common forms frequently escaped from gardens, to agricultural fields of cultivars of the thornless cactus called Indian fig, *Opuntia ficus-indica*, to federally protected species that should never be harvested. Prickly pear species imported all over the world have sometimes proven to be a poor idea, an example of the folly of indiscriminate movement of plants.

Caution

Forage prickly pear with caution, to avoid the thorns and glochids piercing your skin. A guideline from the Chumash tribe specifies that the thorns and glochids be removed from the fruit and pads before they are gathered into a container. In a Chumash story, Coyote got thorns in his eyes through violation of this sensible rule. When removing thorns with a utensil, such as a knife or vegetable peeler, wipe off the implement after each use. Use only glass or ceramic containers for preparation and storage.

purple sage

Salvia leucophylla

EDIBLE leaves, seeds, flowers

The silvery leaves of purple sage are pleasingly pungent in fragrance and taste, and the flowers are mintlike and purple. They both call out for use as tea or seasonings.

Purple sage is a beautiful many-branched shrub of the coastal sage scrub plant community. The brown seeds are similar to chia seeds, with a bit more pungency, and have been referred to as chia by some. They can be used to make pinole or as seasoning. This vigorous shrub provides a long gathering window, ease of collection, and a reliable harvest. The leaves have a future in edgy cuisines, since they are attractive and tasty when lightly fried to garnish pasta or eat as appetizers. The hint of bitterness will please those interested in re-introducing such complex tastes to their palate. Tea is another use for both flowers and leaves.

How to identify

Purple sage has intriguing wrinkled leaves 3 inches long growing opposite each other. The leaves are gray above and white and

Purple sage is an attractive shrub that produces edible seeds and leaves.

densely woolly below. The shrub forms neat mounds growing from 4 to 6 feet tall and equally wide. Three to five light purple flowers grow in compact clusters at the end of flowering stems, producing light brown nutlets, four per flower. The shrubs spread through underground rhizomes.

Where and when to gather

Found in the chaparral of California's central coast south to Orange County below 2,000 feet, purple sage grows with other members of the southern coastal scrub plant community like California sagebrush. The leaves are best gathered before the plant blooms in April and May, and the seed harvest begins in June and may continue into August.

How to gather

Cut the flowering stalks into a basket or bag and leave them to dry, roughing them up occasionally. Or later in the summer, tip them over so the seeds drop out on their own, straight into your waiting container.

How to use

The seeds are used as any edible seed, like golden chia, but take into account a bit of added pungency. They are not mucilaginous. Use the seeds and the leaves for seasoning. The leaves make a strong, interesting tea and can be fried as a garnish, like the leaves of the culinary sage.

Future harvests

This tough shrub can benefit from tip pruning by the harvester gathering leaves for seasoning.

purslane

Portulaca oleracea

portulaca, verdolaga, pigweed, moss rose, Mexican parsley

EDIBLE leaves, stems, flower buds

Well known as a garden flower, an agricultural crop, and an invasive weed, purslane is an annual wild green that is now recognized as a true super-food.

Used for years in Latin American cooking and with a long-time culinary presence in North America, possibly dating back to the pre-Columbian era, purslane is easily adapted to all styles of cooking. Its slightly salty and somewhat sour taste, present in stems, leaves, and flower buds, is a prominent feature in Greek, Asian, Middle Eastern, and Mexican food. Next time you are pulling purslane out of your garden, stop and think: nutrition! For starters, it contains an astounding amount of omega-3 fatty acids. And it has substantial amounts of vitamins A, B, C, carotenoids, antioxidants, calcium, and potassium.

Purslane, considered a weed by many gardeners, is a highly nutritious and edible vegetable, a fact well-known in other parts of the world.

How to identify

Purslane is a ground-hugging, prostrate, succulent annual plant with smooth reddish stems and simple, alternate leaves shaped like a flattened club. It blooms throughout the year, with pretty, short-lived, five-petaled yellow flowers. It has a taproot that can penetrate difficult soils, sometimes allowing other plants to follow suit.

Where and when to gather

Purslane grows throughout California but particularly in the hotter, drier parts. It can survive in infertile, heavy soils, waiting out the drought as seeds, which are long-lived. It grows with heat and moisture and is harvested in July and August.

How to gather

Snip stems with leaves. Keep dry and refrigerated until ready to use.

How to use

Eat raw in salads, stir-fried, or steamed. Use in soups and stews. It is sometimes pickled.

Future harvests

Purslane is a weed to be held in high esteem but not underestimated. Harvest and control make all the difference. Purslane produces a prodigious amount of seeds, so snip off most of the flowers before they set seed. It is more of a problem in the hotter, drier parts of California than along the coast.

pussy ears

Calochortus tolmiei

cat's ears, Tolmie's startulip

`EDIBLE` bulbs

Like other *Calochortus* species, the bulbs of pussy ears can be eaten raw, though cooking brings out their sweetness.

This plant, with its diminutive purplish bloom, is a young child's delight. Growing close to the ground as pussy ears does, a little person might be the only one able to easily see the flower's exquisite details. The petals, in their shape and fuzziness, resemble cat's ears. Found widely from California to Washington and Idaho, it favors grasslands, where its small bulbs have been considered delicacies for hundreds of years. Everyone who sees it feels lucky, even without tasting it. This dainty little beauty does not mind poor soil, and it is still sometimes found in masses, a thrilling sight.

The grasslike leaves of pussy ears are lost amidst the weedy grasses, but the distinctive flower is unmistakable.

How to identify

Pussy ears is a short member of the lily family, growing from 8 to 15 inches tall. The flower has white to pale purple petals with a distinctive fuzziness. Its three petals have a particularly graceful shape, rounded at the base and ending with a sudden taper at the tip. The petals' bases together form a beautiful and somewhat varied design. The flower's coloration is startlingly varied, but the plant's hairs and the minute stature are the tip-offs, rarely seen in native bulbs. The basal leaf persists after flowering.

Where and when to gather

Found near the coast as well as inland in the north Coast Ranges, from deep shade to sun, pussy ears has many different incarnations, depending on where it is growing, from openings in evergreen woodlands to sunny meadows, from foggy coastal bluffs to inland valleys. Dig before it blooms or after it sets seed, from April through June.

How to gather

It can benefit from the same careful handling that other Indian potatoes receive (see page 54). Dig circumspectly once the intriguing three-cornered seed capsules begin to ripen at the top of the flower stems. A digging stick or crowbar is a good implement for carefully removing a few bulbs of this dainty species without harming it.

How to use

These tiny bulbs can be eaten raw but are usually preferred boiled or roasted at least twenty minutes. Boil until soft and well cooked, then sauté in hot oil, and add salt for a delicately delicious hors d'oeuvre.

Future harvests

Take only a few bulbs, and replant the small cormlets in the loosened soil for future harvests.

red huckleberry

Vaccinium parvifolium

red bilberry

`EDIBLE` berries

From the Alaska Panhandle to Washington state to northern California, the red huckleberry is a highly sought after, tart but tasty wild treat.

High in antioxidants, red huckleberries are a treasured trailside snack and ingredient for delicious pies. My mother-in-law in Seattle once made a red huckleberry pie before she went to work one day that was gone by the time she returned. It became a legendary incident, because those small, wild, laboriously gathered, jewel-like berries make a pie fit for the gods, and she was looking forward to having a piece.

How to identify

Red huckleberry is a graceful, deciduous shrub at least 10 feet high, with bell-like

The graceful small leaves of this deciduous shrub make a nice tea.

flowers from pink to white or green. The small green leaves are rounded or oval in shape, with fuzzy undersides. The green branches and twigs are ridged. The smallish, light red fruit dries to a dark purple.

Where and when to gather
More well-known in the states of the Pacific Northwest, red huckleberry in California is found in the California Floristic Province, north coast, Klamath Ranges, northern and southern Sierra Nevada, and the San Francisco Bay Area. It grows on the western sides of the Sierra Nevada and Cascade Range, in redwood, Douglas fir, and other Pacific Coast forest communities. Gather in August and September.

How to gather
Use the fingers as a "berry-rake," use a real berry rake, or pluck the berries one by one. You may need to peer under the leaves to find the red berries. It will be worth it.

How to use
Use to flavor ice cream, in muffins, cakes, pies, and cookies, to make wine and fruit syrups. Can or freeze, or, easiest of all, turn into raisins. Thaw frozen berries briefly in the microwave to retain nutrients. Jams and jellies, smoothies, and sorbets made of red huckleberries are popular as well. The leaves make good tea; pour boiling water over them and let steep for half an hour.

The rich red berries of red huckleberry are popular with hikers and pie bakers.

Future harvests
Patches can be revived through mowing or burning. Tip-pruning is also useful to increase the number of fruit-bearing stems. Leave some berries for the birds and bears. Red huckleberry stems, twigs, and leaves are important winter food for many animals, from deer to mountain beaver.

red maids

Calandrinia ciliata

redmaids, fringed red maids, desert purslane

EDIBLE seeds, leaves, flowers

An annual wildflower of modest proportions, red maids is yet a mighty producer of edible seeds, leaves, and flowers.

To the native peoples of California, the glistening, jet-black seeds of red maids were a boon, a valued ingredient for pinole, used both ceremonially and as a trade item. They have been frequently found in archaeological sites, still tasting good. From February through May, the bright magenta edible flowers of red maids open sequentially from the bottom of the flower stalk to the top. They ripen into a startling quantity of shiny black seeds, tiny and tasty, which are among the most easily and pleasurably collected and cleaned of all the pinole plants. Its shiny leaves are also edible, with an arugulalike bite.

A mass of red maids is a cheerful sight when the flowers open in the sun, a portent of a good seed harvest.

Tiny hairs make a neat fringe on leaf edges, giving the other common name of fringed red maids.

How to identify

When the sun causes the five-petaled flowers of red maids to open fully, the sight is memorable. The deep pink-magenta blooms, ½ to 1 inch wide, have numerous bright golden stamens in the center. The simple, alternate, lance-shaped leaves arising from the stems are fleshy, succulent, and somewhat shiny. With a low-growing, ground-hugging habit, red maids make a neat ground cover, usually growing no more than 8 inches tall.

Where and when to gather

Red maids has a wide distribution in California, in hot, sunny, dry areas from southern California to Del Norte County, the Modoc Plateau, and parts of the Sierra Nevada. Growing in both the inner and outer Coast Ranges and in the valleys, it likes open lean soil and prefers sparsely vegetated and rocky outcroppings, where the growth of tall grasses and other weeds will not outcompete it. Leaves can be picked as early as January, the flowers bloom March through May, and the seeds begin ripening in April and May.

How to gather

Pick the edible leaves before the plant begins to flower, snipping them off with your fingernail. For harvest of seeds, see page 62. The sepals surrounding the seeds of red maids remain green even when the seeds inside are black and ripe, so pick them before the sepals dry and turn brown. Otherwise, you'll lose the seed.

The seed of red maids is ready to be stored or toasted, ground, and eaten.

How to use

The leaves can be eaten raw in a salad, steamed, or nibbled as a trailside snack. The deep pink flowers when rubbed on the cheek leave a natural-looking blush. Quickly toast the cleaned seed in a frying pan no more than one layer deep for thirty to sixty seconds. When seeds are ground in a blender or pounded with a stone, enough oil is released to form seed balls. The toasted whole or ground seeds can be added to rice, other grains, cookies, muffins, and other baked goods. Or the toasted seeds can be ground into flour, which can be substituted for some of the wheat flour in baked goods.

The seeds of red maids, if properly cleaned, can be stored in jars in a cool dry place for ten years or probably much longer. The presence of viable stored red maids seeds in numerous archaeological sites throughout California attests to their long lives.

Future harvests

Leave about 80 percent of the plants in place to reseed, and scatter some seed nearby. You will frequently have the satisfaction of seeing new colonies appear. While other annual wildflowers are in trouble, this valuable food source is remarkable for its resilience. Red maids made a much appreciated appearance in my garden on its own, somehow finding its way through miles of weedy territory.

redwood sorrel

Oxalis oregana

wood sorrel, oxtail

EDIBLE leaves, flowers

Redwood sorrel's sour taste and pleasing texture make it a welcome ingredient of raw salads, trailside snacks, and cooked greens.

In the redwood forests, where time can seem suspended, the summer drought is held at bay by fog drip, and redwood sorrel can retain its juicy edibility even into July and August, when wild greens still tender and mild become rare. From Santa Cruz County north into southern Oregon, the ground is carpeted with masses of low-growing, redwood-adapted, nonwoody plants that love the moisture and shade provided by the big trees. Redwood sorrel is one of the most common of these.

How to identify

Growing close to the ground, the leaves of redwood sorrel grow directly from the base of the plant, emerging from underground roots that account for their carpet-forming habit. The heart-shaped, bright green new leaflets are arranged in threes and have a

In the dim light of a redwood grove, redwood sorrel flowers peek through the edible leaves.

distinctive white-striped midvein. As the leaves age, they become darker green. Single flowers from white to pale and dark pink rise just above the leaves on short stalks. When struck by direct light, the leaflets close along that central vein.

Where and when to gather

In central and northern California's coastal redwood groves and Douglas fir forests, these vigorous plants spread through underground rhizomes, most actively in the rainy season. The best time to harvest the leaves is December through March. Some think the plant is tastier once it begins to flower.

How to gather

Pluck the lighter green younger leaves by hand, or clip with small, sharp scissors.

How to use

Wash, chop, and add the leaves to salads, soups, or salsas. They also can be baked or steamed. Use to accompany dried salmon. The flowers can garnish salads and desserts.

Future harvests

Harvest modestly, taking small amounts of leaves and flowers from different plants within the mass, so that they may quickly grow back into the solid cover the trees' roots appreciate.

redwood violet

Viola sempervirens

evergreen violet

EDIBLE flowers, leaves, stems

Both the leaves and flowers of redwood violet are edible raw or cooked. They make a mild, succulent green and a pleasingly woodsy tea.

Under redwoods and other conifers, in shady, moist woods, this dainty but sturdy ground cover forms dense patches of crisp, round leaves layered tidily over each other. The leaves neatly cover rough edges in banks and slopes next to trails and in openings in the woods in such a pleasing manner that the golden-yellow flowers seem an extra gift. Both leaves and flowers are edible raw or cooked. The tea made from the cooking water of the redwood violet greens, served in old-fashioned flowered teacups, is the perfect ending to a delicate forest meal.

How to identify

This herbaceous perennial hugs the ground, rising no more than 2 or 3 inches.

This delicate mass of redwood violet thrives in the deep shade of the coastal forest.

The deep green, round leaves, 1 or 2 inches wide, are a contrasting lighter green when young. Redwood violet sends down tiny, thin, feeder roots from impressive shallow, horizontal stolons (roots) to establish a colony that is surprisingly impervious to weeds.

Where and when to gather

The yellow flowers appear in March and April over a long period and begin to set seed in April and May. The greens can be collected early in the rainy season from November through April or May; the more rain and shade, the longer the leaves will keep growing, remaining tender and mild.

How to gather

Because they are small and grow close to the ground, collecting large quantities of this green is fairly tedious, which is how it should be—only gather small quantities. Just one-third of a handful, taken from many different patches in the woodland, should suffice, so no harvesting is apparent afterward. Use small, sharp scissors to snip the extremely thin leaf stems and the flowerbuds, which can be eaten also.

How to use

Boil the leaves for at least fifteen minutes until they soften, and serve with rice or chicken, or use to thicken soup. Add the flowers to salads or use to decorate desserts or candy. Use both greens and flowers for tea.

Future harvests

It would require a hard heart to overharvest redwood violet, or any native violet. The care required to snip the leaves is a strong reminder to honor the sweet presence of these plants and the woods they grace. Harvesting a small quantity of leaves and flowers while carefully leaving the roots intact helps to preserve the colony.

salal

Gaultheria shallon

Oregon wintergreen, shallon, gaultheria

`EDIBLE` berries

Among the leathery, green leaves of thicket-forming salal in the coniferous forest, you will find abundant large, blue-black berries.

In many coastal berry patches, salal snuggles right up to evergreen huckleberry. Together, they enjoy the cool, foggy climate and the shelter of various conifers. The larger, darker, softer, blander berries of salal make a natural contrast with the firm, intensely flavored berries of evergreen huckleberry, so they are good eaten together. Patches vary as to berry sweetness, so experiment. With salal, the picking is easy and painless. In full sun, salal grows twice the size that it does in shady patches, and forms more and tastier fruit. The farther north salal grows, the sweeter and more abundant the berries seem to be. Salal grows near the coast in coniferous forests from Santa Barbara County north along the Pacific Coast to Alaska.

How to identify

An upright, evergreen plant with attractive, glossy, thick leaves 2 to 4 inches long,

Salal's evergreen leaves have long been a mainstay of the floral trade.

The pale bell-like flowers of salal hang from bright pink stems.

salal is hard to mistake for anything else. The leaves are simple and alternate. In the sun, it grows upright to 6 feet tall, while in the shade its stems stay under 3 feet tall. Its pale pink bell-shaped flowers hang down from one side of the stem, to be followed by the soft, large, dark berries.

Where and when to gather

Salal and huckleberries share the same foggy experience in the Bishop pine forest in Point Reyes National Seashore, and in forests up and down the coast of California. Frequently found in clear-cuts, salal occurs with red alder, salmonberry, vine maple, tanoak, and either Bishop pine, Douglas fir, redwood, western hemlock, or coyote bush and northern coastal scrub species. It persists in sun or shade. Salal flowers in late spring, and the berries are ripe from mid-August to September.

How to gather

The best way to gather the berries in quantity is to clip the whole flower stalk off, then remove the berries in your home kitchen. If you are eating the berries from the bush, sometimes a tiny insect rests at the base of the fruit, so squeeze the base between thumb and first finger, and only allow the berry to enter your mouth.

How to use

Salal berries are often consumed on the spot, but are sometimes dried, mashed into cakes, and used to make fruit leather. Because the berries are naturally soft, fruit leather is a good way to preserve them. They sweeten as they dry.

Future harvests

Salal likes renewal, and since fire usually isn't an option for you, use the pruning shears where feasible to keep them producing well. Also remove potential or competitive overstory plants. Deer and elk are only moderately enthusiastic about eating salal leaves unless it's cold outside, though with the fruit, it's a different story. Numerous birds enjoy and spread its berries as well. As a thicket-former, it has actually become a troublesome weed in Great Britain, where it was planted for game birds. Schemes to get rid of salal in some timber-producing situations often don't work, even with herbicides, so salal's future, in most situations, looks bright.

saltbush

Atriplex lentiformis

coast saltbush, quail bush, orach, spinach orache, big saltbush

EDIBLE leaves, shoots, seeds

The new leaves of this evergreen shrub are edible and tender, and they can provide enough salty flavor for a whole wild greens stir-fry.

The silver-gray color of saltbush, not usually associated with edibility, is the result of the plant's strategy of depositing salt on the leaves to protect them from munchers. The young shoots are delicious, and the seeds are also eaten. This shrub is frequently recommended as quail food or for other game, but don't let that put you off. Share with the quail, but don't miss this useful pre-salted (gray) green.

How to identify

The goosefoot-shaped leaves of saltbush species, ranging from the desert to the coast, appear grayish because of the tiny hairs on the surface of the leaf, which catch the salt excess secreted onto the leaf surfaces. These concentrations of salt ultimately kill the hairs, and their deposit of salt crystals remains on the leaves' surface. This strategy provides a protective deposit

Saltbush is an attractive silver-leaved shrub often valued as forage for wildlife.

This rugged shrub surprises with its tender new growth, a useful way to add salt to a dish.

to reflect back the intense light that would otherwise overload the photosynthetic system. Saltbush grows from 6 to 8 feet tall and equally wide, making a dense mass that provides good habitat for a multitude of creatures.

Where and when to gather

The genus includes many desert and seashore species, growing in both extremely dry and moist situations. Their ability to grow in high salt locations makes them useful in areas affected by soil salination. Gather young leaves in early to late spring, February through May. The seeds of different species can be gathered from May to July.

How to gather

Ample amounts of saltbush leaves can easily be gathered by snipping. The seeds are also easily collected.

How to use

Eat the tender leaves as a trailside nibble or steam or boil them, especially as they mature. Use them to salt and season other dishes. Dry the leaves thoroughly, then crumble them and store to use as a vegetable salt.

Future harvests

One of the toughest shrubs, saltbush is regarded as drought insurance by cattle ranchers. Deer and other ungulates rely on it, but your moderate harvest will not be missed.

sheep sorrel

Rumex acetosella

red sorrel, sour weed, field sorrel

`EDIBLE` leaves, stems

Sheep sorrel is another member of the fairly large group of weeds spread throughout California and the world whose distinguishing flavor is a refreshingly tart, lemony one.

Resulting from the presence of oxalates, the sour flavor of sheep sorrel's leaves, combined with their sturdy texture, gives the plant a number of culinary uses. Concerns about oxalates in the diet, such as with spinach, have largely proven to be unnecessary, unless massive quantities are continually consumed. This plant turns up frequently in gardens. You can make a fancy French soup out of it, or at the other end of the spectrum, you can eat it raw as a gardening snack, providing a welcome juicy, sour-sweet interlude.

How to identify

Sheep sorrel is a weedy perennial that reproduces both from many tiny seeds and from underground rhizomatous roots. The

The arrowhead-shaped leaves and red seed leaves of sheep sorrel can be seen in July on the coast.

presence of sheep sorrel is easily ascertained when it blooms in early summer. The tiny orange-red or mahogany-colored flowers are closely pressed to the flower stalk. They make a colorful blur from a distance. The dull-green arrowhead-shaped leaves, usually growing fairly close to the ground, are also distinctive, with two lobes at the base pointing downward. The lemony taste is the final distinguishing characteristic.

Where and when to gather

Sheep sorrel grows throughout California, preferring but not requiring areas with some natural moisture. It is best in February through April, before it flowers in May or June. Along the coast, it can emerge again in midsummer, June through July.

How to gather

Pull sheep sorrel up by the roots, which will be snipped off and discarded. Immerse in water and dry quickly. Do not try to compost, since this plant will regrow from its roots right in your compost heap.

How to use

Sheep sorrel can be used as a garnish, as a tea, in small quantities in a chopped salad, and in French sorrel soup, a classic vegetable soup. It's a tasty nibble as well, quenching the thirst and eliminating dry mouth.

Future harvests

Sheep sorrel turns up reliably every spring and disappears in the dry summer. Control it by pulling it up from the roots while the soil is still moist in early and mid-spring. But when the soil is dry, the roots will usually snap off, leaving some behind to regrow with the next year's rains. To control its spread, sheet mulching is recommended rather than hand-weeding. With sheet mulching, a good strategy for many perennial weeds that grow from roots that spread laterally, place sheets of recycled cardboard directly over the weedy area. Spread wood chips or other kinds of mulch over the cardboard to hold it down, to look presentable, and to create a good area for planting the following year. Without the cardboard, the sheep sorrel will simply regrow and emerge through the mulch.

Sierra mint

Pycnanthemum californicum
mountain mint, California mint

`EDIBLE` leaves

This attractive evergreen mountain ground cover packs a minty punch. Strongly scented and pungent, Sierra mint is used by mountaineers for cooking and for beverages.

Sierra mint can provide for the mountain hiker what yerba buena does for the low-land hiker. This herb makes a tea that has benefits you have to drink to understand. Both of these wild teas have a refreshing, hydrating quality that brings you back for more and will soothe an upset stomach. Sierra mint thrives in wetter and higher areas than yerba buena. As with yerba buena, the fragrance of its scented leaf is part of the joy of encountering this plant.

How to identify

Like other members of the mint family, this perennial herbaceous species has square stems, opposite leaves, and two-lipped

The energetic spread of this low-growing mint plant in the mountains ensures the availability of fresh cups of herbal tea.

flowers. The plant's shiny gray foliage and dense clusters of small white flowers with lavender dots are an attractive component of coniferous woodlands and wetter parts of the chaparral. It grows about 2 feet tall.

Where and when to gather

Sierra mint is endemic to California, favoring canyons and slopes in most of the state's mountain ranges. It ranges from sea level to 5,500 feet. Sierra mint blooms from June to September and can be harvested for its leaves until it sets seed.

How to gather

Carefully snip a few leaves and stems from each plant, leaving the area so that nothing looks disturbed. Lightly prune the tops so that they will return more thickly, and use the trimmings for tea.

How to use

Sierra mint can be used like any other mint and is particularly good as a soothing minty tea before bedtime or to settle the stomach. Pour boiling water over stems and leaves and let steep for half an hour, or boil directly in the water for ten minutes.

Future harvests

With moderate gathering practices, Sierra mint can continue to thrive.

Caution

Avoid if pregnant.

silverweed

Potentilla anserina subsp. *pacifica*
potentilla, wild sweet potato
`EDIBLE` roots, leaves

This pretty yellow perennial flower has an illustrious worldwide history, being a plant whose roots and leaves have been of great culinary importance to many peoples.

For many centuries in our Pacific Northwest, silverweed has been grown by native tribes in well-tended estuary gardens with other moisture-loving root foods like springbank clover and chocolate lily. These root foods had a special prestige—they were thought to be the food that was eaten in heaven. The roots of silverweed were also an important staple food in Ireland after the failure of the potato crops, and possibly before. The plant's amino acid profile is said to complement that of barley to produce whole proteins, and has been used to prevent starvation in Tibet. Though I had never seen it mentioned in California ethnographies or heard that it was used within our borders, I was intrigued to find it growing in northern California in seasonal wetlands, available for my own personal discovery of its unique, slender roots for carbohydrates and of its tasty leaves for tea or salads.

The five-petaled yellow flower and the deep-green compound leaves with silvery undersides identify this species.

How to identify
Silverweed is distinguished by its toothed compound leaves, which are deep green on the top, silvery on the underside, and 8 to 12 inches long. It hugs the ground in moist places. The attractive yellow five-petaled flowers are about 1 inch wide and grow at the top of a leafless stem. Silverweed spreads by means of red aboveground horizontal runners that root at the nodes, like strawberries. This plant goes dormant in late fall and reappears in late spring.

Where and when to gather
Silverweed grows from the Pacific Northwest down into the north Coast Ranges.

Silverweed spreads through its red aboveground runners, which root at the nodes, like strawberries.

It's found where the ground stays wet into summer, so if you see a small pond or seep with moisture in August, check for the yellow flowers of this attractive species. The roots can be harvested in October to December, when the foliage dies back, as well as in spring, when the leaves emerge, beginning in March. The leaves are best gathered before the plant blooms.

How to gather

When you find this plant, dig carefully around its stem until you come across the roots, which may be long and straight, or curved. Centrally located plants seem to be less productive than those at the edges of a group. Harvest the longer, fleshier, older roots and replant the shorter pieces. Leaves can be snipped off with small scissors.

How to use

Snip the roots, which should be as thick as a pencil, into 4-inch-long strips before cooking. The roots were traditionally steamed, which was necessary to remove the bitterness, or you can boil them in water until soft. Season and eat with butter or olive oil, using the long, slender roots as you would a starch in your meal. The leaves can be used to make a tea, in salads, or in stews and stir-fries.

Future harvests

Silverweed makes an attractive wetland garden plant, though it can be aggressive. This attribute will not be a problem if you develop a taste for this ancient root food. It is easily grown from seed, and can be propagated by replanting the shorter, narrower roots in the ground or in large containers.

singleleaf pinyon pine

Pinus monophylla

singleleaf pinyon, monophylla

EDIBLE nuts

Comprising an astonishing forty million acres of rich and productive nut-orchards throughout the Great Basin and into California, the singleleaf pinyon pine epitomizes the grace that nature can offer on agriculturally marginal lands.

The open, nut-heavy cone of singleleaf pinyon pine is an appealing sight, with its plump brown nuts held by the thinnest membrane to each of the woody scales. Each cone, producing about thirty large nuts, is pretty enough to be an arid-land Christmas tree ornament. Among the pine nuts, this nut has the softest shell, easily cracked with the teeth. The nut can be eaten, shell and all. Nutrient rich, it is almost the equivalent of butter in its energy-producing fats and carbohydrates, containing 10 percent protein (same as the pecan), 23 percent high-quality unsaturated fats, and 54 percent carbohydrates.

How to identify

The singleleaf pinyon pine has apple-sized cones that are distinctively bright green in the summer, turning brown by fall. In

The nuts produced by singleleaf pinyon pine are sweet and tasty. They release easily from the cones.

The foothills of Mount Pinos in southern California are rich habitat for singleleaf pinyon pine.

a good year, they litter the ground. Each scale displays two nuts nestled together, staggered so that the contents of each scale are visible. The sharp, pointed needles are in groups of only one, a distinctive feature of the singleleaf pinyon. These trees are relatively small, 30 to 45 feet tall, and therefore the cones are more accessible than on some other nut pines.

Where and when to gather

Growing frequently with Utah juniper, rabbitbrush, sagebrush, grasses, and forbs, singleleaf pinyon spreads into California on the east side of the Sierra Nevada, where it covers the foothills at 3,000 to 8,000 feet. They are also found in the Tehachapi Mountains, and the pine nut forest frames the southern end of the Central Valley, favoring the middle elevations and foothills of those semiarid mountains, usually on south-facing slopes. The seeds are ripe by Labor Day, though the cones that enclose them may still be green. The harvest extends from September to early October.

How to gather

If the cones are still green, pull branches down with a hook and twist them off. Place green cones in a sunny spot, where they will open in about a week, revealing ripe nuts that slide out on their own. Usually but not always, dark brown nuts will prove to be full and healthy, while the light tan seeds are empty. Since the nuts are easily separated from the cone, they are frequently gathered during their fall to the ground or from blankets spread on the ground beneath the tree. Or extract nuts by shaking the cones in a bag or box, or shake the tree itself. The ease with which they

Singleleaf pinyon pine is a dense, shrubby conifer with prized pine nuts.

nuts are delicious. Roasting and toasting brings out their flavor. Use in pesto, pasta, salads, and baked goods. Pine nut "butter" was served as a gruel by native peoples to infants and the elderly, and was considered an essential component of the larder.

To store, remove the nuts from the cone to avoid the formation of mold. Storing in the shell preserves the nuts for two or three years. Cure before storing by letting them shrivel slightly in a cool, dry place. They can be stored at room temperature, in the refrigerator, or frozen.

Future harvests

A complex ecology, including squirrels, pinyon jays, chipmunks, sawflies, bears, and bighorn sheep, as well as humans, requires that we exercise temperance in collecting these precious nuts. Boom and bust cycles are common. Gather carefully, without breaking the brittle limbs of the tree. "Chaining," the wholesale removal of nut pines to convert desert shrublands to pasture, is one of the more painful chapters in our land-use history. Honor the singleleaf pinyon.

release and are gathered is a joy to a pine nut harvester used to more recalcitrant species.

How to use

Remove the shell using a table-mounted or hand nutcracker, applying light pressure. Or roll over lightly with a rolling pin until all are slightly cracked, then peel. These

soaproot

Chlorogalum pomeridianum

soap lily, soap plant, amole, wavyleaf soap plant

EDIBLE leaves, bulb

Soaproot has a unique history of traditional usefulness, from its edible leaves to its bulbs that produce soap.

Though soaproot is a fairly common species, it was always a welcome sight to California's tribes. This plant of many practical uses makes a sturdy handsome brush to help with food preparation, soap to wash hair and clothes, glue for arrow making, and poison to stun fish. And it also has edible parts, like the distinctive, straplike leaves that are good to eat raw or cooked when just emerging from the large edible starchy bulb. The bulb can be given the same long, slow cooking as camas, to emerge caramelized, sweet, and no longer soapy. In the late afternoons and evenings of May and June, the star-shaped, spidery-looking white blossoms open up and down its long stems, waiting to be pollinated by moths that only appear with the fading light.

Soaproot opens its spidery white blossoms toward the end of an early summer day.

The wavy basal leaves of soaproot are tender and sweet when eaten young.

How to identify

The large bulb, the size of a baked potato, is covered by dark brown, coarse hairs. The wavy-edged leaves, up to 15 inches long, begin the season lying flat along the ground. The leafless flowering shoots, three to six per plant, rise from the plant's center in April and May, from 2 feet to an impressive 6 feet tall. They bloom in May and June, with six-petaled, slender white flowers with dark veins on the outside of the recurving petals and six noticeably prominent stamens. Their twilight opening is a characteristic used to distinguish this species from others in the genus.

Where and when to gather

Soaproot grows throughout the California Floristic Province, from San Diego County to Oregon, in dry open hills and grasslands, in coastal sage scrub, and in foothill woodland. The bulbs can be gathered April through June while the soil is still moist in spring until the flowers begin to set seed in July and August. Leaves can be gathered as early as October as they emerge from summer dormancy, continuing till just before they bloom in May through June.

How to gather

The mature leaves remain for many months, and indicate where the plant's bulbs can be dug. Harvest the bulb by digging up the plant, breaking it off above the root, and replanting the offsets from the root crown. For greens, cut leaves at base of plant.

How to use

The ideal way to cook the bulbs is in earth or pit ovens for three days, but in their absence, try a slow cooker. As they cook, taste small bits, and if they are still bitter, continue cooking until they're not. They can also be steamed. The leaves can be eaten raw or cooked when just emerging in the early spring. Like the root, they become very sweet when slowly baked. Roast in an oven with a bit of water, or boil, changing and discarding the cooking water several times.

Future harvests

This species is reassuringly prolific. Compared to other native bulbs, it produces a substantial amount of biomass, and it is easily propagated through root division and reseeding. Watching soaproot divide and slowly conquer an area, even without human intervention, gives one confidence in its future. When harvesting, deposit seeds in the hole or nearby. Five other species and a number of subspecies of soaproot are found in California, but a number of these have a limited distribution and should not be harvested.

Caution

As with all plants containing saponins, the foaming substance found in soap, long cooking is required to render the bulb harmless and palatable. Do not eat raw.

sourberry

Rhus aromatica

three-leaf sumac, skunkbush, skunkbush sumac, lemonade berry

`EDIBLE` berries

Native peoples from Oregon to Baja California enjoyed eating sour-berry's fruits, as well as using the plant in basketry and the berries as a dye. The red-orange berries were eaten raw, dried, and used to make a pink lemony drink.

Some plants are or were so valuable to certain indigenous tribes that they identified their culture with the use of the plants. Sourberry is an example. In the same genus as poison oak, it has none of that plant's well-known unpleasant qualities. It was intensely managed, usually by burning, to provide the straight, strong twigs known in basketry as "sticks"; almost 700 sticks were needed to make one Chukchansi Yokuts cradleboard. The plants are hardy and can grow in sun or partial shade. Their main ornamental features are the orange to red fall foliage and berries at the end of summer. As soon as the fruits ripen in the fall, they are gathered, eaten, and preserved, sometimes continuing harvest through the winter.

These bright red berries are harvested in the fall before the leaves turn scarlet and drop off.

The gently lobed leaves of sourberry cradle the scarlet waxy fruits, used in a variety of concoctions.

How to identify

This deciduous shrub has "leaflets of three," like its relative poison oak, but there is nothing to be feared from touching these leaves. A distinctive "skunky" smell results from crushing them. The shrub is thicket-forming and grows to 8 feet tall. Tiny, five-petaled yellow flowers with five orange to reddish flower leaves bloom before the leaves appear. Sticky red-orange berries, about ¼ inch long, appear on the female plants.

Where and when to gather

In the California Floristic Province and in the desert mountains, sourberry grows under 7,200 feet. The berries ripen in the fall and may hang on until early spring.

How to gather

Pluck or snip the berries from the twigs.

How to use

Traditionally, the berries were mashed and cooked to make rich fruit sauces to accompany meat or to be used as dessert. Modern taste buds require that the berries be sweetened. The berries can be cooked in water to make cooling drinks, used to make a refreshing sourberry soup for summer days, made into jam, or dried .

Future harvests

An important species for revegetation projects, sourberry is frequently planted to provide shelter and food for wildlife, so its future looks secure. Sourberry is doing well on its own.

Caution

It has been reported that some people are allergic to the fruits. As with all new foods, try a small amount first.

springbank clover

Trifolium wormskioldii

cows clover, coast clover, sand clover, seaside clover, Wormskjold's clover

EDIBLE roots, leaves, flowers

Springbank clover, one of the most intriguing traditional root foods, thrives in California, producing edible roots, flowers, and leaves.

In the Pacific Northwest, springbank clover was extensively farmed in native-managed estuaries and harvested to be transported in canoes for gifts, trade items, and festival food. It is one of the few perennial clovers, and spreads rapidly when it gets the moisture it needs. Springbank clover is aptly named, for it can indeed be found on banks from which springs flow. The pink-purple flowers are edible, as are the deep green leaves. The leaves retain their sweetness even when the flowers, which make a nice tea, are blooming. Most important to native peoples were the slender white horizontal roots, or rhizomes. Ducks and geese are also fond of the tender rhizomes, which were used as bait to catch them.

How to identify

Springbank clover's lance-shaped leaflets with rounded corners are about 1/3 inch long. Like all members of the clover

The perennial springbank clover, producing flowers that make a pleasant tea, blooms as long as it has moisture.

The edible leaves of springbank clover are tasty when young.

family, leaflets of three make up one leaf. The pink-purple or deeper magenta flower forms heads 1 to 2 inches wide and has bristly, white tips. A matted form growing from rhizomes is present along the coast, where it makes an appealing flowering ground cover. If you see a clover growing in moist places, it may be springbank clover.

Where and when to gather

Springbank clover grows in many different situations throughout the California Floristic Province, particularly in open, moist, and marshy places, from beaches to mountain meadows to coastal prairies, preferring but not requiring full sun. It's found at the edges of seasonal wetlands and ponds. A wet winter will find it thriving, and the leaves can be gathered as soon as it makes good growth with the rains, from November to May. It frequently goes dormant in late summer, leafing out again after the winter rains. Hugging the ground as closely as it does, this plant may not be noticeable until its pretty flowers appear in May to July, when they can be harvested. Springbank clover roots are best while still growing. This occurrence depends on the nature of the moisture supply and the rainfall in a particular season, but usually takes place from December through June.

How to gather

Pick the greens and flowers by hand or snip with scissors. Dig down to at least 1 foot to find the roots, using a spade or digging stick. Gently separate roots from the soil.

This perennial native clover was particularly valued for its edible roots, from which it spreads.

How to use

Springbank clover roots are said to grow sweeter with storage, in a cool, dry, dark place. Steam or boil the supple white roots, which also can be eaten raw. Eat separately or add to stews. Eat greens raw or steamed, soaked in salt water, or eaten with bay nuts. Steep the flowers, dried or fresh, in hot water for healthful teas.

Future harvests

Like many rhizomatous plants, springbank clover grows easily from small sections of root. Harvest the larger roots to eat and replant the smaller root sections in the loosened soil. Home clover gardens, loosely modeled after the estuary gardens of the Northwest, are easy to establish if small root sections are replaced in the ground and allowed to grow with appropriate watering.

stinging nettle

Urtica dioica

burning nettle, wild nettle, Indian spinach

EDIBLE leaves, stems

The intense green color of cooked nettles looks like health itself, and it is indeed a nutrient-dense cooking green, astoundingly high in vitamin A, calcium, magnesium, and iron.

As the days shorten and the rains of autumn begin, inhabitants of much of California remember their connection to the great rain forests of the Northwest. One of the plants most of California shares with Washington, Oregon, Canada, and Alaska is the stinging nettle. The nettle pizza served at a nearby upscale restaurant is only one example why you might want to find and frequent your own wild nettle patch. Cooked, this perennial loses its sting and is reminiscent of cooked spinach, but even milder and healthier.

How to identify

The easiest way to identify stinging nettle is to walk by it and get stung. But otherwise, look for the telltale hairs on the

This stand of stinging nettle is just right for harvesting.

The flowers of stinging nettle indicate that it's too late to harvest this crop.

and can be treated the same. In California, nettle eating begins soon after the first fall rains and into the spring. Most years, you'll be eating fresh nettle soup and stir-fried lemony nettles on rice by Halloween. Depending on the rains, harvesting continues into the spring.

How to gather

In the California Floristic Province, nettle is tenderest in late fall and early spring. Harvest only the new leaves at the top of the plant, the top 4 to 6 inches. Avoid insect-eaten or older leaves. Place in a sturdy cardboard box or canvas bag for transporting. Put in cool water as soon as possible.

How to use

Stinging nettle loses its sting as soon as it is cooked or dried. Wash nettles, place in a large pot with 2 inches of water, and steam. Boil like spinach, or microwave with a small amount of water. Use in soups, lasagnas, and stews. A dehydrator is useful for drying nettles, which can be stored for use in teas or reconstituted for use with pasta. Cooked nettles can be frozen. Dried nettles, as well as fresh, make a popular tea.

Future harvests

Stinging nettle, having spread here from Eurasia and being perennial, is not in much danger of disappearing, but still, harvest with an eye to the future of your sacred nettle patch. Harvesting the tops can lead to bushier plants with a longer harvest time for you.

leaves and stem, the opposite arrangement of leaves, and the drooping clusters of tiny leaves at the leaf axils. The leaves are heart-shaped with jagged edges and prominent veins from the stem.

Where and when to gather

This most valued of potherbs sprouts and grows along creeks, in openings in moist forests, and at the woodland edges, especially in those places where the soil has a chance to accumulate humus. The species, naturalized from Eurasia, is found all over the California Floristic Province. The American stinging nettle, *Urtica dioica* subsp. *gracilis*, is similar in most ways

sugar bush

Rhus ovata

lemonade tree, sugar tree

EDIBLE coating of fruit

Similar to lemonade berry in everything but location, sugar bush, an elegant shrub, has fruits that can replace lemons in beverages and can be made into a concentrate for use in other dishes.

The distribution of sugar bush in the western edge of California's Sonoran Desert makes the plant of potential use to thirsty wanderers. Put the ripe fruits in your water bottle, or, if you run out of water, put the fruit directly in your mouth. Your thirst will be quenched.

How to identify

Sugar bush is an evergreen shrub growing 8 to 12 feet tall and equally wide. It has small pale pink or white flowers that ripen into small, hard-seeded fruits coated with a sweet-and-sour waxy substance. The flower and fruit are slightly smaller than

The tiny flowers of sugar bush will each ripen into fruit with a sweet, rough, waxy coating that has a distinct flavor of lemon.

those of lemonade berry, and the leathery oval leaves fold along the midrib, which distinguishes them from lemonade berry leaves.

Where and when to gather

Sugar bush is found in dry hills, somewhat back from the coast, from Santa Barbara south. It flowers from February through May, and ripens fruit from the end of May to June; fruits remain on the bush for some time after that.

How to gather

Remove ripe fruits from the bush with your fingers and store in a glass or other slick-surfaced container.

How to use

The fruit can be simmered in water until the liquid is sweet and flavorful, with a lemony taste. Cold water can also be used but will take longer. As with lemonade berry, sugar bush could revolutionize the lemonade stand.

Future harvests

Gather circumspectly, with the uses of wildlife in mind. The strongly flavored fruits can be used sparingly.

Caution

Those who are allergic to the cashew, or sumac, family might also be allergic to the fruit of sugar bush.

sugar pine

Pinus lambertiana

big pine, great sugar pine

`EDIBLE` nuts, resin, needles

The sugar pine tree produces the largest and most flavorful of pine nuts.

Famed as the tallest pine in the world, and the fourth largest tree in California, sugar pine is a renowned timber tree. It has provided wood for staggering numbers of shakes and shingles, fences, houses, barns, fruit boxes, and even pipes in church organs. Perhaps less well known is the record it holds for the longest pinecone, and even more to the point, the biggest, most tasty pine nuts. The Indians had another pleasant use for this tree of superlatives. The sweet, gummy resin exuding from the trunk was thought by John Muir to be "the best of sweets—better than maple sugar." Perhaps most important, the large sweet nuts slip easily from the open scales of the long and slender cone, feeding animals and people alike. The only problem, and one worth solving, is gaining access to the cones themselves.

How to identify

Young sugar pines grow closely together in groves, slender and triangular in shape, and similar to one another. Mature sugar pines, about 200 years old, have a graceful, flexible, palmlike top and a diameter near the ground of 6 to 9 feet. In old age, the pines assume the prerogative of the elderly, taking on varied, picturesque forms that

reflect their history of wind, snow, and wild weather. Dull blue-gray bark also marks this period. Most distinctive are the cones,

A young sugar pine tree begins its long life with a graceful, triangular shape.

which hang and are 15 to 24 inches long, green shaded with dark purple where the sun reaches them. Each cone scale carries two dark brown seeds about ½ inch long, with broad wings 1 inch long. Needles are five to the bundle and about 4 inches long.

Where and when to gather

Sugar pine grows most consistently down the Sierra Nevada and up into Oregon, from 3,000 to 7,000 feet elevation. It also grows in smaller amounts in the Klamath Ranges, the north Coast Ranges to Sonoma and Napa, the Cascade Range and the Modoc Plateau, the Transverse Ranges, and down the Peninsular Ranges as far south as Baja. The cones ripen in September and October, when the scales open and release the winged seeds. Subsequently, the cone scales turn yellow-brown, and the cones continue to hang on the tree all winter and through one more summer. Mast years of good production occur every few years, separated by years of moderate production.

How to gather

These tantalizing nuts are not easy to harvest. You may find cones on the ground, but the nuts may be already harvested. Or you can climb 100 feet to get at branches you can shake so that the cones twirl around and eventually detach. Removing the nuts from the tough cone is similar to the technique described for gray pine, in which the cone is smashed end first with a rock, hammer, or hatchet. Splitting the cone in sections by smashing it in quarters, though brutal, seems the best way to coax the nuts out from between the scales. To harvest the resin, slice it off the bark with a sharp knife.

How to use

Fresh resin hanging from the bark, white and delicious, can be eaten, but with restraint, as it can have a laxative effect and was used for this purpose by some indigenous Californians. Resin made from tree wounds caused by fire will be golden to dark brown and hardened, but still edible. The nuts can be eaten like any other pine nuts, cracked, cleaned, and eaten raw or toasted, in pesto, salads, or as snacks. Roasting and then grinding the nuts until they form a thick paste makes a sublime nut butter, a treat that traditionally was called *lopa* by the central Miwok. Because the shells are relatively soft, they can be ground up along with the nutmeats.

Future harvests

The uses of sugar pine in the timber industry are the biggest threats to its survival, along with the advent of the white pine blister rust. Breeding programs aimed at conifers resistant to this disease may help. Protecting local groves and helping to start new ones is required to ensure that the beauty of sugar pine and its delicious nuts stay with us.

swamp onion

Allium validum

tall swamp onion, wild onion, Pacific onion, Pacific mountain onion

EDIBLE leaves, bulb, flowers

This relatively common wild onion is found growing in large masses in the foothills of the Sierra Nevada, where its delicate blossoms belie its powerful punch as a seasoning and cooked vegetable.

Unlike the domesticated onion, the bulb of the swamp onion is a thickened portion of the underground root, but in every other respect, it can be used like a green onion, raw or cooked. A widely harvested wild vegetable, the swamp onion can be viewed but not harvested in Yosemite National Park, where it is the most common wild onion. It is a favorite of wildflower enthusiasts and cooks alike.

How to identify

A small dense head of rose to purple to almost white blossoms is held on flowering stalks from 1 to 3 feet tall. Each plant has three to six flat, somewhat juicy, succulent, bright green, pungent stems growing from 1 to 2 feet tall. The bulb is about 1 inch wide.

A closeup of swamp onion's flowers reveals beauty matched with a strong, oniony smell and taste.

Where and when to gather

Swamp onion grows in the Sierra Nevada from 4,000 to 11,000 feet, favoring moist meadows, seasonally wet seeps, creek banks, and sometimes even creeks. It is found in the Warner Mountains, east of the Sierra Nevada, and in northern California from the mountains to the coast. At its most tender in the spring from March through May, it can also be harvested while the plant is in flower from June to August.

How to gather

The entire plant is edible, but if you want to preserve the plant where it grows, try cutting off portions of the top of the stalk as you would green onions or chives from your garden. When it is growing in loose, sandy soils, you can often easily pull the entire plant out of the ground, but in this case, be extremely careful to harvest lightly, and only from large colonies. In more compacted soils, either dig the bulb cluster, replanting some of the small bulblets, or snip the tips of the leaves.

How to use

Add to egg dishes, stews, stir-fries, and other dishes that benefit from the addition of these sulfurous compounds, without which much of our cuisine would be sadly diminished. All parts can also be used raw; chop and rinse in water just before serving. Cook long and slow to sweeten the taste and increase the digestibility, as for all members of the onion family. The uncooked flowers can also be used as a garnish.

Future harvests

Spreading through short, thick rhizomes, the swamp onion is easy to gather so that it's hard to tell you've been there. Harvest from the middle of the colony. One plant should be enough to flavor your meal.

Caution

Swamp onion may grow with the toxic death camas, which has no oniony odor at all and has white flowers. Let your nose and eyes be your guide. As with camas, only harvest when you can see the bloom, for identification purposes.

tall coastal plantain

Plantago subnuda

plantain, broad-leaved plantain, naked plantain, water plantain

EDIBLE seeds, leaves

An attractive perennial, tall coastal plantain produces a remarkable amount of small brown-black edible seed on its tall, narrow seed stalks.

Neither the bananalike fruit called plantain used in Latin American cooking nor the common weedy European herb of the same name, tall coastal plantain is one of several plantains native to California. One plant can produce one cup of seed, an impressive performance for a wild plant. Tall coastal plantain is one of the easiest native plants from which to gather seed in quantity. The English plantain, *Plantago lanceolata*, is a much smaller plant, producing a smaller amount of seed that is more difficult to collect.

Reproducing readily, lasting many years, and requiring no care, these plants are astonishingly useful. Their seeds can be toasted and ground, and are a nutritious addition to baked goods and breakfast

The seed stalk of this native plantain is substantial, producing a significant amount of edible, healthful seed.

Tall coastal plantain seeds can be roasted, ground, and incorporated into many dishes.

porridges. Like other plantain seeds, they are somewhat mucilaginous, a quality that is reputed to be an aid to glycemic digestion. The leaves when young are eaten fresh or cooked, contain calcium, and a single portion can provide as much vitamin A as a large carrot.

How to identify

Tall coastal plantain is a striking perennial with fleshy, oval-round, pink-veined, basal, pointed leaves resting on the ground and growing from 3 to 8 inches long, depending on soil and moisture. A sturdy, hairy, narrow flowering spike, up to 1 foot long, contains tiny inconspicuous flowers densely adhering to the stalk. When the plant sets seed, the flowering spike resembles a tight ear of dried corn, and contains a substantial amount of black seeds when ripe.

Where and when to gather

Tall coastal plantain is found in a thin band along the north coast, the central coast, the San Francisco Bay Area, the south coast, and the northern Channel Islands. Occasionally growing in salt marshes and moist banks, tall coastal plantain blooms May through September, setting seed about a month after bloom time. It may germinate and grow along the coast as long as moisture is present.

How to gather

Cut the seed stalks and lay them in a paper bag. The seeds will fall out on their own. Gather the leaves to eat well before the flower stalks develop.

How to use

Toasting and grinding make the seeds suitable additions to muffins, breads, trail mix, and cookies. Add to breakfast porridges. Use as a garnish for baked casseroles or for breading. The leaves can be steamed, added to stir-fries, and eaten raw when young.

Future harvests

The sporadic appearance of tall coastal plantain is somewhat surprising, given how well it spreads on its own. Sowing seed nearby doesn't seem to be necessary.

tanoak

Notholithocarpus densiflorus

tanbark oak

EDIBLE acorns

Tanoak is the gracious provider of what some consider the best of all of California's acorns.

Called "the beautiful tree" by some Pomo people, tanoak is one of northern California's glorious hardwood trees. It's hard to know whether this affectionate name refers to the beauty of its leaves, nuts, and trunk or to the splendor of its acorn crop. Tanoak bears tasty acorns, which are high in oil and protein, and are among the easiest acorns to process and store. The tree has the valuable ability to provide good crops while growing as an understory tree in part shade, while other oak trees require full sun to yield good acorn crops. Though tanoak is far less widespread in California than black oak and valley oak, its attributes make it very popular.

How to identify

Tanoaks can grow up to 150 feet tall, with a pyramidal shape achieved when they reach maturity at 100 to 200 years old. The long lance-shaped leaves, simple and

These tanoak acorns were stored for five years without deteriorating.

The unusual acorn cap of tanoak was said in a Pomo story to represent a girl's uncombed hair. The handsome leaves have silvery, pale green undersides.

alternating, grow from 2 to 5 inches long and 2½ inches wide. The leaves are distinctive for their jagged edges, the rich green color on the top, and the fuzzy, pale green underside. In spring, the pale green new growth makes such a contrast to the deep green mature leaves that it is sometimes mistaken for flowers. Tanoak acorns are easily identified by the scraggly cap, in which nests the plump, first pale green, then beige, acorns, covered with tiny hairs. Tanoak, the only member of the genus *Notholithocarpus*, is not a real oak, which is in the genus *Quercus*. The beautiful tree stands alone.

Where and when to gather

Tanoaks are found as understory trees with redwoods and Douglas firs in the Coast Ranges from Ventura County north to Oregon, on slopes to 4,500 feet. They also grow in pure stands. Their acorns are gathered in the fall, from September through November.

How to gather

Pluck acorns from the tree before they are fully ripe. Harvesting from the ground after they have fallen often results in acorns that are invaded by insects. Tanoak acorns take two years to ripen. Accordingly, the tree carries ripe acorns as well as those that will ripen the following year. Therefore, harvest individually by hand rather than knocking all the acorns off at the same time. One large, old tree can produce from 200 to 1,000 pounds of tanoak acorns during a gathering season.

How to use

Tanoak acorns can be ground into flour that can be used in soup, mush, pancakes, and bread. It makes excellent biscuits mixed half and half with wheat flour, a New Year's Eve tradition for us. These acorns are among the easiest ones to shell, with one firm tap on the side rendering the tough shell peelable. The papery skin comes off easily as well. Like all acorns, they require leaching before use (see Acorn Processing, page 85).

Another asset of tanoak acorns is their ability to store well. While the acorns of some species of oak trees can decay in two to three months after harvest, tanoak acorns can emerge from the most casual storage conditions in good shape. Like all acorns, they need to be dried before storage by spreading them out in the sun on trays. Store unshelled in a cool, dry, dark area. Or, peeled nuts may be frozen for later thawing and processing.

Future harvests

Some lumber companies do not have much affection for tanoak, even attempting to eliminate them through aerial spraying of herbicides, to make room for the more valuable and easily harvested conifers like Douglas fir. Tanoak, however, has the resilient ability to crown sprout (send up shoots from the stump), even after being cut.

It needs that resilience, now that the disease called sudden oak death has appeared in northern California. In some areas, this tough and formerly disease-resistant tree has become almost extinct. Be careful when handling and transporting oak and tanoak acorns and wood to avoid moving infected materials and spreading the disease. Disinfect tools and acorns with chlorine (see Resources).

Caution

Never eat an unleached acorn. It isn't poisonous, but the tannins will give you an unpleasant stomachache.

thimbleberry
Rubus parviflorus

EDIBLE berries

When fully ripe, as indicated by their deep red, almost maroon color, and softened texture, thimbleberries taste like an intense raspberry.

With their powerful, somewhat acidic tang, it doesn't take many thimbleberries to add sweet savor to a bowl of mixed fruit. The fruit forms a thin, fleshy coating over a raspberrylike seed structure. Usually found in openings in woodlands, these berries may be all the more sought after when their harvest is spare. Growing up to 8,000 feet in the mountains, thimbleberry is thought to improve in flavor at altitude, like a number of other species.

How to identify
Thimbleberry is a widely distributed deciduous shrub with no thorns. The bushes spread strongly through underground rhizomes. Like those of many woodland understory shrubs, the green

Thimbleberry is a graceful woodland berry with a unique, strong fruity flavor.

leaves, which drop in late summer, are large, thin, flexible, and palmately lobed like a maple leaf. The flowers are composed of five large white petals and are 2 to 4 inches across and translucent. After the petals drop, the sepals form an attractive and noticeable starlike pattern, with the developing fruit in the center. The fruit is dark red and perfectly round-looking, large in diameter but thin and not very fleshy.

Where and when to gather

Found in moist woodlands throughout North America, in California, thimbleberry can be found throughout the California Floristic Province and in the Sierra Nevada. It grows in full sun where moisture is present. The plant blooms March through April, and the fruit ripens from June through late July.

How to gather

Thimbleberries are delicate, with a fragile structure, and are easily squashed. The riper they are, the easier it is to slide the cap of drupelets off the rigid seed core of the berry.

How to use

These berries are rarely found in quantities large enough for preserving, but they can be used to spark the flavors in a bowl of more abundant fruits. They are a special trailside treat. Add to other berries in a fruit bowl, to fruit drinks, jams, and jellies. The flowers, with their elegant structure, can be used for decorating a spring birthday cake.

Future harvests

Thimbleberry can be relied on to spread through its own vigorous underground root system and with the help of birds. Pruning to the ground every four years or so is also helpful.

thistle sage

Salvia carduacea

chia

`EDIBLE` seeds

When you become acquainted with thistle sage, you'll no doubt want to add its tasty seeds to your repertoire of seed foods.

This spring-blooming desert wildflower has a striking appearance. Its large, lavender-blue flowers, and its leaves with a strong sage odor and covering of white woolly hairs will also help you in identifying it. Sometimes thistle sage is referred to as one of the chias, and its seeds are used in the same way. They have a mild, nutty taste similar to that of golden chia, but they are larger and even more nutritious, with 26 percent protein and 32 percent oil.

How to identify

All plant parts of this annual are covered in dense white wool. Like all members of the mint family, it has squarish stems and opposite leaves, and it is rich in volatile oils. The white basal leaves resemble a thistle's, with long spines, while the flowers grow in whorls on calyces that are spiny-tipped and woolly. The foliage is pungent, with a scent similar to citronella.

Where and when to gather

Found in sandy, loose soils in hot, arid parts of California below 4,500 feet, thistle sage sometimes grows profusely over several acres, a stunning sight when it's in bloom. Look for thistle sage in the Carrizo Plains, Death Valley, the upper Sonoran Desert, and the Mojave Desert. Locate and identify the plant while it is blooming in the spring, March through May. The seed will be ripe and ready to harvest for a surprisingly long time, May through November.

How to gather

Avoid the spiny leaves at the base. Wear gloves or use tongs to bend the seed stalk over, letting the ripe seed fall into your bag or basket. The seed is easy to clean, since it sinks to the bottom of the container and the leafy debris can be lifted off the top. Do so right away, to eliminate any interested insects.

How to use

The edible seeds can be toasted in a frying pan or roasted in an oven, then ground in a food blender. Use on rice, in muffins, cookies, and crackers, or mixed with other seeds to make a breakfast mush.

Future harvests

Add this plant to desert gardens. Its seed can be easily grown for your own breakfast cereal. Scatter some of the seed at the outlying edges of the patch, to extend its domain.

The unmistakable, graceful flowers of thistle sage are easily recognized in spring.

tidy tips

Layia platygloss
coastal tidy tips

EDIBLE seeds

Tidy tips is one of the numerous members of the aster family that produces sought-after edible seeds, tasting somewhat like sunflower seeds.

With a wide distribution throughout California, tidy tips' name is derived from the flower's white tips on the yellow petals. Its cheerful, easily identifiable appearance in the spring is always heartening, blending with other members of the aster family (Asteraceae), such as goldfields. Together, this duo forms beautiful and fragrant wildflower meadows that to this day stretch for miles, particularly in southern California. Watching tidy tips through the seasons, as the sturdy plants make early growth in the winter, come into bloom in the spring, and then as the petals fall and the seeds ripen, is a wildflower education in itself.

These annual wildflowers are a well-known component of spring wildflower displays throughout California.

How to identify

Tidy tips has alternating leaves that are narrow and toothed. The plants grow from 5 to 16 inches tall, depending on moisture and soil. They can grow upright or sprawl. The line between the yellow and white in the daisylike flower petals is distinct and "tidy." The yellow disk flowers have a black stamen in the center.

Where and when to gather

Tidy tips grow all over California, from the coast to the desert, in grasslands and inland valleys, and in the western foothills of the Sierra Nevada to 4,500 feet. Good displays can be found in the Central Valley and in the Carrizo Plain, as well as in the Grapevine. Bloom begins in March and is usually over by the end of April. Seeds ripen from April through May.

How to gather

When the ray flowers (the white-tipped yellow petals) have dropped off, begin to examine the center, probing to see if the seeds have turned from light beige to black. Frequently, seeds will be ripe in flowers blooming on lower stems before those blooming on upper stems.

How to use

Removing the chaff from flowers in the aster family is the interesting part of the pinole-making process. With tidy tips, it can be burned off as part of the parching process. Rubbing between the hands and then winnowing off the chaff is the usual procedure (see Pinole: California's Seed Foods, page 62). Toast and grind the seeds, incorporating the flour into baked goods or adding to other grain flours.

Future harvests

Gather only the seeds from each flower that are ripe at the time of your harvest, leaving the rest to mature for next year's crop, and for wildlife.

Torrey pine

Pinus torreyana
soledad pine

`EDIBLE` nuts

Torrey pine, with a limited distribution in California, is one of the least known producers of some of the best edible pine nuts.

Torrey pine is one of the rarest pines in the world, naturally occurring only along the coast in San Diego and on the Channel Islands. It is a protected species, and the seed should be harvested only outside of its protected range in and around San Diego, which may mean only if you find a tree planted by a gardener. Because it is such a beautiful tree and grows readily, many have been planted elsewhere along the coast. Since the nuts are large and easily gathered, it has real possibilities for a semiwild nut orchard along the coast, where nut crops are not easily grown. The nuts make a delicious addition to wild protein sources here in California.

How to identify

In southern California, there are no other native pines found right at the coast. So if you see a short to medium-sized pine tree with tufts of 10-inch long needles, usually

The long, slender needles of Torrey pine make it a graceful addition to the nut pine world.

though not always in bundles of five, and particularly if you are within the extremely limited range of the Torrey pine, identification will be easy. The cones are 3 to 6 inches long, and each may contain about 100 seeds up to 1 inch long. The tough scales of the cones have sharp, pointed tips. In protected areas, the trees can grow up to 70 feet tall, while on exposed bluffs, they assume much shorter, contorted or semiprostrate habits.

Where and when to gather

There are perhaps only 9,000 to 10,000 Torrey pines in existence, found mostly in the sea bluffs of northern San Diego, the nearby community of Del Mar, and on one side of Santa Rosa Island. The cones don't open all at once, so they can be checked for ripe seeds throughout the summer and fall.

How to gather

The large, noticeable cones have a characteristic that may account for their inability to spread, and that also must be considered while collecting. The cones open very slowly and may remain on the trees for up to fifteen years. The seeds are not released all at once, a way of hedging their bets, which makes it difficult to harvest a bountiful crop. But some seeds can usually be gathered throughout the summer. Like its relative the gray pine, Torrey pine's sharp-scaled cones need vigorous smashing to release the seeds. You may want to wear gloves while collecting the pine nuts. Heat can also be used to open the mature cones, either roasting them in an outside fire or in the oven.

Torrey pine is one of the few nut pines that grow right on the coast.

How to use

Use as any edible pinyon nut—eat it raw or toasted, in pastas, in pesto, in nut butters, and in salads. Pine nut cookies, cakes, and muffins made with Torrey pine nuts are true delicacies.

Future harvests

Such a rare tree should only be harvested where wise homeowners have planted them and then given you permission. Trees can be found, for example, in parks and other areas in Monterey County. Outside their natural range, they are not protected and are likely to be available for harvest.

tree mallow

Lavatera assurgentiflora

California tree mallow, mission mallow, malva real (royal mallow)

`EDIBLE` immature seeds

Of the many members of the mallow family that are appreciated for their immature seeds, called mallow peas, tree mallow's are among the largest, about ½ inch in diameter.

Tree mallow is an unusual semiwoody evergreen shrub with a very limited original distribution in the Channel Islands off the coast of Santa Barbara. This large-flowered, fast-growing member of the mallow family has made itself at home up and down the coast of California. Bright green when picked at the right stage, mallow peas taste very much like English peas. The calyx can be removed or eaten. Since tree mallow produces its showy dark pink flowers for a long season, it keeps producing mallow peas as well. Add to that its perennial nature, and you have the Queen of the Mallow Peas. A flowering hedge of tree mallows is a good place to find a pleasant vegetable snack.

How to identify

An erect shrub growing 7 to 12 feet tall and 3 feet wide, tree mallow is notable for its quick growth and its large, flexible,

The large ripening fruit to the right of the tree mallow's flower is the delicacy known as a mallow pea.

With a long period of bloom along the coast, tree mallow produces mallow peas continuously through the summer.

maple-leaf-shaped, alternate dark green leaves that are 3 to 5 inches long. The leaves partially conceal showy, bright reddish pink flowers that are 2 to 3 inches wide. The large flowers look suitable for tucking behind your ear while sipping mai tais in the tropics.

Where and when to gather

Tree mallow is found along the California coast, from Santa Barbara north. Its main bloom time is from April through August, but it produces some flowers all year long, so there are some mallow peas available all year long as well. The main harvest time is May through August.

How to gather

Examine each pea before twisting it off the stem, to see if it has developed enough to fill up at least half of the area surrounded by the calyx. Before that, harvesting is not worthwhile. Also, examine the pea to make sure that all the segments are still light green and soft. Once the peas begin to ripen into seeds, they become tan and bitter and shouldn't be eaten raw.

How to use

To eat raw, peel off the calyx (the united leaves enclosing the seed), and eat. To cook, either boil in water or steam briefly as you would garden peas. There is no need to peel off the calyx first if you are going to cook them.

Future harvests

Tree mallow is irresistible to deer and to gophers and other rodents. Once, beaten and battered by its predators, it completely disappeared from my coastal north-central California area, only to reappear twelve years later for reasons of its own. Because it grows fast and produces lots of seed, its presence among us seems ultimately secure.

tule

Schoeneoplectus californicus, formerly *Scirpus californicus*
California bulrush, bulrush

EDIBLE shoots, rhizomes, seeds, pollen

Tule is a source of material for building, clothing, and bedding, as well as easily prepared and harvested aquatic shoots.

Tules resemble cattails in many ways. Both frequently rim ponds and freshwater swamps with their long, dramatic-looking stems, and are hiding places for wildlife. Both are esteemed for providing delicate, mild vegetables from roots to seeds throughout their life cycle. Both are well worth the mud boots or positive attitude toward wet feet they require. They both have an inner core to the leaf stalk that has been called Cossack asparagus.

I've often wondered why cattails are so much more popular as edibles than tules. Perhaps it's because the male flower at the top of the cattail has been equated with an ear of corn, a vegetable recognizable to us, and one to which we can add butter and salt. Tule's white shoots arising anew each

Tule frequents freshwater wetlands and pond edges in California.

The seeds of tule help to distinguish it from the hot-dog-shaped flowers of cattail, but both grow in wetlands and have many edible parts.

season from the rhizomes are sweet and tender inside, even sweeter than those of cattail. They are ready to eat sooner, too; put your mud boots on in January to get your first tule sprouts.

How to identify

There are seventeen different species of tule in California. Tule has flowers that are quite different from cattails. They do not look like a cat's tail but are borne in reddish or light brown, somewhat ragged-looking clusters at the end of the stalk, darkening to brown as they ripen seed. Unlike cattail, tule has a hollow stem of a rich deep green, up to 10 feet tall but triangular in cross-section.

Where and when to gather

Tule grows throughout California in marshes and swamps, wherever there is standing fresh water. The phrase "in the tules" refers to the Central Valley, where complex freshwater wetlands included many miles of tules, rich habitat for quantities of migratory birds. Gather the shoots sprouting up from the horizontal rhizomes in January through April.

How to gather

Pull up the stem and examine the rhizome for new shoots. Or feel into the muck at the base of the plant and along the horizontal rhizome to a new shoot. Snap off this shoot. If it won't snap, it's too old and tough to eat. The first 3 inches are the best for eating.

How to use

Wash carefully. Eat the leaf shoots peeled and raw, sliced into ½-inch rounds, used in salads, or quickly sautéed. They are an excellent addition to a stir-fry, but shouldn't be cooked more than two or three minutes.

Future harvests

The future of tule is as secure as the future of clean, freshwater ponds and seeps in California. Like cattails, tules are known to become overexuberant, requiring control to prevent the disappearance of other aquatic delicacies that the pond or lake may hold, such as yellow pond lily or wapato. In such situations, harvesting tule for food can be helpful to preserve diverse wetland vegetation.

Caution

Thoroughly wash any aquatic plants you intend to eat. Though they may be delicious eaten raw, heat them enough to kill any bacteria that may be present.

valley oak

Quercus lobata

California valley oak, California white oak, mush oak, water oak, swamp oak, roble

EDIBLE acorns

The acorns of valley oak are among the most abundant, versatile, and sweet of California's acorn harvest.

Valley oak is the classic oak of California's sunny savannah grasslands. Large and picturesque, the tree's black limbs spread and twist and rise to the sun, often in places where soil is deep, moist, and fertile. The huge old oaks can grow as much as 8 feet in

A large valley oak can take your breath away with the beauty of its sculptural limbs, its graceful leaves, and most of all, its large and delicious acorns.

diameter. To early farmers, their presence indicated a good place to grow field crops. The crop the oaks themselves produce by the millions of pounds, the acorn, was all too rarely taken into account or given value by those farmers. Being the largest of all acorns, those of valley oak make picking in quantity relatively easy. They grow in so many parts of California that they were and are widely used. Unlike tanoak and California black oak, valley oak's acorns ripen in one year.

How to identify

Valley oaks can be identified by their irregularly lobed leaves with no spines at the tips of the lobes, their beautiful fall color, and their growth habit, which is wide and round. Their tapered acorns are 1½ to 2½ inches long and a bit less than 1 inch wide, with acorn caps that enclose about one-third of the nut. A huge tree, valley oak grows in full sun and does not, unlike the tanoak, tolerate shade. Neither does it crown sprout, so once it is cut down, its life is over.

Where and when to gather

California's valley oaks grow throughout the California Floristic Province, and also in the Central Valley. The acorns ripen in October and November.

How to gather

Either pluck the acorns from the tree, shake from the tree, or pick them up from the ground as soon as possible after they drop.

How to use

Valley oak acorns don't store as well as those of tanoak, and will germinate in the fall as soon as moisture surrounds them. They were traditionally used to make porridge, known as acorn soup (see Acorn Processing, page 85).

Future harvests

Valley oaks, and oaks of all species in California, lose territory on a daily basis, living as they do where people like to farm, build, and live. Their acorns germinate in humus-rich spots where they drop or are cached by jays, squirrels, and other animals. To ensure future acorn harvests, we can support oaks by protecting the existing trees and supporting restoration projects for new young ones.

vetch

Vicia species

EDIBLE leaves, stems

Most vetches are delicious greens, sweet and without bitterness when the leaf tips are eaten young.

Many vetches, both dainty natives and coarser, vigorous non-native weedy species, trail over other herbaceous species on our roadcuts and slopes. These members of the pea family also produce beans that can, with processing, be eaten, but it's safer to stick to eating the leaves. Before they flower, vetch tips are a delicacy, and it's easy to find ones that you like.

How to identify

Vetches have characteristic compound leaves, six to eight sets, in opposing leaflets along the leaf stem. Pealike irregular flowers range from almost white to cream, pale pink, rose, magenta, lilac, and deep purple. Identification of species can be tricky, but it doesn't matter, as none of them is toxic.

This vetch is typical of species in the genus *Vicia*, most of which have edible leaves.

Where and when to gather

Vetches grow all over California in full sun to part-shade. Harvest in winter to early spring.

How to gather

Leaf tips of the entire leaf can be plucked or snipped off when young.

How to use

Use raw in salads, as trailside nibbles, or boiled briefly.

Future harvests

Please do harvest weedy vetches, which can be found growing in rambunctious masses, overcoming other species of a similar height. The native vetches are usually smaller and found individually, not in large masses; with them, be more circumspect.

vine maple

Acer circinatum

mountain maple, bois du diablo

EDIBLE flowers

Though not a major supplier of nutrients, the exquisite and diminutive flower of vine maple is edible and sweet.

Vine maple grows from British Columbia to northern California. Its small size and graceful leaves brilliantly light up the autumn forest with buttery golden and scarlet hues. When it begins to leaf out in the spring, a dainty flower, somewhat resembling a fuchsia, can be observed in the leaf nodes. This small edible flower supplies a shot of sweetness for those living in northern parts of California, ready for winter to end. This small tree is altogether so exquisite that it feels appropriate to be able to eat some part of it.

How to identify

This deciduous shrub grows from 15 to 23 feet tall, and about half that wide, with small, opposite, lobed leaves, almost fan-shaped in outline, that turn spectacular shades of yellow, red, and maroon in the

IIn the spring, the new leaves of vine maple are just unfolding, and the fuchsialike flowers make a sweet delicacy.

Vine maple is a multistemmed shrub that typically grows in the understory of conifer forests.

fall, depending on how cold the nights are. The leaves are smaller by half than those of bigleaf maple. Light green new leaves and edible thumb-sized greenish white flowers appear in the spring. The winged fruits (samaras) that follow are hairless and of a reddish hue.

Where and when to gather

Vine maple frequents stream banks and can withstand deep shade. It grows from sea level to 5,000 feet. The flowers appear in April to May, when the leaves open.

How to gather

Pluck the flower between your fingers.

How to use

Eat the flowers raw as is, or use them in salads as an unusual, sweet-tasting garnish. They can also be used to decorate cakes.

Future harvests

Each flower you eat is a potential tree, so harvest in moderation.

wapato

Sagittaria latifolia

tule potato, arrowhead, duck potato, katniss

`EDIBLE` tubers, leaves, flower stalks

Wapato is a well-known traditional potatolike root food throughout the United States.

Found in lakes and swampy places where tule grows, wapato was traditionally valued for its easily digestible starch, which was frequently used as food for babies and elders. Wapato can be found in staggering quantities in some places, though the numbers of plants have seriously diminished in many parts of California. Traditional methods of gathering, which involved walking through lakes digging up the tubers with the toes, required a dexterity of the feet which is perhaps beyond our current abilities. But use a rake and give it a try; it is worth it for this easily prepared and enjoyable starch.

How to identify

The leaves of wapato, which float on the top of the water, are easy to spot. The common name arrowhead is a good clue to

The arrowhead-shaped leaves of wapato are distinctive.

the shape of the leaves, which are pointed with two lobes at the base pointing sharply downstem. The large white flowers are most attractive, with maroon blotches at the base surrounded by a pale yellow area with multiple stamens. Notable hand-shaped veins radiate out from the mid-point to the lobes. The roots are about the size of a walnut.

Where and when to gather

Wapato grows in lakes and wet meadows throughout northern California, includ-ing high-country lakes. It is best dug in the late fall and early winter, but it can be dug year-round. The young leaves should be harvested in early summer while still rolled up. Flower stalks should be harvested well before flower buds have opened.

How to gather

You may want to give the toe-digging method a try, but if it doesn't work for you, a pitchfork or rake can be used. The dis-advantage of those modern approaches is that more soil is disturbed, muddying the waters. But keep digging, because the tubers are present at different levels in the soil. The easiest way to gather wapato is to harvest in places where the waters recede, uncovering wapato root-digging areas.

How to use

The tubers of wapato are bitter until cooked. First peel off the bitter outer skin. They can be roasted, boiled, baked, steamed, or fried. They do not store well.

Future harvests

Disturbing beds of wapato can be good for their future if you leave some of the bulbs to float around and embed themselves anew in the mud.

Caution

Be sure that the plant you are identifying as wapato has an arrowhead-shaped leaf with veins that meet at the bottom of the midrib, then run to the tip of each lobe, in a palmate, or hand-shaped, or spidery pattern. If three main veins extend from the midrib as though from the trunk of a tree, with lateral veins branching like tree limbs, or like a child's drawing of a feather, you have found green arrow arum, *Pelt-andra virginica*, which will cause a burn-ing sensation in your mouth and shouldn't be eaten. This plant, another water lover, has leaves that are similar in shape except for the venation, but it has tiny greenish white flowers on a spike held in a long nar-row leaf cradle (spathe). Remember that wapato has large white flowers.

watercress

Nasturtium officinale

garden cress, water radish, water rocket, hedge mustard

`EDIBLE` leaves, stems, seeds

A famous French soup is made out of the leaves of this widespread water-loving European herbaceous species, one of the oldest wild greens still being widely eaten.

Watercress is considered both a weed and a gourmet wild green, being the required ingredient for watercress soup; its intense peppery savor is thought to create a strong craving. Watercress contains some calcium, iodine, folic acid, and iron, but it is notably high in vitamins A and C. Used historically as a remedy for scurvy, currently it is being studied for the many health applications of its phytonutrients, and many claims are being made. It has spread to many parts of the world and is cultivated commercially as well. It is one wild crop that is marketed on a large scale today. It even has its own festivals, and one town in England claims to be the watercress capital of the world.

Watercress has white flowers in clusters and long, narrow seed capsules growing at right angles from the main stems.

How to identify

Watercress is a hardy perennial growing from 1 to 3 feet tall. It can be identified by its mustardlike compound leaves from 6 to 12 inches tall and the small, white, four-petaled flowers growing in clusters. The rounded leaves have one leaflet at the top that is significantly larger than all the other leaflets arranged along the stem. The seed capsules are long and narrow, jutting out at right angles from the main stem. This water-lover has hollow stems that help it float.

Where and when to gather

Watercress is found throughout the California Floristic Province, growing near or in streams, bogs, and other wet places. It withstands frost, and is in flower from May to October. The seeds ripen from July to October. It blooms in May, so try to gather it before that, in February through April. Like many greens, wild and domesticated, it is best before it blooms.

How to gather

Snip the leaves and plunge them into cold water as soon as possible, since they wilt quickly. Store in a vase filled with water until ready to use. Even when it is growing in what seems to be a pure stream, do not use it if there is any possibility of livestock upstream. Gather the watercress seeds in their characteristic mustard family pods.

How to use

There are many uses for watercress, such as making a sour, peppery sauce to accompany meat. It is also used in sandwiches and salads. Try the delicious French soup, which incorporates a rich stock, onion or leek, and cream. The seeds are gathered to be sprouted and used in salads.

Future harvests

Water quality is the main concern for the future of edible wild watercress, which was able to make its way over here from England and spread from east to west, though it has also probably been introduced by gardeners. Watercress is considered an ecologically damaging weed, so when you harvest, remove it by the roots.

Caution

Be very careful that the water from which you gather watercress is unpolluted. It is not always an easy task to ascertain the purity of a watershed, especially where grazing animals may be present upstream unbeknownst to you. Don't take a chance. Once you establish a safe harvest, always wash any aquatic vegetables with care, using one cup of vinegar for two gallons of cold water.

western serviceberry

Amelanchier alnifolia var. *semiintegrifolia*

Saskatoon serviceberry, Pacific serviceberry, shadberry, dwarf shadbush, chuckley-pear, juneberry

`EDIBLE` berries

Serviceberry, a large shrub or small tree, is esteemed for its sweet, dark berries, reminiscent of blueberry with an added hint of almond, and even healthier.

A tree laden with these ripe berries seems somewhat miraculous, and you may wonder why this wild fruit, high in iron and copper, is not more widely known in California. Most who try it, especially dried or as jelly, become fans. Like the blueberry,

The fragrant western serviceberry flowers in April.

These western serviceberry leaves are toothed on the lower half and smooth above, seen here with the newly forming berries.

well established as a super-food, western serviceberry scores high in polyphenol antioxidants. Native tribes and early settlers used the berries for many preparations, from pemmican to puddings, and serviceberry jam or jelly is still prized.

How to identify

In early spring, April through May, this thicket-forming deciduous plant, growing from 8 to 30 feet tall, creates a fairyland effect, with lacy clusters of fragrant white flowers on its branches. Each flower is almost 1 inch long and consists of five long, sometimes twisted white petals. The flowers, with their many stamens (3 to 20), resemble blackberry blossoms. The bright green, 1-inch-long leaves are oval to lance-shaped, alternating, and woolly when the plant is flowering, with margins that are smooth on the lower half and toothed on the upper half. The leaves turn a brilliant orange-red before dropping in the fall. Young branches and buds are reddish brown and smooth, while older twigs are gray. The round fruits are fleshy with two or three seeds each. The berries are first red, then deep blue-purple or black.

Where and when to gather

Different subspecies of western serviceberry grow from near sea level to subalpine conditions, in many different soil types, from California to Alaska. It is used in creek and riverside revegetation, but it does require good drainage. It can be found in sun or part-shade at woodland edges. The fruit ripens from early to late July, and its quality varies from tree to tree.

Serviceberries are deep red before ripening to dark blue.

How to gather

It's easier to harvest berries from the shrubby specimens of western serviceberry than the treelike ones. Because of their size, the berries are easy to gather quickly and in quantity. Because of the birds, the berries are available for only one or two weeks a year. For this reason, locating nearby stands in advance is desirable. Or grow your own.

How to use

Eaten fresh and raw, western serviceberries, when totally ripe, are a treat. They can be used in pies, ice cream, syrups, and smoothies. As with other wild fruits, drying concentrates the sweetness and flavor. The dried fruit can be used wherever currants and raisins are used, such as in muffins and scones. The fresh berries can be processed into sauces, jams and jellies, wine, and fruit compotes, after you strain out the seeds.

Future harvests

These berries deserve to be more widely appreciated, both for the delight and health of humans and for the sustenance of wildlife. Since they can grow in difficult circumstances, they deserve a place in our gardens. They do, however, take up to ten years to bear fruit. So plant now! Perhaps this is the reason they are somewhat rare in the horticultural trade, though commercial orchards do exist in the Pacific Northwest.

wild ginger

Asarum caudatum

western wild ginger, longtail wild ginger

`EDIBLE` leaves, stems, roots

Though this wild ginger is not closely related to the tropical ginger purchased at the market, the uses are the same, and the gingery taste is also similar, with a delightful, indescribable difference.

The large, heart-shaped leaves and the long, fragrant roots of wild ginger mark many a woodland scene in California. Use it to flavor ice cream, puddings, soups, stews, and stir-fries, and for teas, and you may not want to go back to conventional store-bought ginger.

How to identify

With large, deep green leaves the size of your palm, heart-shaped with a notch where the stem connects to the leaf, wild ginger is easy to identify. It grows in colonies in moist tree-covered areas, from redwood to oak woodlands. You usually have

The handsome leaves of the shade-seeking wild ginger are heart-shaped.

to lift the leaves and peer down into the duff in June to catch sight of the elegant maroon flower with its three graceful elongated tubular horns.

Where and when to gather

Wild ginger grows all over California except in the desert. It can be harvested throughout the year.

How to gather

Snip lengths of the horizontal rhizomes, which may lie barely beneath the surface. Cut leaves and stems from the center of the colony.

How to use

The root can be chopped into 1-inch-long pieces and candied, or used in a stir-fry. It can be made into a tea that makes irresistible ice cream and pudding. The leaves also make a good tea, and can be boiled and left to soak in water or milk to use to flavor puddings. Remove the leaf after the infusion is strong enough.

Future harvests

It's good news for wild ginger that its leaves are even more flavorful than its roots. A few leaves can be harvested without disrupting or even disturbing a wild ginger colony. I grow a wild ginger colony that thrives with no care under an oak tree. It's hard to imagine living without it. A colony under redwood trees, or in any woodland, is attractive year-round, and this way you can study its ways and learn to help it by harvesting.

Wild ginger's unusual, intricate flower hides below the ginger leaves.

Caution

Wild ginger contains aristolochic acid, which became newsworthy when a number of people sickened through ingesting it in great concentrations in Chinese herbs touted as diet pills. It's a diuretic and can be hard on the kidneys. An analysis of the science by blogger Hank Shaw suggests that enormous amounts of the western wild ginger would need to be consumed before reaching toxic levels. If, however, you have kidney problems, or are risk-averse, don't eat the actual plant, but make an infusion and use the tea as a concentrate to flavor foods. The aristolochic acid is barely water-soluble; by avoiding eating the actual plant, either its roots or its leaves, you avoid almost all of the risk. Some say that since this plant has been eaten for generations by various native peoples, the risk is still extremely low.

wild hyacinth

Triteleia hyacinthina

fools onion, white brodiaea, white triteleia, hyacinth brodiaea, milk lily

EDIBLE corms

For a real California wedding, include wild hyacinth in the bridal bouquet, then serve the roasted or sautéed corms as hors d'oeuvres at the reception.

Wild hyacinth's showy cluster of flowers is a vision of pure white loveliness. Beautiful aboveground and with delicious roots belowground, as with all the plants used as Indian potatoes, increase is the name of the game. My experience with real potatoes can be summarized, "Plant a peck, harvest a peck." With Indian potatoes, it's different: plant one, get four to twelve cormlets. The small cormlet-sized babies, however, will be ¼ to ½ inch in diameter the first year, but you can eat the mother corm and replant the cormlets for next year's harvest, when they will emerge as large mother corms or bulbs. The larger cormlets make a tasty appetizer, a sublime form of Tater Tots.

Wild hyacinth has funnel-shaped white flowers,

How to identify

The deep green grasslike stems of wild hyacinth appear in early spring, growing to 16 inches tall. This species has funnel-shaped white flowers, sometimes flushed purple, with green veins on the back. Each flower has six stamens with white, yellow, or blue anthers.

Where and when to gather

Found in grasslands and seasonally wet meadows in full sun, wild hyacinth has a wide distribution throughout California and north to British Columbia. It flowers and goes to seed in mid to late summer and should be gathered while the seed stalk is still connected to the underground corms, so you will know what you are gathering and can find the corm, July to September. If it rains, the bulbs will begin to sprout, so gather them in the dry season.

How to gather

As with all Indian potatoes (see page 54), carefully dig alongside the flower stalk, to at least 5 inches below the ground, then feel at the base of the plant to find the corm. Bring it gently to the surface. Remove cormlets clinging to the corm's side, and replant them nearby.

How to use

Remove the bulb's rough, hairy coat. Boil for five to thirty minutes, depending on size, or roast at 300°F for thirty minutes to an hour, until soft. They can then be sautéed in hot oil and seasoned. Or mash and season. The bulbs also can be baked until dry and then stored. Make sure you

Wild hyacinth produces delicious corms, some of which are just beginning to sprout.

thoroughly cook them, for the best flavor and texture.

Future harvests

While gathering, plant or replant the cormlets in late summer and early fall, from 3 to 4 inches deep. Whether it rains or not, sprouts will appear above the soil in about a month, but you should irrigate if the rains are late or erratic in order to keep the leaves and flowering stalk growing.

To protect the corms and cormlets from tunneling underground critters, plant 4 to 8 inches deep in deep wooden boxes or large ceramic containers, at least 18 inches deep. In wetter areas, the gardener may find that seasonal flooding holds down the gopher population, as fire also used to do.

Make some practice digs down to 8 inches deep to make sure you're harvesting all there are, loosening the soil at the same time. Early settlers reported finding 200 corms in 1 square foot.

wild radish

Raphanus raphanistrum
jointed charlock, radish

`EDIBLE` leaves, flowers, seed pods, seeds, root

The leaves and new flowers of wild radish make excellent greens when young. The immature seedpods are spicy and good right off the stem or steamed later.

Wild radish, an annual weed from Europe, has spread so thoroughly throughout California that I am frequently asked for the name of "that beautiful pastel-colored wildflower," growing in miles-long patches of foamy blossoms in spring. Wild radish wreaks havoc on many an indigenous wildflower field, but kept within bounds by foraging, it can be a valuable addition to your diet. Wild radish is a probable hybrid

Flowers from white to yellow to pink and purple mark the wild radish.

Gather the wild radish pods while they are still green.

between domesticated radish and a plant called jointed charlock. Neighborhood children are no doubt knowledgeable consumers of the young seedpods, spicy and good right off the stem.

How to identify
Because they are both in the mustard family, wild radish and wild mustard are similar in many ways, though the latter is much taller, growing from 3 to 5 feet tall. Wild radish usually is no more than 2 to 3 feet tall, and instead of intensely golden flowers, it has blooms in a range from yellow to pink to white, sometimes all growing together. The flowers are four-petaled, with six stamens and a pistil in the middle. The seedpods show constrictions around each seed within the pod. The lobed leaves are about 8 inches long.

Where and when to gather
The east side of California is so far without wild radish. It likes fallow agricultural lands, roadsides, and vacant lots in full or mostly full sun. On the coast, wild radish germinates with the rains in the fall, grows through the winter, and blooms in spring. Gather the seedpods while still tender and green. When using the seeds for seasoning, they should be ripe and hard. Gather the leaves before the plant flowers from September through January. Flowers bloom from January through March. Dig the roots while still young in April and May.

How to gather

Harvest the leaves before flowering. The rough leaves may feel uncomfortably prickly, so bring scissors or shears and boxes with you to the harvest. That roughness disappears with cooking.

How to use

The leaves and flowers when boiled in plenty of water for ten minutes are easy to like and lose their peppery taste. Or cook in hot grease or oil. The young seedpods can be eaten whole and raw, or cooked for a milder taste. They can also be pickled and the seeds used as flavoring. The mature hard seeds can be toasted and ground for a mustardy flavoring. The roots, cooked in boiling salty water for up to an hour, will become mild and tender.

Future harvests

Do not hold back in your desire to harvest and eat wild radish. Make sure that when you harvest, you dig up the entire plant, including the root, preferably before it goes to seed, because wild radish is negatively impacting the flora of California. But eating wild radish in all its parts can positively impact your health.

woodland strawberry

Fragaria vesca, formerly *Fragaria californica*
woods strawberry, wild strawberry, California strawberry

EDIBLE berries, leaves

When California's woodland strawberries ripen to perfection, they soften, sweeten, and turn a rich, deep red color.

Each strawberry species has its own proponents, but to me, California's woodland strawberry is the sweetest and most flavorful in the world. Harvesting these tiny berries, the diameter of a dime, or sometimes, if you're lucky, a nickel, is a form of meditation. Every year, with pride in our ability to delay gratification, we pick enough to freeze for strawberry shortcake for one winter holiday dessert. The leaves are also edible, and make an enjoyable tea.

How to identify

Woodland strawberry has flexible, thin leaves and looks like a smaller version of the domesticated strawberry, while coast strawberry has shiny, waxy, deep green leaves and hugs the ground more closely. It's always a thrill to find woodland strawberry's flat white petals opening close to the ground, and to anticipate the fragrant red berries that will follow. With leaves divided into three nonshiny, only slightly

Woodland strawberry has five-or six-petaled white flowers and handsome, flexible, deep green leaves.

These soft berries are small, but intensely fragrant and flavorful.

hairy, leaflets, woodland strawberry has white five- or six-petaled flowers that open flat to the sun. They are succeeded by typical but tiny, not shiny strawberries. In the right conditions and with enough moisture, the berry plants spread to form masses of plants in full sun at the coast and in part-shade inland.

Where and when to gather

Woodland strawberry is found in open woods and on woodland edges throughout the California Floristic Province. It blooms February through May, and the fruit ripens from late March through June. In the mountains of California, you can find another native strawberry called mountain strawberry, *Fragaria virginica*, which can be harvested similarly.

How to gather

Native strawberries are a prime fruit to gather. You can do this from a sitting or lying position, welcoming the time spent with these generous plants. If you are looking down on the plants, the ripe berries may have turned to face the ground and all you can see from above are the sepals. Turn them over to see if a ripe berry is waiting for you. Don't ignore berries that have begun to dry up, because strawberry raisins can be extremely sweet.

How to use

Few will need this explained, but the berries that make it back to the house can be used in any way that the domesticated strawberry can. If removing the calyx is too tedious, some make a mush of the entire berry, strain it, and use the purée in cooking. Eat them fresh or freeze them for later use. Adding a small number of these intensely flavored berries to a dish of the blander domesticated species elevates the flavor of the whole bowl. The leaves, fresh or dried, can be used to make a pleasant tea. Pour boiling water over the leaves and steep for one-half hour.

Future harvests

Lying close to the ground as they do, woodland strawberries need freedom from the encroachment of taller species, such as Himalayan blackberry, that can crowd them out. Their survival strategy lies in the long aboveground runners that root at the nodes, making new plants, and also, in their ability to withstand shade from taller plant neighbors.

wood rose

Rosa gymnocarpa

redwood rose, California woodland rose, bald-hip rose, little wood rose

`EDIBLE` flowers, fruit

Unlike most sun-loving roses, wood rose is able to produce fragrant, edible flowers and rose hips in the deep shade of California's woodlands.

The dainty wood rose has a delicate, fleeting bloom, lasting only a few weeks in the woods. But each slender petal has a sweetness, even when slightly wilted, that lends itself to puddings, jellies, and forest snacks, as well as deserving a place in your water bottle. The spicy fragrance of this rose is something special, and becomes an indistinguishable part of the taste of the rose petals. The rose hips are powerful providers of vitamins C, A, and E. You may not even notice this subtle shrub until it blooms and fruits. The bright red fruits decorating the slender twigs draw your eyes and fingers.

How to identify

Wood rose grows 3 to 5 feet tall and is sprinkled with sweetly fragrant, single, five-petaled pink flowers. The fruit that follows is a small, delicate, elongated, hairless salmon-red rose hip. Alternate leaflets, often four per side, face each other on stems 3 to 5 inches long. Prickles are straight and slender, sometimes even sparse, and less vicious than those of other native rose species. Unlike the Nootka rose, this wild rose is not thicket-forming and the leaflets are doubly toothed.

Where and when to gather

Found in part-sunny openings or deep in the shady woods, the wood rose impresses with its ability to flower in woodsy shade, where it tolerates both drought and moisture. It grows in northern California and into Oregon and also south along the coast. Its more widespread sun-loving relative, the California wild rose, *Rosa californica*, is less restricted in distribution, thornier, and altogether larger. The flowers of wood rose bloom in April for just a few short weeks. The hips form in May and June.

How to gather

The rose petals will still be sweet even when slightly wilted, and can be removed without interfering with the production of rose hips. The hips form in May and June and persist into winter. This species of rose is gathered somewhat more easily than other species, because the hip separates itself from the dried sepals (flower leaves) so you don't need to remove those

Wood rose, a gentle wild rose, favors shady openings in the forest.

manually. The hips are best after a few nights of light frost or cold in September.

How to use

The flowers can be eaten as snacks or made into delicate products like rose petal jam, tea, or jelly. Add petals to sandwiches, salads, and ice water. The fruit is eaten raw or boiled whole with sweetener for teas, jams, jellies, and syrups. Split open and remove the seeds if eating the entire hips, though some don't bother when making dried fruit used as raisins. Dried, they are good added to cereals, candied, or in soup.

Future harvests

The farther north in California you go, the more vigorous the wood rose seems to be, sometimes appearing as a shorter, stockier type. As one of the few non-thicket-forming wild roses, it merits more restraint in the harvest of its rose hips.

yellow pond lily

Nuphar luteum subsp. *polysepala*
cow lily, wokcas, wocas, pond collard

`EDIBLE` roots, seeds

The large seeds of yellow pond lily are sometimes referred to as wilderness popcorn because they crack and expand slightly when cooked in hot oil and are tasty.

Known for both its edible roots and seeds, yellow pond lily is easily identifiable by its glossy green leaves, large yellow flowers, and serene appearance floating on ponds. One is loathe to disturb these beautiful lilies by harvesting their roots. Root harvest requires diving into the mud in which they are buried, splashing around with a digging stick or crowbar, and stirring up the muck. Instead, come back in two or three months to harvest the famous seeds when they have ripened. They are reachable from a canoe, are relatively large, and are very tasty. Klamath and Modoc Indians were known to harvest from 10,000 solid acres of yellow pond lily seeds, a huge

Find the yellow flower in July, then return to harvest the seed, for wilderness popcorn, from August to September.

undertaking requiring weeks. One observer remarked, "It is such a favorite food with the tribe [the Klamath] that its use is likely never to be wholly given up."

How to identify

If you see large yellow flowers with lush, waxy, nearly circular green leaves up to 12 inches long, floating tranquilly on the surface of a shallow pond or slow-moving stream, it is probably yellow pond lily. The yellow flower parts are actually sepals (flower leaves) almost 2 inches long, seven to nine of them clustering around the reddish stamen. The leaves lie on the water, while the flowers rise slightly above the water.

Where and when to gather

Yellow pond lilies are found growing in slow-moving or still freshwater wetlands from Alaska to central California. You will see them in the Sierra Nevada, the Cascade Range, the San Francisco Bay Area, and south to San Luis Obispo County. The seeds ripen from August to October.

How to gather

You may need a canoe to reach the seeds, but not if the pond is shallow. Clip the mature green seed capsules. Pour into a burlap sack and pound until the seeds have been released from the capsules. Soak in water until the refuse rises to the top. Dry the cleaned seeds on a tarp.

How to use

Pop in hot oil as you would popcorn. They won't absorb air the way that modern popcorn does, but the seed coat cracks open, expands, and softens somewhat. Serve with butter and salt, or grind and use as an ingredient in baked goods and mush, and to thicken stews and soups.

Future harvests

Harvest enough for no more than two or three movies' worth of supreme wilderness popcorn.

yerba buena

Clinopodium douglasii
wild savory

`EDIBLE` leaves, stems

"Refreshing" is a word that is used frequently, but I never really knew what it meant until I started drinking yerba buena tea.

The eye takes delight in the sight of yerba buena, a ground-hugging member of the mint family. Its verdant, rounded, scalloped foliage is pleasingly elegant as it follows the drip line of oak trees or neatly borders the edge of the trail in chaparral or coastal scrub. The sight of it elicits gratitude at the memory of the many occasions that yerba buena tea has enhanced. With its more than minty scent and taste, a sprig or two of yerba buena also prevents water from tasting stale in a water bottle on a hike. Hot or cold, yerba buena makes one of the world's greatest herbal teas.

Spanish senoritas in Old California used to drape the hems of their ball gowns with swags of yerba buena, which would remain fresh and fragrant through a festive evening of dancing.

Yerba buena spreads its light green leaves by means of rooting at the nodes of its sprawling stems.

How to identify

Like other members of the mint family, yerba buena is perennial and has square stems. It grows along the ground, rooting itself as it goes. In winter or late summer, depending on moisture and temperature, it may go dormant. Tiny white two-lipped flowers appear in early spring in the crooks of the leaves. It could be mistaken for modesty, another small woodland ground cover, but modesty has no fragrance.

Where and when to gather

This little plant is present in chaparral, in oak woodlands, in coastal scrub, and in mixed evergreen woodlands from Santa Barbara to Del Norte County. It can be found everywhere except in mountains and deserts. It likes shade but can be found in full sun along the coast if its roots are shaded by rocks or other plants. Yerba buena leaves can be gathered from early spring and into the summer.

How to gather

Snip the stems with scissors or your fingernail. The plant responds to careful tip-pruning, which will cause it to send out more new growth, the most flavorful part for tea. It produces tiny white flowers in April thru June, which can be gathered along with the leaves.

How to use

Rinse dust off the leaves with cold water. Pour boiling water over stems in a teapot and leave for ten or fifteen minutes, depending on how strong you like your tea. Or fill a mason jar with leaves and water

The tiny white flower is barely visible, but the leaves are the thing, for one of the world's great herbal teas.

and leave in the sun for the day, to make sun tea. Or simmer the leaves and stems in the water. It seems impossible to ruin yerba buena tea. It keeps for weeks in the refrigerator, and can be kept in concentrated form and diluted with fresh water. Once steeped, the leaves can be removed, redried, and used again. Some say that if you wish to enjoy the health benefits, don't use it regularly, but save it for that inevitable winter cold. Such restraint is beyond me.

Future harvests

By clipping off the ends of the long, lax stems, you cause the plant to become thicker and healthier. Don't uproot the plant as you clip. Harvest from within the colony.

yerba santa

Eriodictyon californicum

palo santo, mountain balm, California yerba santa

EDIBLE leaves, stems, flowers

The resinous leaves of yerba santa, the "holy herb," make a distinctive tea with a heady savor of native sage and mint.

Once so esteemed medicinally that it was listed in the official pharmocopeia as a cure for bronchitis, yerba santa has slipped back into medicinal semi-obscurity, except for those who welcome the intense tea made from its handsome, dark green, fragrant leaves. An extensive list of medical uses for yerba santa is found in historical documents but they remain unproven. It is mostly frequently used now for easing chronic respiratory ailments, particularly coughs, and for dry mouth. Enjoying a comforting pot of this tea, however, diluted until it's just right, need not be limited to the onset of a cold.

Yerba santa's leathery dark-green leaves make a pleasing background for its flowers.

How to identify

Yerba santa is an evergreen shrub growing 3 to 6 feet tall and equally wide. The lance-shaped leaves are thick, leathery, and as dark a green as there is in the plant kingdom. A condition called sooty fungus frequently infects older leaves with a powdery, black substance. Funnel-shaped flowers in shades from lilac to purple appear at the ends of the stems.

Where and when to gather

Yerba santa is a member of the chaparral plant community in California. Look for it in sunny spots with good drainage, such as roadcuts and canyon walls. It blooms from April through July and can be gathered before and during its bloom time. Sooty fungus may become prominent after that.

Funnel-shaped flowers in shades of lilac to purple appear in spring at the stem ends of yerba santa, providing nectar for bees and butterflies.

How to gather

Prune the plant by cutting off the upper 4 to 6 inches of the twigs, which contain the new leaves, before they become susceptible to sooty fungus. Pull the leaves off the stem to use for tea.

How to use

The leaves, flowers, and stems can be boiled, or left to steep after boiling water is poured over them. They can be used either fresh or dried. If steeped too long, the tea can become bitter, so dilute it with water until it reaches the right balance.

Future harvests

Yerba santa, with its ability to grow in adverse conditions and its bitter-tasting leaves discouraging to herbivores, is an impressively tough plant. Harvest small amounts from a number of plants rather than a large quantity from one plant. As always when harvesting for tea, never strip the leaves while leaving the twig or stem on the plant, but cut back the end of the entire stem as a way of pruning to encourage new growth.

Metric Conversions

Inches	Centimeters		Feet	Meters
¼	0.6		1	0.3
⅓	0.8		2	0.6
½	1.3		3	0.9
¾	1.9		4	1.2
1	2.5		5	1.5
2	5.1		6	1.8
3	7.6		7	2.1
4	10		8	2.4
5	13		9	2.7
6	15		10	3
7	18			
8	20			
9	23			
10	25			

Temperatures

degrees Celsius = $\frac{5}{9} \times$ (degrees Fahrenheit − 32)

degrees Fahrenheit = ($\frac{9}{5} \times$ degrees Celsius) + 32

To convert length:	Multiply by:
Yards to meters	0.9
Inches to centimeters	2.54
Inches to millimeters	25.4
Feet to centimeters	30.5

Resources

Plant identification websites

Calflora
Berkeley, CA
calflora.org

The Jepson Herbarium
Jepson eFlora
University of California
Berkeley, CA
ucjeps.berkeley.edu/IJM.html

United States Department of Agriculture
   Plants Database
plants.usda.gov/java/factSheet

Gardens and museums

Botanical Garden
University of California
200 Centennial Drive
Berkeley, CA 94720
botanicalgarden.berkeley.edu

Chaw'se
Indian Grinding Rock State Historic Park
14881 Pine Grove-Volcano Road
Pine Grove, CA 95665

College of Marin California Indian Studies
   Certificate Program
In partnership with the Miwok Archeologi-
   cal Preserve of Marin and the National
   Park Service
mapom.org
marin.edu/communityeducation/
   CAIndianStudiesCertProgram.html

Dorothy Ramon Learning Center
Morongo Community Center
13000 Fields Road
Banning, CA 92220

Effie Yeaw Nature Center
Ancil Hoffman County Park
2850 San Lorenzo Way
Carmichael, CA 95609

Grace Hudson Museum
431 South Main Street
Ukiah, CA 95482

Kumeyaay-Ipai Interpretive Center
   at Pauwai
13104 Ipai Waaypuk Trail
Poway, CA 92064
poway.org

Larner Seeds
230 Grove Road
Bolinas, CA 94924
larnerseeds.com

Maidu Museum and Historic Site
1970 Johnson Ranch Drive
Roseville, CA 95661
maidumuseum@roseville.ca.us

Malki Museum
11795 Malki Road
Morongo Reservation
Banning, CA 92220

Rancho Santa Ana Botanical Garden
1500 N. College Avenue
Claremont, CA 91711
rsabg.org

Regional Parks Botanical Garden
Native Plants of California
Tilden Regional Park
Berkeley, CA 94708
nativeplants.org

Santa Barbara Botanical Garden
1212 Mission Canyon Road
Santa Barbara, CA 93105
sbbg.org

Santa Barbara Museum of Natural History
2559 Puesta Del Sol
Santa Barbara, CA 93105
sbnature.org

Sierra Mono Museum
North Fork Recreation Center
33507 Road 230
North Fork, CA 93643

Strybing Arboretum and Botanical Gardens
Golden Gate Park
1199 9th Avenue
San Francisco, CA 94122
sfbotanicalgarden.org

UCLA Mildred E. Mathias Botanical
  Garden
100 Stein Plaza Driveway
Los Angeles, CA 90095
botgard.ucla.edu/bg-home.htm

University of California Botanical Garden
Riverside, CA 92502
gardens.ucr.edu

Helpful organizations
California Invasive Pest Plant Council
cal-ipc.org

California Native Plant Society
cnps.org

California Oak Foundation
californiaoaks.org

California Oak Mortality Task Force
suddenoakdeath.org

Chaparral Institute
californiachaparral.com

News from Native California
newsfromnativecalifornia.com

Occidental Arts and Ecology
oaec.org

Society of Ethnobiology
ethnobiology.org

References

Anderson, M. Kat. *Tending the Wild: Native American Knowledge and the Management of California's Natural Resources*. Berkeley: University of California Press, 2005.

Baldwin, Bruce G., et al., eds. *The Jepson Manual: Vascular Plants of California*. 2nd ed. Berkeley: University of California Press, 2012.

Barrows, Prescott David. *Ethno-Botany of the Coahuilla Indians*. 2nd ed. Banning, California: Malki Museum Press, 1977.

Deur, Douglas, and Nancy J. Turner, eds. *Keeping It Living: Traditions of Plant Use and Cultivation on the Northwest Coast of North America*. Seattle: University of Washington Press, 2005.

Goddard, Earl Pliny. *Life and Culture of the Hupa*. Berkeley: University of California Press, 1903.

Harlow, Nora, and Kristin Jakob, eds. *Wild Lilies, Irises and Grasses: Gardening with California Monocots*. Berkeley: University of California Press, 2003.

Haskin, Leslie L. *Wildflowers of the Pacific Coast*. Portland: Binfords & Mort, 1959.

Hodgson, Wendy C. *Food Plants of the Sonoran Desert*. Tucson: The University of Arizona Press, 2001.

Howell, John Thomas, et al. *Marin Flora: An Illustrated Manual of the Flowering Plants, Ferns, and Conifers of Marin County, California*. San Francisco: California Academy of Sciences and the California Native Plant Society, 2007.

Ingram, Steven. *Cacti, Agaves and Yuccas of California and Nevada*. Los Olivos, California: Cachuma Press, 2008.

Moerman, Daniel E. *Native American Ethnobotany*. Portland, Oregon: Timber Press, 1998.

Nabhan, Gary Paul. *Gathering the Desert*. Tucson: University of Arizona Press, 1986.

Ortiz, Bev, as told to Julia F. Parker. *It Will Live Forever: Traditional Yosemite Indian Acorn Preparation*. Berkeley, California: Heyday Press, 1996.

Rea, Amadeo M. *At the Desert's Green Edge: An Ethnobotany of the Gila River Pima*. Tucson: University of Arizona Press, 1997.

Tallamy, Douglas W. *Bringing Nature Home: How You Can Sustain Wildlife with Native Plants*. Portland, Oregon: Timber Press, 2007.

Thayer, Samuel. *Nature's Garden: A Guide to Identifying, Harvesting and Preparing Edible Wild Plants*. Birchwood: Forager's Harvest Press, 2010.

Timbrook, Jan. *Chumash Ethnobotany: Plant Knowledge Among the Chumash People of Southern California*. Santa Barbara, California: Santa Barbara Museum of Natural History, 2007.

Vizgirdas, Ray S., and Edna M. Rey-Vizgirdas. *Wild Plants of the Sierra Nevada*. Reno: University of Nevada Press, 2006.

Acknowledgments

Gratitude to the descendants of the many different native tribes who preserve and use innumerable California native plant species.

Thanks to my family and friends for support and help through the writing of this book. A major chunk of gratitude to ethnobiologist Dr. M. Kat Anderson of the Natural Resources Conservation Service for help of innumerable kinds, and also to Frederica Bowcutt, Carol Bornstein, Eric Garton, Jack Nisbet, Brock Dolman, Ashley Ratcliffe, Mary Abbott, and Vernon and Doreen Smith.

Doug Deur, ethnobotanist and fellow series author, supplied the leavening humor without which I might not have made it.

Gratitude to my inspiring and essential staff at Larner Seeds, to Ruth Lopez, for her time with us, to Grace Alexander, Tina Kochan, Jeff Manson, Lew Lewandowski, and Ildiko Polony.

I am grateful beyond words for the staunch editorial assistance of Eve Goodman and Ellen Wheat.

Thanks to daughter Molly Koehler and to Matt Koehler for insightful and constant encouragement, and for heartlifting baby videography arriving at just the right moment.

Thanks to Peter Warner and all the other photographers who supplied images, and most of all to my husband, Peter G. Smith, for the years of plant photography and wildland documentation, and even more, for his unflagging, unstinting, and downright unbelievable support and assistance. Remember when we drove into the national seashore and wondered if we could do it?

Photography Credits

Richard Bonnett/Flickr, page 304

Carol Bornstein, pages 113, 175

Tom Brandt/Flickr, pages 219, 220

J Brew/Flickr, page 234

Curtis Clark/wikimedia.org, page 152 right

Teri Corelli/Flickr, page 191

Joe Decruyenaere/Flickr, pages 151, 169, 281

Douglas Deur, pages 72, 73, 139

Noah Elhardt/wikimedia.org, page 170

Dawn Endico/Flickr, page 118

Jim Frazee/SARhounds, page 2

Tom Hilton/Flickr, page 237

Saxon Holt, page 101

Neal Kramer, pages 194, 195, 321

Matt Lavin/Flickr, pages 89, 90, 260, 261

Jeff Manson, page 93

Jean Pawek, page 211

Jane Shelby Richardson/wikimedia.org, pages 157, 158, 200, 201

Stan Shebs/wikimedia.org, pages 58, 147, 148

slatsz, pages 301, 302, 303

Doreen Smith, page 207

Clinton Steeds/Flickr, page 97

Mark Turner, pages 105, 180 left, 235, 252, 320

Nancy Turner, page 265

Phil Van Soelen, page 177

Crow Vecchio/NPS/Flickr, page 305

Miguel Vieira/Flickr, pages 76, 77

Peter Warner, pages 23, 43, 149, 150, 203, 204, 205, 212, 285, 297

Lynn Watson, Santa Barbara, pages 183, 184

All other photos are by Peter G. Smith and Judith Larner Lowry.

Index

About the Author

MOLLY KOEHLER

A beloved expert and award-winning writer on California's native plants, **Judith Larner Lowry** has spent the last thirty-five years in their company. As proprietor of Larner Seeds, specialists in California's native plants, she has sought out edible wild plants throughout the Golden State, in their inland, coastal, desert, and woodland homes. Her previous books include *Gardening with a Wild Heart* and *The Landscaping Ideas of Jays*. Author of "The Real California Cuisine" and numerous related articles as well as cofounder of the West Marin Commons' Ethnobotany Group, Lowry shares her passion with a wide range of devoted customers and readers. She invites you to join her on this tour of the edible wild plants of the Golden State.